Bhagavad Gita

Translation and Selected Commentary

Saligrama C. Subbarao, Ph.D.

Saligrama Publishing | Newark, Delaware

Copyright © 2010 by Saligrama C. Subbarao. All rights reserved.
Published by Saligrama Publishing.
Contact the author at saligrama_subbarao@yahoo.com
ISBN 978-0-9843812-0-3
Printed in the United States of America

Dedicated to my parents

Smt. Lakshmidevamma Saligrama
1913-2009
Sahukar Saligrama C. Channappaiah
1907-1987

Acknowledgments

I would like to offer my humble prayers to Lord Ganesha, Lord Krishna, and Maharishi Vyasa.

Shuklaam baradharam vishnum shashivarnam chaturbhujam;
Prasanna vadanam dhyaayet sarva vignopa shaantaye.

Prapanna paarijaataaya totra vetraika paanaye;
Jnaana mudraaya krishnaaya gitaamritaduhe namah.

Namostute vyaasa vishaala buddheh, phullaaravindaayata patra netra;
Yena tvaya bhaarata taila poornah, prajvaalito jnaanamayah pradipah.

I would like to offer my profound gratitude and appreciation to my parents for helping me to learn both Sanskrit and English, and for encouraging me to develop a solid background in science. They led a pure, dharmic life and were excellent role models for me.

I consulted a number of translations, commentaries and essays on the Bhagavad Gita while preparing this book. I owe the authors (listed in the bibliography) a deep debt of gratitude. The phonetic transliterations for the verses were adapted from the Divine Life Society publication of *The Bhagavad Gita*, 2000: http://www.dlshq.org/download/bgita.htm

A number of my friends and family members, including my brothers, sisters and their family showed keen interest in this work and I thank them. Now I would like to mention a few people who contributed directly.

Dr. Linda Stine

I am deeply indebted to my friend Dr. Linda Stine, Professor at Lincoln University, who went through the final version of the manuscript meticulously and with amazing efficiency.

Dr. Robert Langley

I thank my friend Dr. Robert Langley, Professor at Lincoln University, for patiently and skillfully snapping picture after picture as my family looked for just the right photo to put on the back cover.

Mr. Srinivas Udupa and Mr. Ranganath

These friends invited me into a spiritual atmosphere in Bangalore and guided me to obtain valuable material for the book.

Mr. Hiranya Bhatta Saligrama

My friend Hiranni (son of our family friend, Smt. Gundamma and Mr. Ganapati Shastri) read the entire book critically and provided valuable input in the interpretation. I thank him.

Dr. A. V. Nagasampige

I thank Dr. A. V. Navasampige of Poornaprajna Vidyapeetha in Bangalore for clearing some of my doubts.

Deepika Sharma

Deepika (daughter of my late younger brother Athri Sharma) engaged me in a scholarly discussion on the Bhagavad Gita at her residence in Bangalore.

Sushma Narayan

I extend my deep appreciation and sincere thanks to my niece Sushma Narayan (daughter of my younger sister Vasudha Narayan) for typing the first three chapters of the translation.

Lakshmi Subbarao (my daughter), Abhiram Vijayasarathy (son of my younger sister Shambhavi Vijayasarathy), Madhuri Saligrama (daughter of my younger brother Vamadeva Saligrama), and Manoj Laxminarasimhiah (son of my younger sister Manjula Laxminarasimhiah)

These individuals read and reflected on the book in depth, raised thought-provoking questions, and suggested a number of changes. Their inquisitive eyes, fresh perspective, and candid feedback were instrumental in improving the quality of the translation and in selecting verses for commentary. I thank them sincerely.

Meghanath Laxminarasimhiah

Megha (Manjula's second son) accompanied me to Kurukshetra, the place where the Bhagavad Gita was delivered, and also to Mathura, Lord Krishna's birthplace. Tapping his skills as a mechanical engineer, he designed the centerpiece of the front cover – the eighteen steps to Illumination that represent the eighteen chapters of the Bhagavad Gita. It is very difficult for me to convey my appreciation for his immense contribution.

Jagannath Govindaraju
Jag (son of my elder sister Vedavathi Govindaraju) was a great help to me in Bangalore. He connected me with a number of knowledgeable people and helped me to obtain insightful books from libraries and bookstores. I would like to thank him greatly.

Mythili Subbarao
Mythili (my wife) kept me on my toes by asking for progress reports very frequently – sometimes twice a day! She did everything she could to support me as I worked to complete this intensive endeavor.

Kartik Subbarao
Kartik (my son) played a pivotal role in completing this work. He brought to bear his considerable talents in the fields of information technology, philosophy, and writing to make this book possible. He designed the organization and layout of the book, and spent many hours typing and editing the manuscript. I thank him for all of his contributions.

Kartik would like to thank the many Open Source developers, notably the Linux, Perl, OpenOffice.org, and GIMP communities, whose works of karma yoga were key building blocks in creating this book.

Table of Contents

Preface..xi
Introduction...xv
  1. Arjuna Vishada Yoga..1
  2. Sankhya Yoga..15
  3. Karma Yoga...37
  4. Jnana Yoga..55
  5. Sanyasa Yoga..67
  6. Dhyana Yoga...77
  7. Jnana Vijnana Yoga...91
  8. Akshara Brahma Yoga...101
  9. Rajavidya Rajaguhya Yoga.....................................109
  10. Vibhuti Yoga..121
  11. Vishvaroopa Sandarshana Yoga...........................133
  12. Bhakti Yoga..149
  13. Kshetra Kshetrajna Vibhaga Yoga........................155
  14. Gunatraya Vibhaga Yoga......................................167
  15. Purushottama Yoga..175
  16. Daivasura Sampadvibhaga Yoga..........................181
  17. Shraddha Thraya Vibhaga Yoga...........................189
  18. Moksha Sanyasa Yoga...197
Bibliography..221

Preface

The Bhagavad Gita is well known all over the world, and a number of translations, commentaries and essays are available in most of the major languages. One may then naturally wonder about my motivation for undertaking yet another translation. My reason for doing so involves a very special person, my mother.

My mother came to the United States for the first time in 1989, when she was 75, for what was to be only a short visit. Three of her daughters and her three sons (including me) all live in the U.S., and we persuaded her to stay. She lived with my youngest sister in New Jersey for about 10 years, after which she moved to Delaware to stay with my family.

My mother was a kind, humble, selfless and generous person. She had exceptional communication skills and the ability to get along well with everyone. She valued education immensely. She had a special knack of bringing out the best in people, touching everyone she came across in her own unique way. She was an inspiration and a role model, showing by word and deed the importance of hard work. She led a highly disciplined life. She would regularly get up early in the morning, take her bath, offer prayer at the family shrine, eat a little breakfast, walk inside the house for a few minutes and retire to her special room to do japa (silent prayer). In the evening, she would have dinner with us, interact with family members, watch television and go to bed at 10 p.m.

Although this schedule was appropriate for her, based on her age and physical condition, she was used to a hectic 16-hour day schedule in India. One day she politely complained that she felt useless since she was not helping us. I did not agree with her. I told her that she was the main pillar of our immediate and extended family. She forged unity among her children and their families. She appreciated my remarks but was not completely satisfied. She always looked for opportunities to help us and seized them as they occurred. Whenever she saw me getting ready to staple papers, she would gently snatch the stapler from my hand and finish the job herself. After my daughter washed and dried her laundry, my mother would fold the clothes meticulously. She often joined my wife in picking flowers from our garden and preparing garlands for our local temple. At the same time, she imparted to my wife her experiential wisdom. She would serve as an enthusiastic audience for my son's lectures on technology and philosophy, and would often make valuable remarks. Her behavior was the same at my sisters' and brothers' places when she visited them. She believed that everyone should do their part, big or small.

One day, I asked her if she would like me to read some spiritual books to her. She was overjoyed. I started with the Bhagavata Purana. Every day I read an hour or two. She listened with interest and devotion, and made excellent observations. She called my brothers and sisters daily and shared her joyful experience with them. We completed the Bhagavata Purana in a year and a half. One by one, we then finished studying the Varaha Purana, Vishnu Parana, Brahmananda Purana, Shiva Purana, Kalika Purana, Markandeya Purana, Ramayana and Mahabharata. We read a few chapters of the Bhagavad Gita every day as well. My mother regularly discussed spiritual topics with family members. I was amazed at her ability to grasp the essence of scriptures and explain them to others in common and comprehendible terms. She enjoyed her opportunity to watch the Ramayana, Mahabharata and several puranas on TV. Six years flew by unnoticed.

On July 23, 2005, my mother suffered a massive stroke, and the prognosis was that she would live only for a few days. By God's grace she survived, but she lost her mobility and the ability to speak. Although completely bedridden, she did not lose her mental prowess nor her cheerful demeanor. She received guests with a heart-warming smile.

I continued reading spiritual books to her, a number of Upanishads and, as before, a few chapters of the Bhagavad Gita every day. We would read together for about 10 hours each day, and her level of interest and alertness remained high. In the evenings, my sister from New Jersey would call and sing and pray with her over the phone, and my sister in Chicago would do the same.

On Friday, August 10, 2007, my mother started singing "Bhagyada Lakshmi Baramma". Gradually, she began also to sing songs of Purandara Dasa, Thyagaraja and others, and she started reciting Bhagavad Gita verses along with me. Whenever I would make a mistake, she would smile to let me know. When I read the Vishvaroopa Sandarshana Yoga, she would automatically close her eyes. It looked as though she were really experiencing the Lord's infinite manifestation. From April-August 2008, we read Bhagavad Gita one hundred times. She performed Vishnu Sahasranama Puja and Lakshmi Ashtothara Puja.

On March 30, 2009, her condition became serious. She was admitted to the hospital, where she received the best care possible. I continued reading Bhagavad Gita and Shiva Sahasranama every day. Although she was conscious, she was no longer interacting with us. She passed away on April 11, 2009 at 11:15 a.m., surrounded by my family and me.

I know that my mother would have shared her experience of the Bhagavad Gita with others if she could speak. For this reason, I started to translate the Bhagavad Gita and circulated it to my immediate and extended family. During this process, the idea of sharing it with my vishva kutumba (universal family) occurred. Thus, on the first anniversary of my mother's death, I offer this nectar of wisdom to you.

Saligrama Subbarao
April 2010

Introduction

The Bhagavad Gita is one of the most revered and cherished Hindu scriptures, but its message is universal and beneficial to all. It is as relevant today as it was over 5000 years ago when it was delivered by Lord Krishna to Arjuna on the battlefield of sacred Kurukshetra.

I got acquainted with the Bhagavad Gita when I was 12 years old. Verses 51 to 71 in chapter 2 were included in my Sanskrit textbook. I memorized the verses along with their meaning, and was able to reproduce them for tests. Later in college, I would frequently search the Gita for quotations to incorporate into my talks. I had no real understanding of what I was saying, but it had the expected effect on the audience. While I was doing my Master's degree in Chemistry at Bhavan's College in Bombay, I studied the Upanishads and a number of diverse commentaries on the Bhagavad Gita. This gave me the strong intellectual foundation on which I built and expanded my knowledge of the Gita over many years. I could now appreciate the complexity inside the simplicity of its message, and could quote the Bhagavad Gita with meaning. But in the back of my mind, I still felt that there was something missing in my understanding.

About ten years ago, when I started to read and translate the Bhagavad Gita to my mother, I noticed something significant. Although my mother did not have much formal education, she absorbed the Gita with ease and enjoyed it every time. I was fascinated by the Gita, but not *captivated* by it like my mother. Its words resonated deeply to her core. After some reflection, I realized that my mother was full of bhakti (devotion) and had surrendered herself to God, whereas I retained a fair amount of skepticism from my long years of training in science. That skepticism was holding me back from a fuller, experiential immersion. I gradually made a paradigm shift from scientific skepticism to bhakti. I accepted Sri Krishna as the Lord of the Universe and as the Jagadguru (universal teacher). I also accepted that the Bhagavad Gita was revealed by Lord

Krishna to Arjuna and that Maharishi Vyasa wrote this for the benefit of the people. I began to enjoy the Gita immensely, seeing it in a new light. I realized that it is an effective *practical* manual that guides one to lead a pure, purposeful and peaceful life in this chaotic world, and then attain Moksha (liberation).

The Bhagavad Gita presents a number of paths which lead the individual to Self-realization. We do not have to run away to the seclusion of a forest to become spiritual. We only have to let our petty self become a magnanimous one. One need not subscribe to any particular Hindu philosophy such as Advaita, Dvaita or Vishishtadvaita. People of all creeds, agnostics, and even atheists can derive immense value from the Gita's wisdom.

The uniqueness of the Bhagavad Gita lies in its emphasis on selfless work for the benefit of all. Our greatest advances in science and technology, and our most inspirational creations of literature and the arts, have come from individuals who have followed this simple principle. Today, we are connected across the world like never before, and can advance the common good in ways that were previously unimaginable. Yet, at the same time, we also see selfishness and greediness on full display. From terrorists who pursue their hate-fueled obsessions to corrupt financial institutions that undermine economies, humanity suffers heavily. Sometimes it seems like there is no light at the end of the tunnel.

The Bhagavad Gita certainly shows us a way out of this mess. My aim has been to provide a translation that is highly relevant to today, using the simplest possible language. I have tried to capture the essence of each verse as I experience it, with both scientific and spiritual eyes.

The life of Mahatma Gandhi was of the greatest embodiments of the Gita in action. He said: "*When doubts haunt me, when disappointments stare me in the face, and I see not one ray of hope on the horizon, I turn to the Bhagavad Gita and find a verse to comfort me; and I immediately begin to smile in the midst of overwhelming sorrow. Those who meditate on the Gita will derive fresh joy and new meanings from it every day.*"

I do hope that you will read this with bhakti, reflect on it and choose the path that brings you joy and enlightenment.

Chapter 1
Arjuna Vishada Yoga

1.01

धृतराष्ट्र उवाच | धर्मक्षेत्रे कुरुक्षेत्रे समवेता युयुत्सवः | मामकाः पाण्डवाश्चैव किमकुर्वत सञ्जय ||	Dhritaraashtra uvaacha: Dharmakshetre kurukshetre samavetaa yuyutsavah; Maamakaah paandavaashchaiva kim akurvata sanjaya.

Dhritarashtra said: O Sanjaya, what did my sons and the sons of Pandu do after gathering on the sacred plains of Kurukshetra with the desire to engage in war?

Commentary: The first four words of the opening verse convey the essence of the entire Bhagavad Gita. When they are rearranged to read "kshetre kshetre kuru dharma", the meaning is: "Wherever you are, perform your duty for the benefit of all".

1.02

सञ्जय उवाच | दृष्ट्वा तु पाण्डवानीकं व्यूढं दुर्योधनस्तदा | आचार्यमुपसंगम्य राजा वचनमब्रवीत् ||	Sanjaya uvaacha: Drishtvaa tu paandavaaneekam vyudham duryodhanastadaa; Aachaaryam upasamgamya raajaa vachanam abraveet.

Sanjaya said: On seeing the Pandava army arranged for battle, King Duryodhana went to his teacher (Drona) and spoke these words:

1.03

| पश्यैतां पाण्डुपुत्राणामाचार्य महतीं चमूम् \| व्यूढां द्रुपदपुत्रेण तव शिष्येण धीमता \|\| | Pashyaitaam paanduputraanaam aachaarya mahateem chamoom; Vyoodhaam drupadaputrena tava shishyena dheemataa. |

O teacher, behold this great army of the sons of Pandu arranged for battle by your smart student, the son of Drupada (Dhrishtadyumna).

1.04-1.06

| अत्र शूरा महेष्वासा भीमार्जुनसमा युधि \| युयुधानो विराटश्च द्रुपदश्च महारथः \|\| धृष्टकेतुश्चेकितानः काशिराजश्च वीर्यवान् \| पुरुजित्कुन्तिभोजश्च शैब्यश्च नरपुंगवः \|\| युधामन्युश्च विक्रान्त उत्तमौजाश्च वीर्यवान् \| सौभद्रो द्रौपदेयाश्च सर्व एव महारथाः \|\| | Atra shooraa maheshvaasaa bheemaarjunasamaa yudhi; Yuyudhaano viraatashcha drupadashcha mahaarathah. Dhrishtaketush chekitaanah kaashiraajashcha veeryavaan; Purujit kuntibhojashcha shaibyashcha narapungavah. Yudhaamanyushcha vikraanta uttamaujaashcha veeryavaan; Saubhadro draupadeyaashcha sarva eva mahaarathaah. |

Here are heroes and expert archers equal in valor to Bhima and Arjuna such as Yuyudhana, Virata, the great warrior Drupada, Dhristaketu, Chekitana, the brave king of Kashi, Purujit, Kuntibhoja, the outstanding Shaibya, Uttamauja, Abhimanyu (the son of Subhadra) and the sons of Draupadi (Shrutasoma, Shrutakeerti, Shataneeka, and Shruthakarma)

1.07

| अस्माकं तु विशिष्टा ये तान्निबोध द्विजोत्तम \| नायका मम सैन्यस्य संज्ञार्थं तान्ब्रवीमि ते \|\| | Asmaakam tu vishishtaa ye taan nibodha dwijottama; Naayakaah mama sainyasya samjnaartham taan braveemi te. |

Revered Brahmana (Drona), for your information, let me give you the names of the most distinguished on our side, the leaders of my army.

Arjuna Vishada Yoga

1.08

भवान्भीष्मश्च कर्णश्च कृपश्च समितिञ्जयः । अश्वत्थामा विकर्णश्च सौमदत्तिस्तथैव च ॥	Bhavaan bheeshmashcha karnashcha kripashcha samitinjayah; Ashwatthaamaa vikarnashcha saumadattis tathaiva cha.

Yourself, Bhishma, Karna, Kripa, Ashwatthama, Vikarna and the son of Somadatta (Bhurisrava) are always victorious in battle.

1.09

अन्ये च बहवः शूरा मदर्थे त्यक्तजीविताः । नानाशस्त्रप्रहरणाः सर्वे युद्धविशारदाः ॥	Anye cha bahavah shooraa madarthe tyaktajeevitaah; Naanaashastrapraharanaah sarve yuddhavishaaradaah.

Also there are many other heroes who are experts in all types of warfare, who are equipped with a variety of weapons, and who are ready to give up their lives for my sake.

1.10

अपर्याप्तं तदस्माकं बलं भीष्माभिरक्षितम् । पर्याप्तं त्विदमेतेषां बलं भीमाभिरक्षितम् ॥	Aparyaaptam tad asmaakam balam bheeshmaabhirakshitam; Paryaaptam tvidam eteshaam balam bheemaabhirakshitam.

The strength of our army protected by Bhishma is unlimited, whereas theirs protected by Bhima is limited.

1.11

अयनेषु च सर्वेषु यथाभागमवस्थिताः । भीष्ममेवाभिरक्षन्तु भवन्तः सर्व एव हि ॥	Ayaneshu cha sarveshu yathaabhaagam avasthitaah; Bheeshmam evaabhirakshantu bhavantah sarva eva hi.

Let each of you stand firm at your strategic positions and support Bhishma from all sides.

	1.12
तस्य सञ्जनयन्हर्षं कुरुवृद्धः पितामहः । सिंहनादं विनद्योच्चैः शङ्खं दध्मौ प्रतापवान् ॥	Tasya sanjanayan harsham kuruvriddhah pitaamahah; Simhanaadam vinadyocchaih shankham dadhmau prataapavaan.

The eldest of the Kurus, Pitamaha (grandfather) Bhishma, roared like a lion and blew his conch forcefully to cheer up Duryodhana.

	1.13
ततः शङ्खाश्च भेर्यश्च पणवानकगोमुखाः । सहसैवाभ्यहन्यन्त स शब्दस्तुमुलोऽभवत् ॥	Tatah shankhaashcha bheryashcha panavaanakagomukhaah; Sahasaivaabhyahanyanta sa shabdastumulo'bhavat.

Then conches, drums, cymbals, and kettle drums were sounded all at once, making a tumultuous noise.

	1.14
ततः श्वेतैर्हयैर्युक्ते महति स्यन्दने स्थितौ । माधवः पाण्डवश्चैव दिव्यौ शङ्खौ प्रदध्मतुः ॥	Tatah shvetair hayair yukte mahati syandane sthitau; Maadhavah paandavashchaiva divyau shankhau pradadhmatuh.

Then Madhava (Krishna) and the son of Pandu (Arjuna), who were stationed in their magnificent chariot drawn by white horses, sounded their divine conches.

	1.15
पाञ्चजन्यं हृषीकेशो देवदत्तं धनञ्जयः । पौण्ड्रं दध्मौ महाशङ्खं भीमकर्मा वृकोदरः ॥	Paanchajanyam hrisheekesho devadattam dhananjayah; Paundram dadhmau mahaashankham bheemakarmaa vrikodarah.

Hrishikesha (Krishna) blew his conch Panchajanya, Dhananjaya (Arjuna) blew his conch Devadatta, and Vrikodara (Bhima), achiever of awesome feats, blew his great conch Paundra.

1.16

अनन्तविजयं राजा कुन्तीपुत्रो युधिष्ठिरः । नकुलः सहदेवश्च सुघोषमणिपुष्पकौ ॥	Anantavijayam raajaa kunteeputro yudhishthirah; Nakulah sahadevashcha sughoshamanipushpakau.

The son of Kunti, King Yudhishthira blew his conch Anantavijaya, and Nakula and Sahadeva blew their conches Sughosha and Manipushpaka.

1.17-1.18

काश्यश्च परमेष्वासः शिखण्डी च महारथः । धृष्टद्युम्नो विराटश्च सात्यकिश्चापराजितः ॥ द्रुपदो द्रौपदेयाश्च सर्वशः पृथिवीपते । सौभद्रश्च महाबाहुः शङ्खान्दध्मुः पृथक्पृथक् ॥	Kaashyashcha parameshvaasah shikhandee cha mahaarathah; Dhrishtadyumno viraatashcha saatyakishchaaparaajitah. Drupado draupadeyaashcha sarvashah prithiveepate; Saubhadrashcha mahaabaahuh shankhaan dadhmuh prithak prithak.

The expert archer Kashiraja (King of Kashi), the mighty warrior Shikhandi, Dhrishtadyumna, Virata, the invincible Satyaki, Drupada, the sons of Draupadi and the powerful son of Subhadra (Abhimanyu), O Prithivipate (lord of the earth, referring to Dhritarashtra), all blew their conches.

1.19

स घोषो धार्तराष्ट्राणां हृदयानि व्यदारयत् । नभश्च पृथिवीं चैव तुमुलोऽभ्यनुनादयन् ॥	Sa ghosho dhaartaraashtraanaam hridayaani vyadaarayat; Nabhashcha prithiveem chaiva tumulo vyanunaadayan.

The dreadful noise echoed through heaven and earth and shattered the heart of Duryodhana's army.

	1.20
अथ व्यवस्थितान्दृष्ट्वा धार्तराष्ट्रान् कपिध्वजः । प्रवृत्ते शस्त्रसम्पाते धनुरुद्यम्य पाण्डवः ॥	Atha vyavasthitaan drishtvaa dhaartaraashtraan kapidhvajah; Pravritte shastrasampaate dhanurudyamya paandavah.

Then, observing your son's army ready for combat and sensing that the war would erupt very soon, Pandu's son (Arjuna), stationed in his chariot flying the banner of the monkey god (Lord Hanuman), lifted his bow.

	1.21-1.22
हृषीकेशं तदा वाक्यमिदमाह महीपते । अर्जुन उवाच । सेनयोरुभयोर्मध्ये रथं स्थापय मेऽच्युत ॥ यावदेतान्निरीक्षेऽहं योद्धुकामानवस्थितान् । कैर्मया सह योद्धव्यमस्मिन् रणसमुद्यमे ॥	Hrisheekesham tadaa vaakyamidamaaha maheepate; Arjuna uvaacha: Senayor ubhayormadhye ratham sthaapaya me'chyuta. Yaavad etaan nireekshe'ham yoddhukaamaan avasthitaan; Kair mayaa saha yoddhavyam asmin ranasamudyame.

O Mahipate (Dhritarashtra), Arjuna then spoke these words to Hrishikesha (Krishna). O Achyuta (Krishna), please position my chariot between the two armies so that I may see those warmongers who are assembled here and with whom I must fight.

	1.23
योत्स्यमानानवेक्षेऽहं य एतेऽत्र समागताः । धार्तराष्ट्रस्य दुर्बुद्धेर्युद्धे प्रियचिकीर्षवः ॥	Yotsyamaanaan avekshe'ham ya ete'tra samaagataah; Dhaartaraashtrasya durbuddher yuddhe priyachikeershavah.

Let me also see those assembled here who are willing to fight to appease the wicked son of Dhritarashtra (Duryodhana).

1.24-1.25

सञ्जय उवाच | एवमुक्तो हृषीकेशो गुडाकेशेन भारत | सेनयोरुभयोर्मध्ये स्थापयित्वा रथोत्तमम् ॥ भीष्मद्रोणप्रमुखतः सर्वेषां च महीक्षिताम् | उवाच पार्थ पश्यैतान्समवेतान्कुरूनिति ॥	Sanjaya uvaacha: Evamukto hrisheekesho gudaakeshena bhaarata; Senayor ubhayormadhye sthaapayitvaa rathottamam. Bheeshmadronapramukhatah sarveshaam cha maheekshitaam; Uvaacha paartha pashyaitaan samavetaan kuroon iti.

Sanjaya said: O descendent of Bharata (Dhritarashtra), having thus been requested by Gudakesha (Arjuna), Hrishikesha (Krishna) parked the magnificent chariot between the armies facing Bhishma, Drona and all the other kings. Krishna said to Partha (Arjuna), look at all the Kurus assembled here.

1.26-1.29

तत्रापश्यत्स्थितान्पार्थः पितृनथ पितामहान् | आचार्यान्मातुलान्भ्रातृन्पुत्रान्पौत्रान्सखींस्तथा || श्वशुरान्सुहृदश्चैव सेनयोरुभयोरपि | तान्समीक्ष्य स कौन्तेयः सर्वान्बन्धूनवस्थितान् || कृपया परयाविष्टो विषीदन्निदमब्रवीत् | अर्जुन उवाच | दृष्ट्वेमं स्वजनं कृष्ण युयुत्सुं समुपस्थितम् || सीदन्ति मम गात्राणि मुखं च परिशुष्यति | वेपथुश्च शरीरे मे रोमहर्षश्च जायते ||	Tatraapashyat sthitaan paarthah pitrin atha pitaamahaan; Aachaaryaan maatulaan bhraatrun putraan pautraan sakheemstathaa. Shvashuraan suhridashchaiva senayorubhayorapi; Taan sameekshya sa kaunteyah sarvaan bandhoon avasthitaan. Kripayaa parayaa'vishto visheedannidam abraveet; Arjuna Uvaacha: Drishtvemam swajanam krishna yuyutsum samupasthitam. Seedanti mama gaatraani mukham cha parishushyati; Vepathushcha shareere me romaharshashcha jaayate.

There, Partha (Arjuna) saw in both the armies paternal uncles, grand uncles, teachers, maternal uncles, brothers, cousins, sons, nephews, grandsons, grand nephews, friends, fathers-in-law and also well-wishers. When Kaunteya (Arjuna) saw all his kinsmen, he was overcome with compassion and spoke with sadness. O Krishna, as I see these kinsmen, assembled here, eager for battle, my limbs are giving in and my mouth is drying up. My whole body is trembling and my hairs are standing on end.

1.30

गाण्डीवं स्रंसते हस्तात्त्वक्चैव परिदह्यते | न च शक्नोम्यवस्थातुं भ्रमतीव च मे मनः ||	Gaandeevam sramsate hastaat tvak chaiva paridahyate; Na cha shaknomyavasthaatum bhramateeva cha me manah.

Gandiva (Arjuna's bow) is slipping from my hand and my skin is burning all over. I have no strength to stand and I feel giddy.

1.31

निमित्तानि च पश्यामि विपरीतानि केशव |
न च श्रेयोऽनुपश्यामि हत्वा स्वजनमाहवे ||

Nimittaani cha pashyaami vipareetaani keshava;
Na cha shreyo'nupashyaami hatvaa swajanam aahave.

O Keshava (Krishna), I see bad omens and do not see any good coming from killing our kinsmen in battle.

1.32-1.34

न काङ्क्षे विजयं कृष्ण न च राज्यं सुखानि च |
किं नो राज्येन गोविन्द किं भोगैर्जीवितेन वा ||
येषामर्थे काङ्क्षितं नो राज्यं भोगाः सुखानि च |
त इमेऽवस्थिता युद्धे प्राणांस्त्यक्त्वा धनानि च ||
आचार्याः पितरः पुत्रास्तथैव च पितामहाः |
मातुलाः श्वशुराः पौत्राः श्यालाः सम्बन्धिनस्तथा ||

Na kaangkshe vijayam krishna na cha raajyam sukhaani cha;
Kim no raajyena govinda kim bhogair jeevitena vaa.
Yeshaam arthe kaangkshitam no raajyam bhogaah sukhaani cha;
Ta ime'vasthitaa yuddhe praanaamstyaktvaa dhanaani cha.
Aachaaryaah pitarah putraastathaiva cha pitaamahaah;
Maatulaah shwashuraah pautraah shyaalaah sambandhinas tathaa.

O Krishna, I have no desire for victory or kingdom or pleasure. O Govinda, (Krishna), what good is kingdom or enjoyment or even life? Our teachers, paternal uncles, sons, nephews, grand uncles, maternal uncles, fathers-in-law, grandchildren, grand nephews, brothers-in–law and other relatives, for whose sake we want these enjoyments, are assembled here on this battlefield ready to give up their lives and wealth.

1.35

एतान्न हन्तुमिच्छामि घ्नतोऽपि मधुसूदन । अपि त्रैलोक्यराज्यस्य हेतोः किं नु महीकृते ॥	Etaan na hantum icchaami ghnato'pi madhusoodana; Api trailokya raajyasya hetoh kim nu maheekrite.

O Madhusudana (Krishna), I do not like to kill them though they are intent on killing me, not even to become the ruler of the three worlds, much less for an earthly kingdom.

1.36

निहत्य धार्तराष्ट्रान्नः का प्रीतिः स्याज्जनार्दन । पापमेवाश्रयेदस्मान्हत्वैतानाततायिनः ॥	Nihatya dhaartaraashtraan nah kaa preetih syaaj janaardana; Paapam evaashrayed asmaan hatvaitaan aatataayinah.

What pleasure can there be in killing the sons of Dhritarashtra. We may incur sin if we kill them, even though they are the aggressors.

1.37

तस्मान्नार्हा वयं हन्तुं धार्तराष्ट्रान्स्वबान्धवान् । स्वजनं हि कथं हत्वा सुखिनः स्याम माधव ॥	Tasmaan naarhaa vayam hantum dhaartaraashtraan swabaandhavaan; Swajanam hi katham hatvaa sukhinah syaama maadhava.

O Madhava (Krishna), therefore it is not proper to kill the sons of Dhritarashtra and other kinsmen. How can we be happy after killing our own kinsmen?

1.38-1.39

| यद्यप्येते न पश्यन्ति लोभोपहतचेतसः ।
कुलक्षयकृतं दोषं मित्रद्रोहे च पातकम् ॥
कथं न ज्ञेयमस्माभिः पापादस्मान्निवर्तितुम् ।
कुलक्षयकृतं दोषं प्रपश्यद्भिर्जनार्दन ॥ | Yadyapyete na pashyanti lobhopahatachetasah;
Kulakshayakritam dosham mitradrohe cha paatakam.
Katham na jneyam asmaabhih paapaad asmaan nivartitum;
Kulakshayakritam dosham prapashyadbhir janaardana. |

O Janardana (Krishna), although these men are corrupted by greed and see no harm in destroying families and being treacherous to friends, we clearly see the harm. Why should we not turn away from committing these heinous acts?

1.40

| कुलक्षये प्रणश्यन्ति कुलधर्माः सनातनाः ।
धर्मे नष्टे कुलं कृत्स्नमधर्मोऽभिभवत्युत ॥ | Kulakshaye pranashyanti kuladharmaah sanaatanaah;
Dharme nashte kulam kritsnam adharmo'bhibhavatyuta. |

With the destruction of family, its sacred traditional practices (dharma) will be lost. When dharma is lost, adharma (corrupt practices) takes over.

1.41

| अधर्माभिभवात्कृष्ण प्रदुष्यन्ति कुलस्त्रियः ।
स्त्रीषु दुष्टासु वार्ष्णेय जायते वर्णसङ्करः ॥ | Adharmaabhibhavaat krishna pradushyanti kulastriyah;
Streeshu dushtaasu vaarshneya jaayate varnasankarah. |

With the prevalence of adharma, the women of the family lose their virtue. O Varshneya (Krishna), when women lose their virtue, intermixing of castes will occur.

1.42
सङ्करो नरकायैव कुलघ्नानां कुलस्य च । पतन्ति पितरो ह्येषां लुप्तपिण्डोदकक्रियाः ॥	Sankaro narakaayaiva kulaghnaanaam kulasya cha; Patanti pitaro hyeshaam luptapindodakakriyaah.

The intermixing of castes leads both the killers of the family and the family itself to hell. The spirits of their ancestors are deprived of the ritual offerings of rice and water.

1.43
दोषैरेतैः कुलघ्नानां वर्णसङ्करकारकैः । उत्साद्यन्ते जातिधर्माः कुलधर्माश्च शाश्वताः ॥	Doshair etaih kulaghnaanaam varnasankarakaarakaih; Utsaadyante jaatidharmaah kuladharmaashcha shaashvataah.

The evil acts of those who destroy the family and cause the intermixing of castes lead to the destruction of the eternal dharma of the caste as well as that of the family.

1.44
उत्सन्नकुलधर्माणां मनुष्याणां जनार्दन । नरके नियतं वासो भवतीत्यनुशुश्रुम ॥	Utsannakuladharmaanaam manushyaanaam janaardana; Narake'niyatam vaaso bhavateetyanushushruma.

O Janardana (Krishna), we hear that persons whose family dharma has been ruined dwell in hell indefinitely.

1.45
अहो बत महत्पापं कर्तुं व्यवसिता वयम् । यद्राज्यसुखलोभेन हन्तुं स्वजनमुद्यताः ॥	Aho bata mahat paapam kartum vyavasitaa vayam; Yadraajya sukhalobhena hantum swajanam udyataah.

Alas, driven by the greed of pleasure of a kingdom, we are prepared to commit the heinous act of killing our kinsmen.

1.46

यदि मामप्रतीकारमशस्त्रं शस्त्रपाणयः ।
धार्तराष्ट्रा रणे हन्युस्तन्मे क्षेमतरं भवेत् ॥

Yadi maam aprateekaaram ashastram shastrapaanayah;
Dhaartaraashtraa rane hanyus tanme kshemataram bhavet.

It is all right with me if the sons of Dhritarashtra kill me with their weapons in battle while I am unarmed and unresisting.

1.47

सञ्जय उवाच ।
एवमुक्त्वार्जुनः सङ्ख्ये रथोपस्थ उपाविशत् ।
विसृज्य सशरं चापं शोकसंविग्नमानसः ॥

Sanjaya uvaacha:
Evamuktvaa'rjunah sankhye rathopastha upaavishat;
Visrijya sasharam chaapam shokasamvignamaanasah.

Sanjaya said: Saying this in the battlefield, Arjuna, overwhelmed with grief, dropped his bow and arrow and slumped in the chariot.

ॐ तत्सदिति श्रीमद्भगवद्गीतासूपनिषत्सु ब्रह्मविद्यायां योगशास्त्रे श्रीकृष्णार्जुनसंवादे अर्जुनविषादयोगो नाम प्रथमोऽध्यायः ।

Om Tat Saditi Srimad Bhagavadgeetaasoopanishatsu Brahmavidyaayaam Yogashaastre Sri Krishnaarjunasamvaade Arjunavishaadayogo Naama Prathamo'dhyaayah.

Thus ends the first discourse entitled Arjuna Vishada Yoga in the Upanishad, the divine Bhagavad Gita, the knowledge of Brahman, the scripture on Yoga and the dialogue between Sri Krishna and Arjuna.

Chapter 2
Sankhya Yoga

2.01

सञ्जय उवाच |
तं तथा कृपयाविष्टमश्रुपूर्णाकुलेक्षणम् |
विषीदन्तमिदं वाक्यमुवाच मधुसूदनः ||

Sanjaya uvaacha:
Tam tathaa kripayaavishtam ashrupoornaakulekshanam;
Visheedantam idam vaakyam uvaacha madhusoodanah.

Sanjaya said: Madhusudhana (Krishna) spoke to Arjuna who was overcome by compassion and grief, and whose eyes were filled with tears.

2.02

श्रीभगवानुवाच |
कुतस्त्वा कश्मलमिदं विषमे समुपस्थितम् |
अनार्यजुष्टमस्वर्ग्यमकीर्तिकरमर्जुन ||

Sri Bhagavaan uvaacha:
Kutastvaa kashmalam idam vishame samupasthitam;
Anaaryajushtam aswargyam akeertikaram arjuna.

Bhagavan (Lord Krishna) said: Arjuna, from where did these impure thoughts come to you at this critical time? This is unworthy of a nobleman. It is disgraceful and does not lead to heaven.

2.03

क्लैब्यं मा स्म गमः पार्थ नैतत्त्वय्युपपद्यते । क्षुद्रं हृदयदौर्बल्यं त्यक्त्वोत्तिष्ठ परन्तप ॥	Klaibyam maa sma gamah paartha naitat tvayyupapadyate; Kshudram hridaya daurbalyam tyaktvottishtha parantapa.

Partha (Arjuna), do not be a coward. It does not suit you, parantapa (scorcher of enemies). Shake off this weakness of heart and stand up.

2.04

अर्जुन उवाच । कथं भीष्ममहं सङ्ख्ये द्रोणं च मधुसूदन । इषुभिः प्रतियोत्स्यामि पूजार्हावरिसूदन ॥	Arjuna uvaacha: Katham bheeshmamaham sankhye dronam cha madhusoodana; Ishubhih pratiyotsyaami poojaarhaavarisoodana.

Arjuna said: Madhusudhana (Krishna), How can I shoot arrows at Bhishma and Drona who deserve my reverence?

2.05

गुरूनहत्वा हि महानुभावान् श्रेयो भोक्तुं भैक्ष्यमपीह लोके । हत्वार्थकामांस्तु गुरूनिहैव भुञ्जीय भोगान् रुधिरप्रदिग्धान् ॥	Guroon ahatvaa hi mahaanubhaavaan Shreyo bhoktum bhaikshyam apeeha loke; Hatvaarthakaamaamstu guroon ihaiva Bhunjeeya bhogaan rudhirapradigdhaan.

It is better to live in this world by begging than to kill these honorable elders. Although they have a vested interest in this battle, by killing them I would have to enjoy pleasures soaked in their blood.

2.06

न चैतद्विद्मः कतरन्नो गरीयो यद्वा जयेम यदि वा नो जयेयुः । यानेव हत्वा न जिजीविषामः तेऽवस्थिताः प्रमुखे धार्तराष्ट्राः ॥	Na chaitad vidmah kataran no gareeyo Yadvaa jayema yadi vaa no jayeyuh; Yaan eva hatvaa na jijeevishaamah Te'vasthitaah pramukhe dhaartaraashtraah.

We do not know which of the two is better for us, to conquer them or to be conquered by them. We would not be happy to live after killing the sons of Dhritarashtra who stand before us.

Sankhya Yoga

2.07

कार्पण्यदोषोपहतस्वभावः पृच्छामि त्वां धर्मसम्मूढचेताः । यच्छ्रेयः स्यान्निश्चितं ब्रूहि तन्मे शिष्यस्तेऽहं शाधि मां त्वां प्रपन्नम् ॥	Kaarpanyadoshopahataswabhaavah Pricchaami tvaam dharmasammoodha chetaah; Yacchreyah syaan nishchitam broohi tanme Shishyaste'ham shaadhi maam tvaam prapannam.

I have completely lost my will and am confused about my duty. Please tell me what is the right course of action. I am your student and have taken refuge in you. Please instruct me.

2.08

न हि प्रपश्यामि ममापनुद्याद् यच्छोकमुच्छोषणमिन्द्रियाणाम् । अवाप्य भूमावसपत्नमृद्धं राज्यं सुराणामपि चाधिपत्यम् ॥	Na hi prapashyaami mamaapanudyaad Yacchokam ucchoshanam indriyaanaam; Avaapya bhoomaavasapatnam riddham Raajyam suraanaam api chaadhipatyam.

I do not know what can relieve me of this sorrow that is burning up my senses. Even sovereignty over a rich kingdom on the earth or lordship over the devas (celestial beings) would not accomplish this.

2.09

सञ्जय उवाच । एवमुक्त्वा हृषीकेशं गुडाकेशः परन्तपः । न योत्स्य इति गोविन्दमुक्त्वा तूष्णीं बभूव ह ॥	Sanjaya uvaacha: Evam uktvaa hrisheekesham gudaakeshah parantapah; Na yotsya iti govindam uktvaa tooshneem babhoova ha.

Sanjaya said: Having thus spoken to Hrishikesha (Krishna), Gudakesha (Arjuna) again said to Govinda (Krishna) "na yotsye" (I shall not fight), and became quiet.

2.10

| तमुवाच हृषीकेशः प्रहसन्निव भारत । सेनयोरुभयोर्मध्ये विषीदन्तमिदं वचः ॥ | Tam uvaacha hrisheekeshah prahasanniva bhaarata; Senayor ubhayor madhye visheedantam idam vachah. |

O Bharata (Dhritarashtra), Hrishikesha (Krishna), smiling as it were, then spoke these words to Arjuna who stood in despair in the midst of the two armies.

2.11

| श्रीभगवानुवाच । अशोच्यानन्वशोचस्त्वं प्रज्ञावादांश्च भाषसे । गतासूनगतासूंश्च नानुशोचन्ति पण्डिताः ॥ | Sri Bhagavaan uvaacha: Ashochyaan anvashochastvam prajnaavaadaamshcha bhaashase; Gataasoon agataasoomshcha naanushochanti panditaah. |

Bhagavan (Lord Krishna) said: You are speaking words of wisdom, and yet you are mourning for those who should not be mourned. The wise do not mourn either for the dead or the living.

2.12

| न त्वेवाहं जातु नासं न त्वं नेमे जनाधिपाः । न चैव न भविष्यामः सर्वे वयमतः परम् ॥ | Na tvevaaham jaatu naasam na tvam neme janaadhipaah; Na chaiva na bhavishyaamah sarve vayam atah param. |

There was never a time when these kings or you or I did not exist. There will never be a time when we shall not exist.

2.13

| देहिनोऽस्मिन्यथा देहे कौमारं यौवनं जरा ।
तथा देहान्तरप्राप्तिर्धीरस्तत्र न मुह्यति ॥ | Dehino'smin yathaa dehe kaumaaram yauvanam jaraa;
Tathaa dehaantara praaptir dheeras tatra na muhyati. |

Just as, in this body, the embodied self passes through childhood, youth, and old age, it also passes into another body after death. The wise are not confused about this.

Commentary: A man in his old age knows that he is the same person he was as an adult and as a child, although his physical features and behaviors have changed significantly. When a child becomes an adult, his childhood dies and his adulthood is born. When the adult becomes an old man, a similar death/rebirth happens. When the old man dies, the embodied self gets a new body, and the cycle of birth and death continues until Self-realization occurs. Observing all of this hoopla, the wise man is not perturbed because he knows the Self remains changeless.

2.14

| मात्रास्पर्शास्तु कौन्तेय शीतोष्णसुखदुःखदाः ।
आगमापायिनोऽनित्यास्तांस्तितिक्षस्व भारत ॥ | Maatraasparshaastu kaunteya sheetoshnasukhaduhkhadaah;
Aagamaapaayino'nityaas taamstitikshaswa bhaarata. |

O Kaunteya (Arjuna), when the senses come in contact with the sensory objects, a person feels cold or heat, pleasure or pain. These feelings come and go and are not permanent. O Bharata (Arjuna), endure them.

2.15

| यं हि न व्यथयन्त्येते पुरुषं पुरुषर्षभ ।
समदुःखसुखं धीरं सोऽमृतत्वाय कल्पते ॥ | Yam hi na vyathayantyete purusham purusharshabha;
Samaduhkha sukham dheeram so'mritatvaaya kalpate. |

O best among men (Arjuna), the wise man who is not affected by happiness and sorrow and remains calm in both situations is fit for immortality.

2.16

| नासतो विद्यते भावो नाभावो विद्यते सतः । उभयोरपि दृष्टोऽन्तस्त्वनयोस्तत्त्वदर्शिभिः ॥ | Naasato vidyate bhaavo naabhaavo vidyate satah; Ubhayorapi drishto'ntastvanayos tattvadarshibhih. |

The asat (unreal) does not exist and the sat (real) does not cease to exist. Seers of truth have clearly seen this.

Commentary: *"The asat does not exist"* means that it will not exist later as it does now, and it does not exist now as it did before. The asat changes spontaneously and continuously. *"The sat does not cease to exist"* means that it remains the same forever without undergoing any changes. Sat is the Self (atman) in the asat (body). Seers of truth (tattvadarshi) have clearly distinguished between sat and asat.

2.17

| अविनाशि तु तद्विद्धि येन सर्वमिदं ततम् । विनाशमव्ययस्यास्य न कश्चित्कर्तुमर्हति ॥ | Avinaashi tu tad viddhi yena sarvam idam tatam; Vinaasham avyayasyaasya na kashchit kartum arhati. |

Know that sat, which pervades the whole universe, is indestructible. Nothing can destroy it.

2.18

| अन्तवन्त इमे देहा नित्यस्योक्ताः शरीरिणः । अनाशिनोऽप्रमेयस्य तस्माद्युध्यस्व भारत ॥ | Antavanta ime dehaa nityasyoktaah shareerinah; Anaashino'prameyasya tasmaad yudhyasva bhaarata. |

The physical body, in which the indestructible, immeasurable and eternal sat dwells, is the one that comes to an end. Therefore, Arjuna, you have to fight.

2.19

| य एनं वेत्ति हन्तारं यश्चैनं मन्यते हतम् ।
 उभौ तौ न विजानीतो नायं हन्ति न हन्यते ॥ | Ya enam vetti hantaaram <br> yashchainam manyate hatam;
 Ubhau tau na vijaaneeto naayam <br> hanti na hanyate. |

One who thinks the Self can kill and the other who thinks the Self can be killed are both wrong. The Self neither kills nor gets killed.

2.20

| न जायते म्रियते वा कदाचिन्
 नायं भूत्वा भविता वा न भूयः ।
 अजो नित्यः शाश्वतोऽयं पुराणो
 न हन्यते हन्यमाने शरीरे ॥ | Na jaayate mriyate vaa kadaachin
 Naayam bhootvaa bhavitaa vaa na bhooyah;
 Ajo nityah shaashvato'yam puraano
 Na hanyate hanyamaane shareere. |

The Self has no birth or death at any time. The Self has never manifested, does not manifest, and will not manifest. The Self is unborn, eternal, ever existing and timeless. The Self is not destroyed when the body dies.

2.21

| वेदाविनाशिनं नित्यं य एनमजमव्ययम् ।
 कथं स पुरुषः पार्थ कं घातयति हन्ति कम् ॥ | Vedaavinaashinam nityam ya enam ajam avyayam;
 Katham sa purushah paartha kam ghaatayati hanti kam. |

Partha (Arjuna), if a person knows that the Self is indestructible, eternal, unborn, and immutable, how can that person kill anyone or cause anyone to be killed?

2.22

| वासांसि जीर्णानि यथा विहाय
 नवानि गृह्णाति नरोऽपराणि ।
 तथा शरीराणि विहाय जीर्णा-
 न्यन्यानि संयाति नवानि देही ॥ | Vaasaamsi jeernaani yathaa vihaaya
 Navaani grihnaati naro'paraani;
 Tathaa shareeraani vihaaya jeernaa
 Nyanyaani samyaati navaani dehee. |

Just as a person replaces worn out clothes with new clothes, the embodied self replaces worn out bodies with new bodies.

2.23

| नैनं छिन्दन्ति शस्त्राणि नैनं दहति पावकः ।
न चैनं क्लेदयन्त्यापो न शोषयति मारुतः ॥ | Nainam cchindanti shastraani nainam dahati paavakah;
Na chainam kledayantyaapo na shoshayati maarutah. |

Weapons cannot cut the Self, fire cannot burn it, water cannot drench it and the wind cannot dry it up.

2.24

| अच्छेद्योऽयमदाह्योऽयमक्लेद्योऽशोष्य एव च ।
नित्यः सर्वगतः स्थाणुरचलोऽयं सनातनः ॥ | Acchedyo'yam adaahyo'yam akledyo'shoshya eva cha;
Nityah sarvagatah sthaanur achalo'yam sanaatanah. |

It is indivisible, incombustible, insoluble, and non-dryable. It is everlasting, all pervading, unchangeable, immovable, and primeval.

2.25

| अव्यक्तोऽयमचिन्त्योऽयमविकार्योऽयमुच्यते ।
तस्मादेवं विदित्वैनं नानुशोचितुमर्हसि ॥ | Avyakto'yam achintyo'yam avikaaryo'yam uchyate;
Tasmaad evam viditvainam naanushochitum arhasi. |

The Self is unmanifest, incomprehensible and unalterable. Knowing this, you need not grieve.

2.26-2.27

| अथ चैनं नित्यजातं नित्यं वा मन्यसे मृतम् ।
तथापि त्वं महाबाहो नैवं शोचितुमर्हसि ॥
जातस्य हि ध्रुवो मृत्युर्ध्रुवं जन्म मृतस्य च ।
तस्मादपरिहार्येऽर्थे न त्वं शोचितुमर्हसि ॥ | Atha chainam nityajaatam nityam vaa manyase mritam;
Tathaapi tvam mahaabaaho naivam shochitum arhasi.
Jaatasya hi dhruvo mrityur dhruvam janma mritasya cha;
Tasmaad aparihaarye'rthe na tvam shochitum arhasi. |

Arjuna, even if you think the Self is subject to birth and death, you should not grieve for it. Death is certain for those who have been born and rebirth is certain for those who have died. You should not mourn over the unavoidable.

2.28

अव्यक्तादीनि भूतानि व्यक्तमध्यानि भारत । अव्यक्तनिधनान्येव तत्र का परिदेवना ॥	Avyaktaadeeni bhootaani vyaktamadhyaani bhaarata; Avyakta nidhanaanyeva tatra kaa paridevanaa.

All beings are unmanifest before birth and after death. They only manifest between birth and death. So what is there to grieve about?

2.29

आश्चर्यवत्पश्यति कश्चिदेन- माश्चर्यवद्वदति तथैव चान्यः । आश्चर्यवच्चैनमन्यः शृणोति श्रुत्वाप्येनं वेद न चैव कश्चित् ॥	Aashcharyavat pashyati kashchid enam Aashcharyavad vadati tathaiva chaanyah; Aashcharyavacchainam anyah shrinoti Shrutvaapyenam veda na chaiva kashchit.

Some look upon the Self with awe. Others describe it as awesome. Still others hear about it and think it is awesome. Regardless of how they learn about it, no one knows it.

Commentary: Self-realization requires proper and relentless efforts over several births. However, some people with limited spiritual knowledge try to visualize the Self and think of it as a wonder. Others talk about it as being wonderful. Yet others hear about it as wonderful. Visualizing, wondering, talking and hearing alone will not unravel the mystery of the Self.

2.30

देही नित्यमवध्योऽयं देहे सर्वस्य भारत । तस्मात्सर्वाणि भूतानि न त्वं शोचितुमर्हसि ॥	Dehee nityam avadhyo'yam dehe sarvasya bhaarata; Tasmaat sarvaani bhootaani na tvam shochitum arhasi.

Arjuna, the Self that exists in the bodies of all beings cannot be killed. Therefore, you need not grieve for any being.

2.31

स्वधर्ममपि चावेक्ष्य न विकम्पितुमर्हसि । धर्म्याद्धि युद्धाच्छ्रेयोऽन्यत्क्षत्रियस्य न विद्यते ॥	Swadharmam api chaavekshya na vikampitum arhasi; Dharmyaaddhi yuddhaacchreyo'nyat kshatriyasya na vidyate.

Considering your Kshatriya (warrior) dharma, you should not waver. For a Kshatriya, there is nothing more sacred than fighting a just war.

2.32

यदृच्छया चोपपन्नं स्वर्गद्वारमपावृतम् । सुखिनः क्षत्रियाः पार्थ लभन्ते युद्धमीदृशम् ॥	Yadricchayaa chopapannam swargadvaaram apaavritam; Sukhinah kshatriyaah paartha labhante yuddham eedrisham.

Arjuna, happy are the Kshatriyas who get the opportunity to fight in a just and unsolicited war. Such a war opens the doors of heaven.

2.33

अथ चेत्त्वमिमं धर्म्यं संग्रामं न करिष्यसि । ततः स्वधर्मं कीर्तिं च हित्वा पापमवाप्स्यसि ॥	Atha chettvam imam dharmyam samgraamam na karishyasi; Tatah swadharmam keertim cha hitvaa paapam avaapsyasi.

If you do not fight in this just war, then you will incur sin for forsaking your dharma and your honor.

2.34

अकीर्तिं चापि भूतानि कथयिष्यन्ति तेऽव्ययाम् । सम्भावितस्य चाकीर्तिर्मरणादतिरिच्यते ॥	Akeertim chaapi bhootaani kathayishyanti te'vyayaam; Sambhaavitasya chaakeertir maranaad atirichyate.

Then people will talk about your disgraceful behavior forever. For an honorable person, dishonor is worse than death.

2.35

भयाद्रणादुपरतं मंस्यन्ते त्वां महारथाः। येषां च त्वं बहुमतो भूत्वा यास्यसि लाघवम् ॥	Bhayaad ranaad uparatam mamsyante tvaam mahaarathaah; Yeshaam cha tvam bahumato bhootvaa yaasyasi laaghavam.

The great warriors who respect you highly now will assume that you ran away from the battlefield out of fear and will disrespect you.

2.36

अवाच्यवादांश्च बहून्वदिष्यन्ति तवाहिताः। निन्दन्तस्तव सामर्थ्यं ततो दुःखतरं नु किम् ॥	Avaachyavaadaamshcha bahoon vadishyanti tavaahitaah; Nindantastava saamarthyam tato duhkhataram nu kim.

Your enemies will say nasty words about you and mock your bravery. What can be more miserable than this?

2.37

हतो वा प्राप्स्यसि स्वर्गं जित्वा वा भोक्ष्यसे महीम्। तस्मादुत्तिष्ठ कौन्तेय युद्धाय कृतनिश्चयः ॥	Hato vaa praapsyasi swargam jitvaa vaa bhokshyase maheem; Tasmaad uttishtha kaunteya yuddhaaya kritanishchayah.

If you are killed in the battle, you will go to heaven. If you win, you will enjoy the kingdom on earth. Therefore arise, Arjuna, and resolve to fight.

2.38

सुखदुःखे समे कृत्वा लाभालाभौ जयाजयौ। ततो युद्धाय युज्यस्व नैवं पापमवाप्स्यसि ॥	Sukhaduhkhe same kritvaa laabhaalaabhau jayaajayau; Tato yuddhaaya yujyasva naivam paapamavaapsyasi.

Consider alike pleasure and pain, gain and loss, victory and defeat and engage in the battle. This way, you will not incur any sin.

2.39

एषा तेऽभिहिता साङ्ख्ये बुद्धिर्योगे त्विमां शृणु । बुद्ध्या युक्तो यया पार्थ कर्मबन्धं प्रहास्यसि ॥	Eshaa te'bhihitaa saankhye buddhir yoge tvimaam shrinu; Buddhyaa yukto yayaa paartha karma bandham prahaasyasi.

So far, I have explained to you the wisdom of Sankhya Yoga. Arjuna, now listen to the wisdom of Karma Yoga. Practicing this, you will cut the bonds of karma (action).

2.40

नेहाभिक्रमनाशोऽस्ति प्रत्यवायो न विद्यते । स्वल्पमप्यस्य धर्मस्य त्रायते महतो भयात् ॥	Nehaabhikramanaasho'sti pratyavaayo na vidyate; Swalpam apyasya dharmasya traayate mahato bhayaat.

On this path, no effort is wasted and there are no adverse effects. Even a little practice of this discipline frees one from great fears.

2.41

व्यवसायात्मिका बुद्धिरेकेह कुरुनन्दन । बहुशाखा ह्यनन्ताश्च बुद्धयोऽव्यवसायिनाम् ॥	Vyavasaayaatmikaa buddhir ekeha kurunandana; Bahushaakhaa hyanantaashcha buddhayo'vyavasaayinaam.

O Kurunandana (Arjuna), the properly cultivated intellect is steady, resolute and focused on a single goal. Whereas the uncultivated intellect is irresolute and wanders in many directions.

2.42

यामिमां पुष्पितां वाचं प्रवदन्त्यविपश्चितः । वेदवादरताः पार्थ नान्यदस्तीति वादिनः ॥	Yaam imaam pushpitaam vaacham pravadantyavipashchitah; Vedavaadarataah paartha naanyad asteeti vaadinah.

Arjuna, there are those with superficial knowledge of the Vedas who enjoy debating its various doctrines in flowery words. They say that there is nothing else in the Vedas besides rituals prescribed to obtain enjoyment.

2.43

| कामात्मानः स्वर्गपरा जन्मकर्मफलप्रदाम् ।
क्रियाविशेषबहुलां भोगैश्वर्यगतिं प्रति ॥ | Kaamaatmaanah swargaparaa janmakarmaphalapradaam;
Kriyaavisheshabahulaam bhogaishwaryagatim prati. |

They are driven by a desire for pleasure and consider the attainment of heaven as the supreme goal of life. They perform Vedic rituals for the sake of pleasure, prosperity and a better rebirth.

2.44

| भोगैश्वर्यप्रसक्तानां तयापहृतचेतसाम् ।
व्यवसायात्मिका बुद्धिः समाधौ न विधीयते ॥ | Bhogaishwarya prasaktaanaam tayaapahritachetasaam;
Vyavasaayaatmikaa buddhih samaadhau na vidheeyate. |

Those whose bewildered mind chases pleasure and power cannot acquire resolute intellect.

2.45

| त्रैगुण्यविषया वेदा निस्त्रैगुण्यो भवार्जुन ।
निर्द्वन्द्वो नित्यसत्त्वस्थो निर्योगक्षेम आत्मवान् ॥ | Traigunyavishayaa vedaa nistraigunyo bhavaarjuna;
Nirdvandvo nityasatvastho niryogakshema aatmavaan. |

The Vedas deal with the three gunas (qualities) of nature (sattva, rajas and tamas). Free yourself of these and also from the dualities of nature. Do not be concerned with acquiring and hoarding material possessions. Stay focused on the Atma (Self).

2.46

| यावानर्थ उदपाने सर्वतः सम्प्लुतोदके ।
तावान्सर्वेषु वेदेषु ब्राह्मणस्य विजानतः ॥ | Yaavaanartha udapaane sarvatah samplutodake;
Taavaan sarveshu vedeshu braahmanasya vijaanatah. |

What purpose does a well serve when pure water is abundantly available? For an enlightened brahmin, the Vedas are as superfluous as that well.

2.47

| कर्मण्येवाधिकारस्ते मा फलेषु कदाचन ।
मा कर्मफलहेतुर्भूर्मा ते सङ्गोऽस्त्वकर्मणि ॥ | Karmanyevaadhikaaraste maa phaleshu kadaachana;
Maa karmaphalahetur bhoor maa te sango'stvakarmani. |

Your right is only to perform your duty, never to the fruits thereof. Let not your motivation for action be the fruits of your action. Also you should not think of avoiding action.

Commentary: This verse may shock a lot of people. One may think, how can anybody ask me to work for free? Am I that stupid to be exploited? The common mindset is that even before starting work, one wants to know what is in it for him. The desire for fruit is generally the motivation for work. Work done this way may produce the desired fruits and deliver momentary happiness. But along with the desired fruits, some unwanted results are also produced. These karmic consequences are initially unmanifest, but later become manifest.

    Furthermore, focusing more on the fruits may distract a person from doing the work efficiently, leading to the loss of productivity. Does this mean that one should not work, to avoid the karmic consequences? The answer is no. Even inaction can have karmic consequences. Here, Lord Krishna is saying to remain focused on the task and do your duty for the benefit of all. Receive whatever share of the fruits that come to you as a gift of God. This way, you will not incur any karmic consequences.

2.48

| योगस्थः कुरु कर्माणि सङ्गं त्यक्त्वा धनञ्जय ।
सिद्ध्यसिद्ध्योः समो भूत्वा समत्वं योग उच्यते ॥ | Yogasthah kuru karmaani sangam tyaktvaa dhananjaya;
Siddhyasiddhyoh samo bhootvaa samatvam yoga uchyate. |

Arjuna, perform your duties with a steady mind without attachment to results. Remain calm in success and failure. This calmness of the mind is called yoga.

2.49

| दूरेण ह्यवरं कर्म बुद्धियोगाद्धनञ्जय ।
 बुद्धौ शरणमन्विच्छ कृपणाः फलहेतवः ॥ | Doorena hyavaram karma buddhiyogaad dhananjaya; Buddhau sharanamanviccha kripanaah phalahetavah. |

Arjuna, ordinary action is far inferior to buddhi yoga. Seek refuge in buddhi. Those who crave for the fruits of their actions are misers.

Commentary: Ordinary action (performed with attachment to fruits) is far inferior to buddhi yoga. Buddhi yoga is a path for liberation that involves performing actions with calmness of mind, without any anxiety about success or failure, and without any selfish motives or attachment to the fruits of action. Lord Krishna urges Arjuna to follow buddhi yoga. He calls those who crave for the fruits of their actions misers. People can become so obsessed with the fruits of actions that they end up hoarding them instead of enjoying them. This makes them utterly miserable

2.50

| बुद्धियुक्तो जहातीह उभे सुकृतदुष्कृते ।
 तस्माद्योगाय युज्यस्व योगः कर्मसु कौशलम् ॥ | Buddhiyukto jahaateeha ubhe sukrita dushkrite; Tasmaad yogaaya yujyasva yogah karmasu kaushalam. |

One who has developed tranquility can rid himself of the karmic effects of good and evil deeds in this life itself. Therefore practice buddhi yoga which is skillful action.

2.51

| कर्मजं बुद्धियुक्ता हि फलं त्यक्त्वा मनीषिणः ।
 जन्मबन्धविनिर्मुक्ताः पदं गच्छन्त्यनामयम् ॥ | Karmajam buddhiyuktaa hi phalam tyaktvaa maneeshinah; Janmabandha vinirmuktaah padam gacchantyanaamayam. |

One who has equanimity of mind and abandons the desire for the fruits of his actions is freed from the bondage of birth and attains a state of no suffering.

2.52

यदा ते मोहकलिलं बुद्धिर्व्यतितरिष्यति । तदा गन्तासि निर्वेदं श्रोतव्यस्य श्रुतस्य च ॥	Yadaa te mohakalilam buddhir vyatitarishyati; Tadaa gantaasi nirvedam shrotavyasya shrutasya cha.

When your intellect overcomes the delusion, then you will be indifferent to what you hear and what you have heard about this world.

Commentary: We live constantly dwelling on our past and imagining our future. We practically live in a world of fantasy. When we develop the intellect that can discriminate between real and unreal, our fantasy world disappears. We drop all of our baggage from the past, along with our daydreams of the future.

2.53

श्रुतिविप्रतिपन्ना ते यदा स्थास्यति निश्चला । समाधावचला बुद्धिस्तदा योगमवाप्स्यसि ॥	Shrutivipratipannaa te yadaa sthaasyati nishchalaa; Samaadhaavachalaa buddhistadaa yogam avaapsyasi.

When your intellect overcomes the confusion created by listening to conflicting opinions, becomes steady, and remains firm in meditation, then you will achieve Self-realization.

2.54

अर्जुन उवाच । स्थितप्रज्ञस्य का भाषा समाधिस्थस्य केशव । स्थितधीः किं प्रभाषेत किमासीत व्रजेत किम् ॥	Arjuna uvaacha: Sthitaprajnasya kaa bhaashaa samaadhisthasya keshava; Sthitadheeh kim prabhaasheta kimaaseeta vrajeta kim.

Arjuna said: O Keshava (Krishna), what are the characteristics of the person who is established in wisdom and is aware of the Self? How does he talk, sit and move?

2.55

श्रीभगवानुवाच । प्रजहाति यदा कामान्सर्वान्पार्थ मनोगतान् । आत्मन्येवात्मना तुष्टः स्थितप्रज्ञस्तदोच्यते ॥	Sri Bhagavaan uvaacha: Prajahaati yadaa kaamaan sarvaan paartha manogataan; Aatmanyevaatmanaa tushtah sthitaprajnastadochyate.

Bhagavan (Lord Krishna) said: When a person has erased all desires from his mind, is aware of his Self and content with his Self, he is called a person of steady wisdom.

2.56

दुःखेष्वनुद्विग्नमनाः सुखेषु विगतस्पृहः । वीतरागभयक्रोधः स्थितधीर्मुनिरुच्यते ॥	Duhkheshwanudvignamanaah sukheshu vigataasprihah; Veetaraagabhayakrodhah sthitadheer munir uchyate.

A person who is not agitated by sorrow, who does not crave for pleasure and who is free from lust, fear and anger, is called a sage of steady wisdom.

2.57

यः सर्वत्रानभिस्नेहस्तत्तत्प्राप्य शुभाशुभम् । नाभिनन्दति न द्वेष्टि तस्य प्रज्ञा प्रतिष्ठिता ॥	Yah sarvatraanabhisnehas tattat praapya shubhaashubham; Naabhinandati na dveshti tasya prajnaa pratishthitaa.

One who is detached from everything, who neither rejoices nor resents pleasant or unpleasant experiences, is considered to have a stable mind.

2.58

यदा संहरते चायं कूर्मोऽङ्गानीव सर्वशः । इन्द्रियाणीन्द्रियार्थेभ्यस्तस्य प्रज्ञा प्रतिष्ठिता ॥	Yadaa samharate chaayam kurmo'ngaaneeva sarvashah; Indriyaaneendriyaarthebhyas tasya prajnaa pratishthitaa.

He who can withdraw his senses from the sensory objects, just like a turtle withdraws its limbs into its shell, has a stable mind.

	2.59
विषया विनिवर्तन्ते निराहारस्य देहिनः । रसवर्जं रसोऽप्यस्य परं दृष्ट्वा निवर्तते ॥	Vishayaa vinivartante niraahaarasya dehinah; Rasavarjam raso'pyasya param drishtvaa nivartate.

The sensory objects are not noticed by a person who has given up sensual pleasure, but the taste of enjoyment still lingers on. Even this taste dissipates in the person who has realized the Self.

	2.60
यततो ह्यपि कौन्तेय पुरुषस्य विपश्चितः । इन्द्रियाणि प्रमाथीनि हरन्ति प्रसभं मनः ॥	Yatato hyapi kaunteya purushasya vipashchitah; Indriyaani pramaatheeni haranti prasabham manah.

Kaunteya (Arjuna), even the mind of a person who is practicing self-control may be swept away by the unruly senses.

	2.61
तानि सर्वाणि संयम्य युक्त आसीत मत्परः । वशे हि यस्येन्द्रियाणि तस्य प्रज्ञा प्रतिष्ठिता ॥	Taani sarvaani samyamya yukta aaseeta matparah; Vashe hi yasyendriyaani tasya prajnaa pratishthitaa.

Having controlled the senses, one should meditate upon Me. One whose senses are under complete control is known to be a person of steady wisdom.

	2.62
ध्यायतो विषयान्पुंसः सङ्गस्तेषूपजायते । सङ्गात्सञ्जायते कामः कामात्क्रोधोऽभिजायते ॥	Dhyaayato vishayaan pumsah sangas teshupajaayate; Sangaat sanjaayate kaamah kaamaat krodho'bhijaayate.

When a person thinks of objects of pleasure, attachment for them develops. Attachment breeds desire. Unsatisfied desires produce anger.

2.63

| क्रोधाद्भवति सम्मोहः सम्मोहात्स्मृतिविभ्रमः । स्मृतिभ्रंशाद् बुद्धिनाशो बुद्धिनाशात्प्रणश्यति ॥ | Krodhaad bhavati sammohah sammohaat smriti vibhramah; Smritibhramshaad buddhinaasho buddhinaashaat pranashyati. |

Anger breeds delusion, delusion affects memory, loss of memory results in impaired reasoning and impaired reasoning causes total destruction.

2.64

| रागद्वेषवियुक्तैस्तु विषयानिन्द्रियैश्चरन् । आत्मवश्यैर्विधेयात्मा प्रसादमधिगच्छति ॥ | Raagadvesha viyuktaistu vishayaanindriyaishcharan; Aatmavashyair vidheyaatmaa prasaadamadhigacchati. |

A self-controlled person who can move around sensory objects without being attracted to them or repelled by them attains tranquility.

2.65

| प्रसादे सर्वदुःखानां हानिरस्योपजायते । प्रसन्नचेतसो ह्याशु बुद्धिः पर्यवतिष्ठते ॥ | Prasaade sarvaduhkhaanaam haanir asyopajaayate; Prasannachetaso hyaashu buddhih paryavatishthate. |

There is no sorrow for a person who has attained tranquility. Such a person is firmly established in wisdom.

2.66

| नास्ति बुद्धिरयुक्तस्य न चायुक्तस्य भावना । न चाभावयतः शान्तिरशान्तस्य कुतः सुखम् ॥ | Naasti buddhir ayuktasya na chaayuktasya bhaavanaa; Na chaabhaavayatah shaantir ashaantasya kutah sukham. |

A person with an unsteady mind cannot meditate. Without meditation, there is no peace of mind. Without peace of mind, how can there be happiness?

2.67

इन्द्रियाणां हि चरतां यन्मनोऽनुविधीयते । तदस्य हरति प्रज्ञां वायुर्नावमिवाम्भसि ।।	Indriyaanaam hi charataam yanmano'nuvidheeyate; Tadasya harati prajnaam vaayur naavam ivaambhasi.

If one allows the mind to follow the fickle senses, they sweep away one's power of reasoning just like a storm blows away a ship off its course on the sea.

2.68

तस्माद्यस्य महाबाहो निगृहीतानि सर्वशः । इन्द्रियाणीन्द्रियार्थेभ्यस्तस्य प्रज्ञा प्रतिष्ठिता ।।	Tasmaad yasya mahaabaaho nigriheetaani sarvashah; Indriyaaneendriyaarthebhyas tasya prajnaa pratishthitaa.

Arjuna, the person whose senses are completely detached from sensory objects is a person of steady wisdom.

2.69

या निशा सर्वभूतानां तस्यां जागर्ति संयमी । यस्यां जाग्रति भूतानि सा निशा पश्यतो मुनेः ।।	Yaanishaa sarvabhootaanaam tasyaam jaagarti samyamee; Yasyaam jaagrati bhootaani saa nishaa pashyato muneh.

When it is night for all other beings, the self-controlled one is awake. When all beings are awake, it is night for the seer.

Commentary: Common people are in the darkness (night) of spiritual ignorance, but a self-controlled individual is awake to the presence of the Self. On the other hand, common people are awake to the sensory objects around them, but a seer is indifferent to the sensory objects as if they are in the darkness of night.

2.70

आपूर्यमाणमचलप्रतिष्ठं समुद्रमापः प्रविशन्ति यद्वत् । तद्वत्कामा यं प्रविशन्ति सर्वे स शान्तिमाप्नोति न कामकामी ॥	Aapooryamaanam achalapratishtham Samudram aapah pravishanti yadvat; Tadvat kaamaa yam pravishanti sarve Sa shaantim aapnoti na kaamakaami.

Rivers flow into the ocean from all sides, but the ocean remains unaffected. Similarly, when a person with steady intellect is exposed to sensory objects, desire for them is not produced in him. Such a person attains peace. A person who seeks to gratify the senses does not attain peace.

2.71

विहाय कामान्यः सर्वान्पुमांश्चरति निःस्पृहः । निर्ममो निरहङ्कारः स शान्तिमधिगच्छति ॥	Vihaaya kaamaan yah sarvaan pumaamshcharati nihsprihah; Nirmamo nirahankaarah sa shaantim adhigacchati.

One who gives up all desires and moves without attachment, selfishness and ego attains peace.

2.72

एषा ब्राह्मी स्थितिः पार्थ नैनां प्राप्य विमुह्यति । स्थित्वास्यामन्तकालेऽपि ब्रह्मनिर्वाणमृच्छति ॥	Eshaa braahmee sthitih paartha nainaam praapya vimuhyati; Sthitvaasyaamantakaale'pi brahmanirvaanamricchati.

Arjuna, this is known as the state of Brahmi (complete oneness with God). One who has attained this state is never again deluded. One who remains in this state at the moment of death attains Brahma Nirvana (everlasting joy).

ॐ तत्सदिति श्रीमद्भगवद्गीतासूपनिषत्सु ब्रह्मविद्यायां योगशास्त्रे श्रीकृष्णार्जुनसंवादे साङ्ख्ययोगो नाम द्वितीयोऽध्यायः	Om Tat Saditi Srimad Bhagavadgeetaasoopanishatsu Brahmavidyaayaam Yogashaastre Sri Krishnaarjunasamvaade Saankhyayogo Naama Dvitiyo'dhyaayah

Thus ends the second discourse entitled Sankhya Yoga in the Upanishad, the divine Bhagavad Gita, the knowledge of Brahman, the scripture on Yoga and the dialogue between Sri Krishna and Arjuna.

Chapter 3
Karma Yoga

3.01

अर्जुन उवाच |
ज्यायसी चेत्कर्मणस्ते मता बुद्धिर्जनार्दन |
तत्किं कर्मणि घोरे मां नियोजयसि केशव ||

Arjuna uvaacha
Jyaayasee chet karmanaste mataa buddhir janaardana;
Tat kim karmani ghore maam niyojayasi keshava.

Arjuna said: Janardana (Krishna), if you consider that the path of knowledge is superior to the path of action, then why do you prompt me to do this horrific deed?

3.02

व्यामिश्रेणेव वाक्येन बुद्धिं मोहयसीव मे |
तदेकं वद निश्चित्य येन श्रेयोऽहमाप्नुयाम् ||

Vyaamishreneva vaakyena buddhim mohayaseeva me;
Tadekam vada nishchitya yena shreyo'ham aapnuyaam.

You confuse me by your ambivalent statements. Please tell me, unequivocally, how I may achieve the highest good.

3.03

श्रीभगवानुवाच |
लोकेऽस्मिन् द्विविधा निष्ठा पुरा प्रोक्ता मयानघ |
ज्ञानयोगेन साङ्ख्यानां कर्मयोगेन योगिनाम् ||

Loke'smin dvividhaa nishthaa puraa proktaa mayaanagha;
Jnaanayogena saankhyaanaam karmayogena yoginaam.

Bhagavan (Lord Krishna) said: In the past, I taught two paths of spiritual discipline: the yoga of knowledge for the contemplative person and the yoga of action for the active person.

3.04

न कर्मणामनारम्भान्नैष्कर्म्यं पुरुषोऽश्नुते |
न च संन्यसनादेव सिद्धिं समधिगच्छति ||

Na karmanaam anaarambhaan naishkarmyam purusho'shnute;
Na cha sannyasanaad eva siddhim samadhigacchati.

One does not become free from the bondage of karma by giving up action completely. No one becomes perfect just by abandoning action.

3.05

न हि कश्चित्क्षणमपि जातु तिष्ठत्यकर्मकृत् |
कार्यते ह्यवशः कर्म सर्वः प्रकृतिजैर्गुणैः ||

Na hi kashchit kshanamapi jaatu tishthatyakarmakrit;
Kaaryate hyavashah karma sarvah prakritijair gunaih.

No one can remain actionless even for a moment. Every creature is compelled to be active by the gunas (qualities) of nature.

3.06

कर्मेन्द्रियाणि संयम्य य आस्ते मनसा स्मरन् |
इन्द्रियार्थान्विमूढात्मा मिथ्याचारः स उच्यते ||

Karmendriyaani samyamya ya aaste manasaa smaran;
Indriyaarthaan vimoodhaatmaa mithyaachaarah sa uchyate.

One who outwardly suppresses the organs of action but constantly thinks of sensuous objects is a deluded person and is called pretentious.

Karma Yoga

3.07

| यस्त्विन्द्रियाणि मनसा नियम्यारभतेऽर्जुन ।
 कर्मेन्द्रियैः कर्मयोगमसक्तः स विशिष्यते ॥ | Yastvindriyaani manasaa niyamyaarabhate'rjuna;
 Karmendriyaih karmayogam asaktah sa vishishyate. |

Arjuna, one who disciplines his senses by the mind and engages his action organs without selfish motive, is superior.

3.08

| नियतं कुरु कर्म त्वं कर्म ज्यायो ह्यकर्मणः ।
 शरीरयात्रापि च ते न प्रसिद्ध्येदकर्मणः ॥ | Niyatam kuru karma tvam karma jyaayo hyakarmanah;
 Shareerayaatraapi cha te na prasiddhyed akarmanah. |

Perform your duty. Action is better than inaction. Without action, even the maintenance of the physical body is impossible.

3.09

यज्ञार्थात्कर्मणोऽन्यत्र लोकोऽयं कर्मबन्धनः । तदर्थं कर्म कौन्तेय मुक्तसङ्गः समाचर ॥	Yajnaarthaat karmano'nyatra loko'yam karmabandhanah; Tadartham karma kaunteya muktasangah samaachara.

All the work not done in the spirit of yajna (sacrifice) traps the person in bondage. Therefore, Arjuna, work without selfish motive in the spirit of sacrifice.

Commentary: Yajna (pronounced YUG-nya) traditionally is a vedic ritual performed to please the devas so that they may fulfill specific desires. For example, a yajna can be performed to obtain rain or progeny. Yajna involves the pouring of oblations (ghee, wooden chips, rice, grains, etc.) into Agni (sacred fire), along with the chanting of appropriate vedic hymns. Food items specially prepared for the occasion are offered to the devas by throwing a small portion into Agni. The leftover food, called prasada (gift of God), is distributed to the assembled guests.

The concept of yajna is very broad, and is not restricted to the description given above. Yajna literally means sacrifice. Any selfless action performed for the benefit of all can be considered yajna. In this verse, Lord Krishna says that only selfless actions performed for the benefit of all do not produce karmic results. He urges Arjuna to perform action free from attachment.

3.10

सहयज्ञाः प्रजाः सृष्ट्वा पुरोवाच प्रजापतिः । अनेन प्रसविष्यध्वमेष वोऽस्त्विष्टकामधुक् ॥	Sahayajnaah prajaah srishtvaa purovaacha prajaapatih; Anena prasavishyadhvam esha vo'stvishtakaamadhuk.

At the beginning of creation, the creator Brahma created the human beings along with the spirit of yajna. Brahma said: through this (yajna) you shall prosper; may this fulfill all your wishes.

Commentary: Yajna is an integral part of creation. It is through yajna that the harmonious world order is maintained. Brahma says that yajna shall fulfill all human desires.

Karma Yoga

3.11

देवान्भावयतानेन ते देवा भावयन्तु वः । परस्परं भावयन्तः श्रेयः परमवाप्स्यथ ॥	Devaan bhaavayataanena te devaa bhaavayantu vah; Parasparam bhaavayantah shreyah param avaapsyatha.

Nourish the devas through sacrifice and let them nourish you. Thus nourishing each other, you will obtain the maximum benefit.

3.12

इष्टान्भोगान्हि वो देवा दास्यन्ते यज्ञभाविताः । तैर्दत्तानप्रदायैभ्यो यो भुङ्क्ते स्तेन एव सः ॥	Ishtaan bhogaan hi vo devaa daasyante yajnabhaavitaah; Tair dattaan apradaayaibhyo yo bhungkte stena eva sah.

Nourished by your yajna, the devas will grant your desires. Those who enjoy their gifts and give back nothing are crooks.

Commentary for 3.11-3.12: Yajna is the connection between human beings and the devas who represent the forces of nature. Through yajna rituals, we provide the devas with what they need, and the devas reciprocate by providing what we need. Universal harmony is maintained by this interdependence. Lord Krishna makes the point "Parasparam bhaavayantah shreyah param avaapsyatha" – by caring for each other, we all reap the maximum benefit.

One may wonder whether yajna rituals actually do any good. We may not understand them by applying the methods of science. However, a common sense approach sheds enough light. Consider the yajna ritual as a symbolic act of thanksgiving to the devas for nature's bounty, which cultivates in us a mindset to preserve and replenish nature.

We have to follow the yajna principle of give and take to maintain a harmonious world. This is not the mercenary type of give and take. We have to enjoy the act of giving and receive whatever we get with happiness. Lord Krishna emphasizes the yajna of selfless giving. A person who cares only to suck everything he can from the system without consideration for putting anything back into the system is branded as a crook.

3.13

| यज्ञशिष्टाशिनः सन्तो मुच्यन्ते सर्वकिल्बिषैः । भुञ्जते ते त्वघं पापा ये पचन्त्यात्मकारणात् ॥ | Yajnashishtaashinah santo muchyante sarva kilbishaih; Bhunjate te tvagham paapaa ye pachantyaatma kaaranaat. |

The pious who eat the leftovers (prasada) of a yajna are freed from all sins. The impious who cook only for themselves accrue sins.

Commentary: The pious people who perform selfless actions as a worship of God and share the fruits of their actions with others do not suffer the karmic consequences of their actions. On the other hand, those who perform actions with selfish motives and enjoy the fruits of their actions without sharing with others suffer the karmic consequences of their actions. Here, food is symbolic of the fruits of actions.

3.14

| अन्नाद्भवन्ति भूतानि पर्जन्यादन्नसम्भवः । यज्ञाद्भवति पर्जन्यो यज्ञः कर्मसमुद्भवः ॥ | Annaad bhavanti bhootaani parjanyaad anna sambhavah; Yajnaad bhavati parjanyo yajnah karma samudbhavah. |

Food sustains all living beings. Food is grown because of rain. The rainfall is caused by yajna. Yajna is the result of action.

3.15

| कर्म ब्रह्मोद्भवं विद्धि ब्रह्माक्षरसमुद्भवम् । तस्मात्सर्वगतं ब्रह्म नित्यं यज्ञे प्रतिष्ठितम् ॥ | Karma brahmodbhavam viddhi brahmaakshara samudbhavam; Tasmaat sarvagatam brahma nityam yajne pratishthitam. |

The prescribed actions for yajna come from the Vedas and the Vedas are revealed by the indestructible (God). Hence the all-pervading God is always present in the sacrifice.

3.16

| एवं प्रवर्तितं चक्रं नानुवर्तयतीह यः ।
 अघायुरिन्द्रियारामो मोघं पार्थ स जीवति ।। | Evam pravartitam chakram naanuvartayateeha yah;
 Aghaayur indriyaaraamo mogham paartha sa jeevati. |

Arjuna, one who does not perform his duties to keep the wheel of creation in motion and indulges in sensual pleasure, that sinful person is a freeloader.

3.17

| यस्त्वात्मरतिरेव स्यादात्मतृप्तश्च मानवः ।
 आत्मन्येव च सन्तुष्टस्तस्य कार्यं न विद्यते ।। | Yastvaatmaratir eva syaad aatmatriptashcha maanavah;
 Aatmanyeva cha santushtas tasya kaaryam na vidyate. |

One who has realized the Self and experiences the joy of Self-realization is at peace. He has no more duty to perform.

3.18

| नैव तस्य कृतेनार्थो नाकृतेनेह कश्चन ।
 न चास्य सर्वभूतेषु कश्चिदर्थव्यपाश्रयः ।। | Naiva tasya kritenaartho naakriteneha kashchana;
 Na chaasya sarvabhooteshu kashchidartha vyapaashrayah. |

Such a person has no reason to perform or abstain from any action. He does not depend on anything or anyone outside.

3.19

| तस्मादसक्तः सततं कार्यं कर्म समाचर ।
 असक्तो ह्याचरन्कर्म परमाप्नोति पूरुषः ।। | Tasmaad asaktah satatam kaaryam karma samaachara;
 Asakto hyaacharan karma param aapnoti poorushah. |

Always perform your duty without attachment. One reaches the supreme goal of life by performing action without attachment.

3.20

| कर्मणैव हि संसिद्धिमास्थिता जनकादयः ।
लोकसंग्रहमेवापि सम्पश्यन्कर्तुमर्हसि ॥ | Karmanaiva hi samsiddhim aasthitaa janakaadayah;
Lokasangraham evaapi sampashyan kartum arhasi. |

Janaka and others attained perfection by doing their duties without attachment. Always do your duty considering the benefit of the world.

Commentary: Janaka was a famous king of the Videha Kingdom whose capital was Mithila. He was the father of Sita (Sri Rama's wife). He was an ideal ruler as well as a great scholar of scriptures. He was well known as a Rajarshi because he was both a raja (king) and a rishi (sage). He attained perfection even while performing worldly actions. His actions were always free from selfish motives, performed for Lokasangraha (universal benefit). Lord Krishna urges Arjuna to follow the path of Janaka.

3.21

| यद्यदाचरति श्रेष्ठस्तत्तदेवेतरो जनः ।
स यत्प्रमाणं कुरुते लोकस्तदनुवर्तते ॥ | Yadyad aacharati shreshthas tattadevetaro janah;
Sa yat pramaanam kurute lokas tad anuvartate. |

Whatever great persons do, common people are likely to do. Whatever standards they establish, the masses are likely to follow.

3.22

| न मे पार्थास्ति कर्तव्यं त्रिषु लोकेषु किञ्चन ।
नानवाप्तमवाप्तव्यं वर्त एव च कर्मणि ॥ | Na me paarthaasti kartavyam trishu lokeshu kinchana;
Naanavaaptam avaaptavyam varta eva cha karmani. |

Arjuna, I have no duty in all the three worlds. There is nothing I have to attain that has not yet been attained. Even so, I engage in action.

3.23

यदि ह्यहं न वर्तेयं जातु कर्मण्यतन्द्रितः । मम वर्त्मानुवर्तन्ते मनुष्याः पार्थ सर्वशः ॥	Yadi hyaham na varteyam jaatu karmanyatandritah; Mama vartmaanuvartante manushyaah paartha sarvashah.

Arjuna, if I were to stop working, human beings would follow my example.

3.24

उत्सीदेयुरिमे लोका न कुर्यां कर्म चेदहम् । सङ्करस्य च कर्ता स्यामुपहन्यामिमाः प्रजाः ॥	Utseedeyur ime lokaa na kuryaam karma ched aham; Sankarasya cha kartaa syaam upahanyaam imaah prajaah.

If I stopped working, the universe would come to an end. I would be the cause of chaos and destruction of all the people.

Commentary for 3.21-3.24: Lord Krishna points out the importance of role models in the world. He directly addresses Arjuna's fear in 1.40 of society breaking down by illustrating how *inaction* can lead to destruction. He conveys to Arjuna how Arjuna can best serve society by performing his duty.

3.25

सक्ताः कर्मण्यविद्वांसो यथा कुर्वन्ति भारत । कुर्याद्विद्वांस्तथासक्तश्चिकीर्षुर्लोकसंग्रहम् ॥	Saktaah karmanyavidvaamso yathaa kurvanti bhaarata; Kuryaad vidvaam stathaa saktash chikeershur lokasangraham.

Arjuna, though the unwise work for selfish gains, the wise work without selfish motive for the benefit of society.

3.26

न बुद्धिभेदं जनयेदज्ञानां कर्मसङ्गिनाम् । जोषयेत्सर्वकर्माणि विद्वान्युक्तः समाचरन् ॥	Na buddhibhedam janayed ajnaanaam karmasanginaam; Joshayet sarva karmaani vidvaan yuktah samaacharan.

The wise should not confuse the ignorant who work with selfish motives. The wise should allow them to act with attachment while themselves performing all work in the spirit of yoga.

Commentary: The idea here is not to keep the ignorant as ignorant forever. On the contrary, it is to help them grow spiritually at a pace that they can handle. The ignorant person only works if he gains something for himself. Otherwise he bums around. Since working to enjoy the fruits of action is better than inaction due to laziness, it is better not to discourage people from working for rewards. Giving them an abstract lecture on the spiritual benefits of detached action may confuse them at best, and reinforce their laziness at worst. At this stage, they do not fully grasp the virtue of selfless service. The wise should serve as role models of detached service, which will, in due course of time, inspire the ignorant to emulate them. This is a practical approach to bring about gradual transformation.

3.27

प्रकृतेः क्रियमाणानि गुणैः कर्माणि सर्वशः । अहङ्कारविमूढात्मा कर्ताहमिति मन्यते ॥	Prakriteh kriyamaanaani gunaih karmaani sarvashah; Ahamkaaravimoodhaatmaa kartaaham iti manyate.

All actions are done by the gunas of prakriti (primordial nature). The person who is deluded by ego thinks he is the doer.

3.28

तत्त्ववित्तु महाबाहो गुणकर्मविभागयोः । गुणा गुणेषु वर्तन्त इति मत्वा न सज्जते ॥	Tattvavittu mahaabaaho gunakarma vibhaagayoh; Gunaa guneshu vartanta iti matvaa na sajjate.

Arjuna, those who truly understand the gunas and their respective functions realize that the gunas urge the senses. They can move around the gunas of sensory objects without developing attachment.

3.29

प्रकृतेर्गुणसम्मूढाः सज्जन्ते गुणकर्मसु । तान्कृत्स्नविदो मन्दान्कृत्स्नविन्न विचालयेत् ॥	Prakriter gunasammoodhaah sajjante gunakarmasu; Taan akritsnavido mandaan kritsnavin na vichaalayet.

Those who are deluded by the gunas of prakriti are attached to the actions of those gunas. The person of perfect knowledge should not disturb these ignorant people.

3.30

मयि सर्वाणि कर्माणि संन्यस्याध्यात्मचेतसा । निराशीर्निर्ममो भूत्वा युध्यस्व विगतज्वरः ॥	Mayi sarvaani karmaani sannyasyaadhyaatma chetasaa; Niraasheer nirmamo bhootvaa yudhyasva vigatajwarah.

Offering all your actions to Me, absorbed in the Self, without any expectations, free from the feelings of ownership and devoid of mental anguish, engage in the battle.

3.31

ये मे मतमिदं नित्यमनुतिष्ठन्ति मानवाः । श्रद्धावन्तोऽनसूयन्तो मुच्यन्ते तेऽपि कर्मभिः ॥	Ye me matam idam nityam anutishthanti maanavaah; Shraddhaavanto'nasooyanto muchyante te'pi karmabhih.

Those who follow my doctrines regularly with full faith and without envy are freed from the bondage of Karma.

3.32

ये त्वेतदभ्यसूयन्तो नानुतिष्ठन्ति मे मतम् । सर्वज्ञानविमूढांस्तान्विद्धि नष्टानचेतसः ॥	Ye tvetad abhyasooyanto naanutishthanti me matam; Sarvajnaanavimoodhaam staan viddhi nashtaan achetasah.

Consider those who regard my doctrines with scorn and who, as a result, fail to follow them diligently, as being totally ignorant, confused and lost.

3.33

सदृशं चेष्टते स्वस्याः प्रकृतेर्ज्ञानवानपि । प्रकृतिं यान्ति भूतानि निग्रहः किं करिष्यति ॥	Sadrisham cheshtate swasyaah prakriter jnaanavaan api; Prakritim yaanti bhootaani nigrahah kim karishyati.

Even a wise person acts according to his own nature. All living beings behave according to their nature. What good can repression do?

3.34

| इन्द्रियस्येन्द्रियस्यार्थे रागद्वेषौ व्यवस्थितौ ।
 तयोर्न वशमागच्छेत्तौ ह्यस्य परिपन्थिनौ ॥ | Indriyasyendriyasyaarthe raagadveshau vyavasthitau; Tayor na vasham aagacchet tau hyasya paripanthinau. |

Feelings of attraction and repulsion start with the senses in relation to their objects. One should not be fixated on them because they are two main obstacles in the path of Self-realization.

Commentary for 3.33-3.34: Our inborn nature strongly shapes our desires and behavioral tendencies. Even the wise are not immune to this karmic relationship. If we act impulsively on our desires, that can be dangerous. Alternatively, if we feel a desire that we dislike, we can repress it. But what good does repression do? Repressed desires end up manifesting in a variety of unhealthy forms over which we have no control. It would seem that we are damned if we do and damned if we don't.

Lord Krishna provides an answer: develop awareness into the nature of our desires, so that we are not ruled by them. He explains that the attraction between the senses and the sense objects is due to the interaction between our gunas and the gunas of the sense objects. Once we become aware of this interaction, we can take steps to guard against negative karmic consequences. These steps are outlined throughout the Bhagavad Gita.

3.35

श्रेयान्स्वधर्मो विगुणः परधर्मात्स्वनुष्ठितात् ।
स्वधर्मे निधनं श्रेयः परधर्मो भयावहः ॥

Shreyaan svadharmo vigunah paradharmaat svanushthitaat;
Svadharme nidhanam shreyah paradharmo bhayaavahah.

It is better to do one's own dharma (duty), though not glamorous, than doing another's dharma well. It is better to die doing one's own dharma because doing another's dharma is dangerous.

Commentary: The word *dharma* comes from *dhri* which means to support. Dharma represents duties human beings have to perform in order to maintain harmony in the world. Some of these duties are common to all, but others are specific to individuals. Based on our prarabdha karma (karmic response from previous lives), we are born with a unique blend of gunas (sattva, rajas and tamas) and into different social circumstances. Our gunas play a significant role in determining our personality. Birth can be considered both as a missed opportunity to attain liberation in our previous life, and as a fresh opportunity to attain liberation in our current life. The path of liberation lies in harnessing the special blend of gunas we have inherited to perform tasks as acts of worship for the benefit of all. This is what it means to follow svadharma (personal dharma).

In the performance of svadharma, nature is aligned with us. The task becomes easy, enjoyable and productive. There is no conflict among what we are capable of doing, what we want to do, and what we are actually doing. Our mind and body work together peacefully. As we follow svadharma, our spiritual awareness becomes stronger, opening up new possibilities for our svadharma to evolve over time.

At the same time, we should not abandon our dharma for *another's* dharma. Our fickle mind can easily get distracted by the idea that someone else's work is more glamorous. The tendency is to jump ship, just like some cows who see the other side of the fence as greener. They go through the thorny fence and get bloodied up in the process, only to discover that it was just an illusion.

The essence of this verse is that through svadharma, we serve society best as well as make the most spiritual progress.

Karma Yoga

3.36

अर्जुन उवाच । अथ केन प्रयुक्तोऽयं पापं चरति पूरुषः । अनिच्छन्नपि वार्ष्णेय बलादिव नियोजितः ॥	Arjuna uvaacha: Atha kena prayukto'yam paapam charati poorushah; Anicchann api vaarshneya balaad iva niyojitah.

Arjuna said: O Krishna, what motivates a person to commit sin even against his will, as though driven by force?

3.37

श्रीभगवानुवाच । काम एष क्रोध एष रजोगुणसमुद्भवः । महाशनो महापाप्मा विद्ध्येनमिह वैरिणम् ॥	Sri Bhagavaan uvaacha: Kaama esha krodha esha rajoguna samudbhavah; Mahaashano mahaapaapmaa viddhyenam iha vairinam.

Bhagavan (Lord Krishna) said: It is lust and anger, products of rajoguna. Lust is insatiable and leads to anger when unfulfilled. It is the worst enemy.

3.38

धूमेनाव्रियते वह्निर्यथादर्शो मलेन च । यथोल्बेनावृतो गर्भस्तथा तेनेदमावृतम् ॥	Dhoomenaavriyate vahnir yathaadarsho malena cha; Yatholbenaavrito garbhas tathaa tenedam aavritam.

Just as the fire is covered by smoke, the mirror by dust, and the embryo by the membrane, so the intellect is obscured by passion.

3.39

आवृतं ज्ञानमेतेन ज्ञानिनो नित्यवैरिणा । कामरूपेण कौन्तेय दुष्पूरेणानलेन च ॥	Aavritam jnaanam etena jnaanino nityavairinaa; Kaamaroopena kaunteya dushpoorenaanalena cha.

Arjuna, the intellect is obscured by the insatiable fire of desire which is the eternal enemy of even the wise.

3.40

| इन्द्रियाणि मनो बुद्धिरस्याधिष्ठानमुच्यते ।
एतैर्विमोहयत्येष ज्ञानमावृत्य देहिनम् ॥ | Indriyaani mano buddhir asyaadhishthaanam uchyate; Etair vimohayatyesha jnaanam aavritya dehinam. |

The senses, the mind and the intellect are said to be the dwelling place of desire. Through these, desire obscures real knowledge and deludes the embodied self.

3.41

| तस्मात्त्वमिन्द्रियाण्यादौ नियम्य भरतर्षभ ।
पाप्मानं प्रजहि ह्येनं ज्ञानविज्ञाननाशनम् ॥ | Tasmaat tvam indriyaanyaadau niyamya bharatarshabha; Paapmaanam prajahi hyenam jnaana vijnaana naashanam. |

Therefore Arjuna, first restrain the senses and then vanquish this enemy desire, which destroys knowledge and wisdom.

3.42

| इन्द्रियाणि पराण्याहुरिन्द्रियेभ्यः परं मनः ।
मनसस्तु परा बुद्धिर्यो बुद्धेः परतस्तु सः ॥ | Indriyaani paraanyaahur indriyebhyah param manah; Manasastu paraa buddhir yo buddheh paratastu sah. |

It is said that the senses are superior to the sensory objects, the mind is superior to the senses, the intellect is superior to the mind and superior to the intellect is the Self.

3.43

| एवं बुद्धेः परं बुद्ध्वा संस्तभ्यात्मानमात्मना ।
जहि शत्रुं महाबाहो कामरूपं दुरासदम् ॥ | Evam buddheh param buddhvaa samstabhyaatmaanam aatmanaa; Jahi shatrum mahaabaaho kaamaroopam duraasadam. |

Realizing that which is higher than the intellect (the Self), conquer this formidable enemy, desire.

ॐ तत्सदिति श्रीमद्भगवद्गीतासूपनिषत्सु ब्रह्मविद्यायां योगशास्त्रे श्रीकृष्णार्जुनसंवादे कर्मयोगो नाम तृतीयोऽध्यायः	Om Tat Saditi Srimad Bhagavadgeetaasoopanishatsu Brahmavidyaayaam Yogashaastre Sri Krishnaarjunasamvaade Karmayogo Naama Tritiyo'dhyaayah

Thus ends the third discourse entitled *Karma Yoga* in the Upanishad, the divine Bhagavad Gita, the knowledge of Brahman, the scripture on Yoga and the dialogue between Sri Krishna and Arjuna.

Chapter 4
Jnana Yoga

4.01

| श्रीभगवानुवाच \|
 इमं विवस्वते योगं प्रोक्तवानहमव्ययम् \|
 विवस्वान्मनवे प्राह मनुरिक्ष्वाकवेऽब्रवीत् \|\| | Sri Bhagavaan uvaacha:
 Imam vivasvate yogam proktavaan aham avyayam;
 Vivasvaan manave praaha manur ikshvaakave'braveet. |

Bhagavan (Lord Krishna) said: I revealed this eternal yoga to Vivasvat (Sun God). Vivasvat imparted it to his son Manu, and Manu taught it to his son Ikshvaku (first King of the Solar Dynasty and ancestor of Sri Rama).

4.02

| एवं परम्पराप्राप्तमिमं राजर्षयो विदुः \|
 स कालेनेह महता योगो नष्टः परन्तप \|\| | Evam paramparaa praaptam imam raajarshayo viduh;
 Sa kaaleneha mahataa yogo nashtah parantapa. |

Handed down this way in regular succession, the saintly kings knew it, but over time, Arjuna, it got lost.

4.03

स एवायं मया तेऽद्य योगः प्रोक्तः पुरातनः । भक्तोऽसि मे सखा चेति रहस्यं ह्येतदुत्तमम् ॥	Sa evaayam mayaa te'dya yogah proktah puraatanah; Bhakto'si me sakhaa cheti rahasyam hyetad uttamam.

This ancient yoga is a supreme mystery. I have explained this to you today because you are my devotee and friend.

Commentary: As we read the Bhagavad Gita, it is important to keep in mind that Krishna moves fluidly through different roles in the conversational dialogue. At times he communicates as Brahman; at times as a personal God; and at times as a human being who is a friend and mentor to Arjuna. This helps us to understand the context for verses like 9.29 where he states that he has no friend or foe, and verses 12.13-12.20 where he mentions how his devotees are dear to him.

4.04

अर्जुन उवाच । अपरं भवतो जन्म परं जन्म विवस्वतः । कथमेतद्विजानीयां त्वमादौ प्रोक्तवानिति ॥	Arjuna uvaacha: Aparam bhavato janma param janma vivasvatah; Katham etadvijaaneeyaam tvam aadau proktavaan iti.

Arjuna said: You were born a long time after Vivasvat. How am I to understand that you taught this yoga to him in the beginning?

4.05

श्रीभगवानुवाच । बहूनि मे व्यतीतानि जन्मानि तव चार्जुन । तान्यहं वेद सर्वाणि न त्वं वेत्थ परन्तप ॥	Sri Bhagavaan uvaacha: Bahooni me vyateetaani janmaani tava chaarjuna; Taanyaham veda sarvaani na tvam vettha parantapa.

Bhagavan said: I have been born a number of times and so have you, Arjuna. I remember them all, but you do not.

4.06

अजोऽपि सन्नव्ययात्मा भूतानामीश्वरोऽपि सन् । प्रकृतिं स्वामधिष्ठाय सम्भवाम्यात्ममायया ॥	Ajo'pi sannavyayaatmaa bhootaanaam eeshwaro'pi san; Prakritim swaam adhishthaaya sambhavaamyaatmamaayayaa.

Although unborn, eternal and the supreme Lord of all beings, I manifest by controlling my prakriti through my yoga-maya.

4.07

यदा यदा हि धर्मस्य ग्लानिर्भवति भारत । अभ्युत्थानमधर्मस्य तदात्मानं सृजाम्यहम् ॥	Yadaa yadaa hi dharmasya glaanir bhavati bhaarata; Abhyutthaanam adharmasya tadaatmaanam srijaamyaham.

Whenever Dharma deteriorates and Adharma breaks out, I manifest.

4.08

परित्राणाय साधूनां विनाशाय च दुष्कृताम् । धर्मसंस्थापनार्थाय सम्भवामि युगे युगे ॥	Paritraanaaya saadhoonaam vinaashaaya cha dushkritaam; Dharma samsthaapanaarthaaya sambhavaami yuge yuge.

To protect the pious, to punish the wicked, and to reestablish Dharma, I appear in every yuga (age).

4.09

जन्म कर्म च मे दिव्यमेवं यो वेत्ति तत्त्वतः । त्यक्त्वा देहं पुनर्जन्म नैति मामेति सोऽर्जुन ॥	Janma karma cha me divyam evam yo vetti tattvatah; Tyaktva deham punarjanma naiti maameti so'rjuna.

One who truly understands my divine appearance and activities is not reborn after death, but attains Me.

4.10

वीतरागभयक्रोधा मन्मया मामुपाश्रिताः । बहवो ज्ञानतपसा पूता मद्भावमागताः ॥	Veetaraagabhayakrodhaa manmayaa maam upaashritaah; Bahavo jnaana tapasaa pootaa madbhaavam aagataah.

Freed from attachment, fear and anger, completely immersed in Me, taking shelter in Me and purified by spiritual knowledge, many have realized Me.

4.11

ये यथा मां प्रपद्यन्ते तांस्तथैव भजाम्यहम् । मम वर्त्मानुवर्तन्ते मनुष्याः पार्थ सर्वशः ॥	Ye yathaa maam prapadyante taamstathaiva bhajaamyaham; Mama vartmaanuvartante manushyaah paartha sarvashah.

In whatever manner people worship Me, I appropriately reward them. All paths people follow reach Me in the end.

Commentary: Lord Krishna says that he is accessible to all beings. Wherever worship is done and in whatever form worship is done, it will reach Him. God appears in a form that matches the worshiper's state of mind. If a devotee thinks of God fondly as a child, He engages him as a child. If a devotee thinks of God as a friend, He will treat him like a friend. God satisfies the aspirations of his devotees appropriately.

4.12

काङ्क्षन्तः कर्मणां सिद्धिं यजन्त इह देवताः । क्षिप्रं हि मानुषे लोके सिद्धिर्भवति कर्मजा ॥	Kaangkshantah karmanaam siddhim yajanta iha devataah; Kshipram hi maanushe loke siddhir bhavati karmajaa.

In this world, people who desire their actions to bear fruit worship devas. In the mortal world, fruitive actions deliver results quickly.

4.13

चातुर्वर्ण्यं मया सृष्टं गुणकर्मविभागशः । तस्य कर्तारमपि मां विद्ध्यकर्तारमव्ययम् ॥	Chaaturvarnyam mayaa srishtam gunakarma vibhaagashah; Tasya kartaaram api maam viddhyakartaaram avyayam.

I created the order of the four varnas (types) of people based on the different gunas and karma. Although I am the founder of the order, you should understand that I am still the eternal non-doer.

4.14

न मां कर्माणि लिम्पन्ति न मे कर्मफले स्पृहा । इति मां योऽभिजानाति कर्मभिर्न स बध्यते ॥	Na maam karmaani limpanti na me karmaphale sprihaa; Iti maam yo'bhijaanaati karmabhir na sa badhyate.

Karma (action) does not bind Me because I have no attachment for its fruits. One who understands Me as such is not bound by his karma.

4.15

एवं ज्ञात्वा कृतं कर्म पूर्वैरपि मुमुक्षुभिः । कुरु कर्मैव तस्मात्त्वं पूर्वैः पूर्वतरं कृतम् ॥	Evam jnaatvaa kritam karma poorvair api mumukshubhih; Kuru karmaiva tasmaat tvam poorvaih poorvataram kritam.

Knowing this truth, the ancient seekers of liberation performed action. Therefore, you do the same.

4.16

किं कर्म किमकर्मेति कवयोऽप्यत्र मोहिताः । तत्ते कर्म प्रवक्ष्यामि यज्ज्ञात्वा मोक्ष्यसेऽशुभात् ॥	Kim karma kim akarmeti kavayo'pyatra mohitaah; Tat te karma pravakshyaami yajjnaatvaa mokshyase'shubhaat.

What is action and what is inaction? Even the wise are confused on this issue. I will explain to you what action is. Knowing this, you will be freed from misfortune.

4.17

| कर्मणो ह्यपि बोद्धव्यं बोद्धव्यं च विकर्मणः ।
अकर्मणश्च बोद्धव्यं गहना कर्मणो गतिः ॥ | Karmano hyapi boddhavyam boddhavyam cha vikarmanah;
Akarmanashcha boddhavyam gahanaa karmano gatih. |

You should know the nature of action, forbidden action, and inaction. The true nature of action is very difficult to comprehend.

4.18

| कर्मण्यकर्म यः पश्येदकर्मणि च कर्म यः ।
स बुद्धिमान्मनुष्येषु स युक्तः कृत्स्नकर्मकृत् ॥ | Karmanyakarma yah pashyed akarmani cha karma yah;
Sa buddhimaan manushyeshu sa yuktah kritsnakarmakrit. |

One who sees inaction in action and action in inaction is a wise person. He is a yogi although he performs all kinds of actions.

Commentary: The common understanding is that all actions (karma) produce karmic consequences and inaction (akarma, renunciation of action) does not have any karmic consequences. This is a misconception and yogis see through it. When an action is performed as an act of worship without attachment to fruits and ego, it does not have any karmic retribution. This is inaction in action. When action is renounced with ulterior motives, it has karmic consequences. This is action in inaction.

4.19

| यस्य सर्वे समारम्भाः कामसङ्कल्पवर्जिताः ।
ज्ञानाग्निदग्धकर्माणं तमाहुः पण्डितं बुधाः ॥ | Yasya sarve samaarambhaah kaamasankalpa varjitaah;
Jnaanaagni dagdhakarmaanam tam aahuh panditam budhaah. |

The person whose endeavors are free from attachment to the results, and whose desires have been destroyed in the fire of spiritual knowledge, is called a sage by the wise.

	4.20
त्यक्त्वा कर्मफलासङ्गं नित्यतृप्तो निराश्रयः । कर्मण्यभिप्रवृत्तोऽपि नैव किञ्चित्करोति सः ॥	Tyaktvaa karmaphalaasangam nityatripto niraashrayah; Karmanyabhipravritto'pi naiva kinchit karoti sah.

He who has relinquished all attachment to the results of his actions, who is always content and self sufficient though engaged in action, is doing nothing at all (karmically).

	4.21
निराशीर्यतचित्तात्मा त्यक्तसर्वपरिग्रहः । शारीरं केवलं कर्म कुर्वन्नाप्नोति किल्बिषम् ॥	Niraasheer yatachittaatmaa tyaktasarvaparigrahah; Shaareeram kevalam karma kurvannaapnoti kilbisham.

One who is without any attachments, who has mind and body under control, who has no sense of any possession though engaged in physical action, does not suffer from karmic consequences.

	4.22
यदृच्छालाभसन्तुष्टो द्वन्द्वातीतो विमत्सरः । समः सिद्धावसिद्धौ च कृत्वापि न निबध्यते ॥	Yadricchaalaabhasantushto dvandvaateeto vimatsarah; Samah siddhaavasiddhau cha kritvaapi na nibadhyate.

One who is content with whatever happens on its own accord, who has transcended dualities such as longing and aversion, who is free from envy, and who treats alike success and failure, is not bound by action even when he is engaged in action.

	4.23
गतसङ्गस्य मुक्तस्य ज्ञानावस्थितचेतसः । यज्ञायाचरतः कर्म समग्रं प्रविलीयते ॥	Gatasangasya muktasya jnaanaavasthitachetasah; Yajnaayaacharatah karma samagram pravileeyate.

There are no karmic retributions for actions performed by a liberated person who has no attachment, whose mind is established in the Self, and who works in the spirit of sacrifice.

4.24

| ब्रह्मार्पणं ब्रह्म हविर्ब्रह्माग्नौ ब्रह्मणा हुतम् | Brahmaarpanam brahmahavirbrahmaagnau brahmanaa hutam; |
| ब्रह्मैव तेन गन्तव्यं ब्रह्मकर्मसमाधिना || | Brahmaiva tena gantavyam brahmakarmasamaadhinaa. |

The act of offering is Brahman. The oblation is Brahman. The person making the oblation is Brahman. The sacrificial fire is Brahman. One who meditates on Brahman in action at all times attains Brahman.

4.25

| दैवमेवापरे यज्ञं योगिनः पर्युपासते | | Daivam evaapare yajnam yoginah paryupaasate; |
| ब्रह्माग्रावपरे यज्ञं यज्ञेनैवोपजुह्वति || | Brahmaagnaavapare yajnam yajnenaivopajuhvati. |

Some yogis worship devas through sacrifice, while others offer the ego as sacrifice in the fire of Brahman.

4.26

| श्रोत्रादीनीन्द्रियाण्यन्ये संयमाग्निषु जुह्वति | | Shrotraadeeneendriyaanyanye samyamaagnishu juhvati; |
| शब्दादीन्विषयानन्य इन्द्रियाग्निषु जुह्वति || | Shabdaadeen vishayaananya indriyaagnishu juhvati. |

Some use self-control as a means to discipline the senses (like hearing). Others use the senses as a means to focus only on pure sensory objects.

4.27

| सर्वाणीन्द्रियकर्माणि प्राणकर्माणि चापरे | | Sarvaaneendriya karmaani praanakarmaani chaapare; |
| आत्मसंयमयोगाग्नौ जुह्वति ज्ञानदीपिते || | Aatmasamyamayogaagnau juhvati jnaanadeepite. |

Others offer all actions of the senses and the life breath in the yoga of self control, illuminated by wisdom.

4.28

| द्रव्ययज्ञास्तपोयज्ञा योगयज्ञास्तथापरे ।
 स्वाध्यायज्ञानयज्ञाश्च यतयः संशितव्रताः ॥ | Dravyayajnaas tapoyajnaa yogayajnaastathaapare;
 Swaadhyaayajnaana yajnaashcha yatayah samshitavrataah. |

Some offer as sacrifice their wealth, or austerity, or yoga practices. Others of disciplined mind take strict vows and offer their study of the scriptures.

4.29

| अपाने जुह्वति प्राणं प्राणेऽपानं तथापरे ।
 प्राणापानगती रुद्ध्वा प्राणायामपरायणाः ॥ | Apaane juhvati praanam praane'paanam tathaa'pare;
 Praanaapaana gatee ruddhvaa praanaayaamaparaayanaah. |

Some who practice breath control offer the incoming breath to the outgoing and the outgoing breath to the incoming. After controlling the movements of the incoming and outgoing breath, they are focused upon the control of the whole breath.

4.30

| अपरे नियताहाराः प्राणान्प्राणेषु जुह्वति ।
 सर्वेऽप्येते यज्ञविदो यज्ञक्षपितकल्मषाः ॥ | Apare niyataahaaraah praanaan praaneshu juhvati;
 Sarve'pyete yajnavido yajnakshapita kalmashaah. |

Others control their diet and offer life-breaths into life-breaths. All these people are knowledgeable in yajna, and their sins are destroyed by yajna.

4.31

| यज्ञशिष्टामृतभुजो यान्ति ब्रह्म सनातनम् ।
 नायं लोकोऽस्त्ययज्ञस्य कुतोऽन्यः कुरुसत्तम ॥ | Yajnashishtaamritabhujo yaanti brahma sanaatanam;
 Naayam loko'styayajnasya kuto'nyah kurusattama. |

Those who eat the nectar-like sacred food (prasada) left over from a yajna attain the eternal Brahman. The person who does not perform any sacrifice is not happy even in this world, Arjuna; how can he be happy in the next?

4.32

एवं बहुविधा यज्ञा वितता ब्रह्मणो मुखे । कर्मजान्विद्धि तान्सर्वानेवं ज्ञात्वा विमोक्ष्यसे ॥	Evam bahuvidhaa yajnaa vitataa brahmano mukhe; Karmajaan viddhi taan sarvaan evam jnaatvaa vimokshyase.

All these different kinds of yajna have been described in the Vedas. All of them are born of action. Knowing them, you shall be liberated.

4.33

श्रेयान्द्रव्यमयाद्यज्ञाज्ज्ञानयज्ञः परन्तप । सर्वं कर्माखिलं पार्थ ज्ञाने परिसमाप्यते ॥	Shreyaan dravyamayaadyajnaaj jnaanayajnah parantapa; Sarvam karmaakhilam paartha jnaane parisamaapyate.

Arjuna, the offering of knowledge is superior to the offering of material. However, all actions that do not bind ultimately become knowledge.

4.34

तद्विद्धि प्रणिपातेन परिप्रश्नेन सेवया । उपदेक्ष्यन्ति ते ज्ञानं ज्ञानिनस्तत्त्वदर्शिनः ॥	Tadviddhi pranipaatena pariprashnena sevayaa; Upadekshyanti te jnaanam jnaaninas tattvadarshinah.

Acquire this knowledge from an enlightened person by serving him with humility and devotion. Inquire of him sincerely and he will guide you to obtain this knowledge.

4.35

यज्ज्ञात्वा न पुनर्मोहमेवं यास्यसि पाण्डव । येन भूतान्यशेषेण द्रक्ष्यस्यात्मन्यथो मयि ॥	Yajjnaatvaa na punarmoham evam yaasyasi paandava; Yena bhootaanyasheshena drakshyasyaatmanyatho mayi.

Arjuna, when you have learned this, you will never again be deluded. This knowledge will enable you to see all beings in yourself and yourself in Me.

4.36

| अपि चेदसि पापेभ्यः सर्वेभ्यः पापकृत्तमः ।
सर्वं ज्ञानप्लवेनैव वृजिनं सन्तरिष्यसि ॥ | Api chedasi paapebhyah sarvebhyah paapakrittamah;
Sarvam jnaanaplavenaiva vrijinam santarishyasi. |

Even if you are the worst of all sinners, you shall sail through the ocean of sins by the ship of wisdom.

4.37

| यथैधांसि समिद्धोऽग्निर्भस्मसात्कुरुतेऽर्जुन ।
ज्ञानाग्निः सर्वकर्माणि भस्मसात्कुरुते तथा ॥ | Yathaidhaamsi samiddho'gnir bhasmasaat kurute'rjuna;
Jnaanaagnih sarvakarmaani bhasmasaat kurute tathaa. |

Arjuna, as the blazing fire burns firewood to ashes, the fire of knowledge destroys all karma.

4.38

| न हि ज्ञानेन सदृशं पवित्रमिह विद्यते ।
तत्स्वयं योगसंसिद्धः कालेनात्मनि विन्दति ॥ | Na hi jnaanena sadrisham pavitram iha vidyate;
Tat swayam yogasamsiddhah kaalenaatmani vindati. |

There is nothing in this world that can purify like spiritual knowledge. One who practices karma yoga attains this knowledge in due course of time.

4.39

| श्रद्धावाँल्लभते ज्ञानं तत्परः संयतेन्द्रियः ।
ज्ञानं लब्ध्वा परां शान्तिमचिरेणाधिगच्छति ॥ | Shraddhaavaan labhate jnaanam tatparah samyatendriyah;
Jnaanam labdhvaa paraam shaantim achirenaadhigacchati. |

One who has faith, who is resolute, and who has total self-control gains this knowledge. Having attained this knowledge, one attains eternal peace.

4.40

अज्ञश्चाश्रद्दधानश्च संशयात्मा विनश्यति । नायं लोकोऽस्ति न परो न सुखं संशयात्मनः ॥	Ajnashchaashraddhadhaanashcha samshayaatmaa vinashyati; Naayam loko'sti na paro na sukham samshayaatmanah.

The ignorant, the faithless and the skeptics waste their lives. They will not be happy in this world or the next.

4.41

योगसंन्यस्तकर्माणं ज्ञानसञ्छिन्नसंशयम् । आत्मवन्तं न कर्माणि निबध्नन्ति धनञ्जय ॥	Yogasannyasta karmaanam jnaanasamcchinnasamshayam; Aatmavantam na karmaani nibadhnanti dhananjaya.

Arjuna, one who has renounced all actions according to karma yoga, whose doubts have been dispelled by wisdom and who is absorbed in the Self, that person will not be bound by karma.

4.42

तस्मादज्ञानसम्भूतं हृत्स्थं ज्ञानासिनात्मनः । छित्त्वैनं संशयं योगमातिष्ठोत्तिष्ठ भारत ॥	Tasmaad ajnaanasambhootam hritstham jnaanaasinaatmanah; Cchittvainam samshayam yogam aatishthottishtha bhaarata.

Arjuna, sever the ignorance that is harbored in your heart with the sword of self-knowledge. Establish yourself in karma yoga and get ready for the fight.

ॐ तत्सदिति श्रीमद्भगवद्गीतासूपनिषत्सु ब्रह्मविद्यायां योगशास्त्रे श्रीकृष्णार्जुनसंवादे ज्ञानयोगो नाम चतुर्थोऽध्यायः	Om Tat Saditi Srimad Bhagavadgeetaasoopanishatsu Brahmavidyaayaam Yogashaastre Sri Krishnaarjunasamvaade Jnaanayogo Naama Chaturtho'dhyaayah

Thus ends the fourth discourse entitled Jnana Yoga in the Upanishad, the divine Bhagavad Gita, the knowledge of Brahman, the scripture on Yoga and the dialogue between Sri Krishna and Arjuna.

Chapter 5
Sanyasa Yoga

5.01

अर्जुन उवाच |
संन्यासं कर्मणां कृष्ण पुनर्योगं च शंससि |
यच्छ्रेय एतयोरेकं तन्मे ब्रूहि सुनिश्चितम् ||

Arjuna uvaacha:
Sannyaasam karmanaam krishna
punar yogam cha shamsasi;
Yacchreya etayorekam tanme broohi
sunishchitam.

Arjuna said: O Krishna, you praise both the renunciation of action and the yoga of action. Please tell me for sure which of these two is the better path.

5.02

श्रीभगवानुवाच |
संन्यासः कर्मयोगश्च निःश्रेयसकरावुभौ |
तयोस्तु कर्मसंन्यासात्कर्मयोगो विशिष्यते ||

Sri Bhagavaan uvaacha:
Sannyaasah karmayogashcha
nihshreyasakaraa vubhau;
Tayostu karmasannyaasaat
karmayogo vishishyate.

Bhagavan (Lord Krishna) said: Renunciation of action and the yoga of action both lead to the supreme, but of the two the yoga of action is more manageable than the renunciation of action.

5.03

| ज्ञेयः स नित्यसंन्यासी यो न द्वेष्टि न काङ्क्षति । निर्द्वन्द्वो हि महाबाहो सुखं बन्धात्प्रमुच्यते ॥ | Jneyah sa nityasannyaasi yo na dveshti na kaangkshati; Nirdvandvo hi mahaabaaho sukham bandhaat pramuchyate. |

Arjuna, one who neither hates nor desires is considered a true sanyasi. He who is beyond dualities is easily released from bondage.

5.04

| साङ्ख्ययोगौ पृथग्बालाः प्रवदन्ति न पण्डिताः । एकमप्यास्थितः सम्यगुभयोर्विन्दते फलम् ॥ | Saankhyayogau prithagbaalaah pravadanti na panditaah; Ekam apyaasthitah samyag ubhayor vindate phalam. |

Only the ignorant and not the learned say that sankhya yoga (path of knowledge) and karma yoga (path of selfless action) produce different results. One who is firmly established in either one of these two paths reaps the benefits of both.

5.05

| यत्साङ्ख्यैः प्राप्यते स्थानं तद्योगैरपि गम्यते । एकं साङ्ख्यं च योगं च यः पश्यति स पश्यति ॥ | Yatsaankhyaih praapyate sthaanam tad yogair api gamyate; Ekam saankhyam cha yogam cha yah pashyati sa pashyati. |

The goal reached by sankhya yogis is also the goal reached by karma yogis. The person who clearly sees the oneness of goal knows the truth.

5.06

| संन्यासस्तु महाबाहो दुःखमाप्तुमयोगतः । योगयुक्तो मुनिर्ब्रह्म नचिरेणाधिगच्छति ॥ | Sannyaasastu mahaabaaho duhkham aaptuma yogatah; Yogayukto munir brahma na chirenaadhigacchati. |

Arjuna, renunciation of action (sankhya yoga) is difficult to achieve without following the yoga of action (karma yoga). The sage who follows karma yoga with his mind fixed on Brahman quickly attains Brahman.

5.07

योगयुक्तो विशुद्धात्मा विजितात्मा जितेन्द्रियः । सर्वभूतात्मभूतात्मा कुर्वन्नपि न लिप्यते ।।	Yogayukto vishuddhaatmaa vijitaatmaa jitendriyah; Sarvabhootaatmabhootaatmaa kurvannapi na lipyate.

A karma yogi who has purified himself by restraining his senses and by performing selfless actions, and who sees the same Self in all beings, is not bound by karma although he is engaged in action.

5.08-5.09

नैव किञ्चित्करोमीति युक्तो मन्येत तत्त्ववित् । पश्यञ्शृण्वन्स्पृशञ्जिघ्रन्नश्नन्गच्छन्स्वपञ्श्वसन् ।। प्रलपन्विसृजन्गृह्लन्नुन्मिषन्निमिषन्नपि । इन्द्रियाणीन्द्रियार्थेषु वर्तन्त इति धारयन् ।।	Naiva kinchit karomeeti yukto manyeta tattvavit; Pashyan shrunvan sprishan jighran nashnan gacchan swapan shwasan. Pralapan visrijan grihnan nunmishan nimishannapi; Indriyaaneendriyaartheshu vartanta iti dhaarayan.

The enlightened person always thinks, "I am not the doer". Even while seeing, hearing, touching, smelling, eating, walking, sleeping, breathing, talking, relieving, holding, opening and closing his eyes, he thinks that he is not doing anything and that only his senses are engaged by their sensory objects.

5.10

ब्रह्मण्याधाय कर्माणि सङ्गं त्यक्त्वा करोति यः । लिप्यते न स पापेन पद्मपत्रमिवाम्भसा ।।	Brahmanyaadhaaya karmaani sangam tyaktvaa karoti yah; Lipyate na sa paapena padmapatram ivaambhasaa.

Just as water does not stick to the surface of a lotus leaf, sin does not stick to a person who acts without attachment and dedicates all his actions to Brahman.

5.11

| कायेन मनसा बुद्ध्या केवलैरिन्द्रियैरपि ।
योगिनः कर्म कुर्वन्ति सङ्गं त्यक्त्वात्मशुद्धये ॥ | Kaayena manasaa buddhyaa kevalair indriyair api;
Yoginah karma kurvanti sangam tyaktvaatmashuddhaye. |

Without attachment, the karma yogi works with the body, mind, intellect and senses only for the sake of self purification.

5.12

| युक्तः कर्मफलं त्यक्त्वा शान्तिमाप्नोति नैष्ठिकीम् ।
अयुक्तः कामकारेण फले सक्तो निबध्यते ॥ | Yuktah karmaphalam tyaktvaa shaantim aapnoti naishthikeem;
Ayuktah kaamakaarena phale sakto nibadhyate. |

The karma yogi, having given up the fruit of action, attains lasting peace, but the non-yogi who is attached to the fruits of action is bound.

5.13

| सर्वकर्माणि मनसा संन्यस्यास्ते सुखं वशी ।
नवद्वारे पुरे देही नैव कुर्वन्न कारयन् ॥ | Sarvakarmaani manasaa sannyasyaaste sukham vashee;
Navadvaare pure dehee naiva kurvan na kaarayan. |

Renouncing all actions by the mind, the dweller of the body who is master of himself rests happily in the city of nine gates (the body), neither acting nor causing others to act.

5.14

| न कर्तृत्वं न कर्माणि लोकस्य सृजति प्रभुः ।
न कर्मफलसंयोगं स्वभावस्तु प्रवर्तते ॥ | Na kartritvam na karmaani lokasya srijati prabhuh;
Na karmaphala samyogam swabhaavas tu pravartate. |

The Lord does not determine the doer or the deed, nor cause and effect. Nature does this all.

5.15

नादत्ते कस्यचित्पापं न चैव सुकृतं विभुः । अज्ञानेनावृतं ज्ञानं तेन मुह्यन्ति जन्तवः ॥	Naadatte kasyachit paapam na chaiva sukritam vibhuh; Ajnaanenaavritam jnaanam tena muhyanti jantavah.

The omnipresent Lord is not responsible for either the sin or the virtue of anyone. Human beings are deluded because their knowledge is covered by ignorance.

5.16

ज्ञानेन तु तदज्ञानं येषां नाशितमात्मनः । तेषामादित्यवज्ज्ञानं प्रकाशयति तत्परम् ॥	Jnaanena tu tad ajnaanam yeshaam naashitam aatmanah; Teshaam aadityavaj jnaanam prakaashayati tatparam.

For those whose ignorance of the Self has been removed by knowledge, that knowledge illuminates the Self like the Sun.

5.17

तद्बुद्धयस्तदात्मानस्तन्निष्ठास्तत्परायणाः । गच्छन्त्यपुनरावृत्तिं ज्ञाननिर्धूतकल्मषाः ॥	Tadbuddhayas tadaatmaanas tannishthaas tatparaayanaah; Gacchantyapunaraavrittim jnaana nirdhoota kalmashaah.

Those whose mind and intellect are completely absorbed in the supreme, who are totally devoted to the supreme, and who have the supreme as the ultimate goal become fully cleansed of their sins and are never born again.

5.18

| विद्याविनयसम्पन्ने ब्राह्मणे गवि हस्तिनि ।
 शुनि चैव श्वपाके च पण्डिताः समदर्शिनः ॥ | Vidyaavinaya sampanne braahmane gavi hastini; Shuni chaiva shvapaake cha panditaah samadarshinah. |

An enlightened person regards all beings equally: a brahmin of learning and humility, a cow, an elephant, a dog or a dog-eating person.

Commentary: An enlightened person sees the same Brahman in a learned brahmin, a cow, an elephant, a dog, and a dog-eater. This does not mean that he ceases to recognize the differences in their appearance and behavior. Nor does it imply that he indiscriminately treats them the same way. For example, he may offer the brahmin fresh fruits and the cow fresh grass. *Samadarshina* simply means recognizing the same Self in all, irrespective of their differences.

5.19

| इहैव तैर्जितः सर्गो येषां साम्ये स्थितं मनः ।
 निर्दोषं हि समं ब्रह्म तस्माद् ब्रह्मणि ते स्थिताः ॥ | Ihaiva tairjitah sargo yeshaam saamye sthitam manah; Nirdosham hi samam brahma tasmaad brahmani te sthitaah. |

Even here in this mortal world, birth and death are conquered by those whose minds are established in sameness. Such people have realized Brahman because Brahman is flawless and is the same in everyone.

5.20

| न प्रहृष्येत्प्रियं प्राप्य नोद्विजेत्प्राप्य चाप्रियम् ।
 स्थिरबुद्धिरसम्मूढो ब्रह्मविद् ब्रह्मणि स्थितः ॥ | Na prahrishyet priyam praapya nodvijet praapya chaapriyam; Sthirabuddhir asammoodho brahmavid brahmani sthitah. |

The person of steady intellect, undeluded, who knows Brahman and who is established in Brahman, neither rejoices on obtaining the pleasant nor grieves on obtaining the unpleasant.

5.21

बाह्यस्पर्शेष्वसक्तात्मा विन्दत्यात्मनि यत्सुखम् । स ब्रह्मयोगयुक्तात्मा सुखमक्षयमश्नुते ॥	Baahyasparsheshwasaktaatmaa vindatyaatmani yat sukham; Sa brahma yoga yuktaatmaa sukham akshayam ashnute.

The yogi with the self detached from external contacts, fully absorbed in the Self, experiences the joy of the Self. Having achieved oneness with Brahman, the yogi enjoys eternal bliss.

5.22

ये हि संस्पर्शजा भोगा दुःखयोनय एव ते । आद्यन्तवन्तः कौन्तेय न तेषु रमते बुधः ॥	Ye hi samsparshajaa bhogaa duhkhayonaya eva te; Aadyantavantah kaunteya na teshu ramate budhah.

Arjuna, the pleasures that arise from sense contacts are sources of suffering. They have a beginning and an end. Therefore, the wise do not revel in them.

5.23

शक्नोतीहैव यः सोढुं प्राक्शरीरविमोक्षणात् । कामक्रोधोद्भवं वेगं स युक्तः स सुखी नरः ॥	Shaknoteehaiva yah sodhum praak shareera vimokshanaat; Kaamakrodhodbhavam vegam sa yuktah sa sukhee narah.

One who can overcome desire and anger in this life before leaving this body is a yogi and a happy person.

5.24

योऽन्तःसुखोऽन्तरारामस्तथान्तर्ज्योतिरेव यः । स योगी ब्रह्मनिर्वाणं ब्रह्मभूतोऽधिगच्छति ॥	Yo'ntah sukho'ntaraaraamas tathaantarjyotir eva yah; Sa yogee brahma nirvaanam brahmabhooto'dhigacchati.

The yogi who is happy within, who rejoices within and who is illuminated from within by the knowledge of the Self, attains Brahman.

5.25

लभन्ते ब्रह्मनिर्वाणमृषयः क्षीणकल्मषाः । छिन्नद्वैधा यतात्मानः सर्वभूतहिते रताः ॥	Labhante brahma nirvaanam rishayah ksheenakalmashaah; Cchinnadvaidhaa yataatmaanah sarvabhootahite rataah.

The seers whose sins have been cleansed, whose doubts have been removed by knowledge, who are self-controlled and who are actively involved in the common welfare, attain Brahman.

5.26

कामक्रोधवियुक्तानां यतीनां यतचेतसाम् । अभितो ब्रह्मनिर्वाणं वर्तते विदितात्मनाम् ॥	Kaamakrodhaviyuktaanaam yateenaam yatachetasaam; Abhito brahma nirvaanam vartate viditaatmanaam.

The saintly persons who are free from lust and anger, self-disciplined and Self realized, experience Brahman's bliss everywhere.

5.27-5.28

स्पर्शान्कृत्वा बहिर्बाह्यांश्चक्षुश्चैवान्तरे भ्रुवोः । प्राणापानौ समौ कृत्वा नासाभ्यन्तरचारिणौ ॥ यतेन्द्रियमनोबुद्धिर्मुनिर्मोक्षपरायणः । विगतेच्छाभयक्रोधो यः सदा मुक्त एव सः ॥	Sparsaan kritvaa bahir baahyaamschakshus chaivaantare bhruvoh; Praanaapaanau samau kritvaa naasaabhyantara chaarinau. Yatendriya manobuddhir munir mokshaparaayanah; Vigatecchaabhaya krodho yah sadaa mukta eva sah.

Shutting out all external contacts and fixing the gaze between the eyebrows, equalizing the outgoing and incoming breaths, with senses, mind and intellect under control, having liberation as the prime goal, free from desire, fear and anger, the sage achieves liberation.

5.29

भोक्तारं यज्ञतपसां सर्वलोकमहेश्वरम् । सुहृदं सर्वभूतानां ज्ञात्वा मां शान्तिमृच्छति ॥	Bhoktaaram yajnatapasaam sarvaloka maheshwaram; Suhridam sarvabhootaanaam jnaatvaa maam shaantim ricchati.

One who realizes Me as the recipient of all sacrifices and austerities, as the supreme Lord of all the worlds and as the friend of all beings, attains peace.

ॐ तत्सदिति श्रीमद्भगवद्गीतासूपनिषत्सु ब्रह्मविद्यायां योगशास्त्रे श्रीकृष्णार्जुनसंवादे संन्यासयोगो नाम पञ्चमोऽध्यायः	Om Tat Saditi Srimad Bhagavadgeetaasoopanishatsu Brahmavidyaayaam Yogashaastre Sri Krishnaarjunasamvaade Sanyaasayogo Naama Panchamo'dhyaayah

Thus ends the fifth discourse entitled Sanyasa Yoga in the Upanishad, the divine Bhagavad Gita, the knowledge of Brahman, the scripture on Yoga and the dialogue between Sri Krishna and Arjuna.

Chapter 6
Dhyana Yoga

6.01

श्रीभगवानुवाच |
अनाश्रितः कर्मफलं कार्यं कर्म करोति यः |
स संन्यासी च योगी च न निरग्निर्न चाक्रियः ||

Sri Bhagavaan uvaacha:
Anaashritah karmaphalam kaaryam karma karoti yah;
Sa sannyaasi cha yogee cha na niragnirna chaakriyah.

Bhagavan (Lord Krishna) said: One who performs one's duty without any interest in its fruits is a sanyasi and a yogi. One does not become a sanyasi just by giving up the sacred fire and does not end up a yogi by dereliction of duties.

6.02

यं संन्यासमिति प्राहुर्योगं तं विद्धि पाण्डव |
न ह्यसंन्यस्तसङ्कल्पो योगी भवति कश्चन ||

Yam sannyaasamiti praahuryogam tam viddhi paandava;
Na hyasannyastasankalpo yogee bhavati kashchana.

Arjuna, what people call sanyasa is really yoga. No one becomes a yogi without renouncing selfish motives.

6.03

| आरुरुक्षोर्मुनेर्योगं कर्म कारणमुच्यते ।
योगारूढस्य तस्यैव शमः कारणमुच्यते ॥ | Aarurukshormuneryogam karma kaaranamuchyate;
Yogaaroodhasya tasyaiva shamah kaaranamuchyate. |

Karma (action) is said to be the means of the sage who wants to advance in yoga. Serenity is the path for those who have already attained yoga.

6.04

| यदा हि नेन्द्रियार्थेषु न कर्मस्वनुषज्जते ।
सर्वसङ्कल्पसंन्यासी योगारूढस्तदोच्यते ॥ | Yadaa hi nendriyaartheshu na karmaswanushajjate;
Sarvasankalpasannyaasee yogaaroodhas tadochyate. |

When one is not attached to either objects of the senses or to actions, and has renounced all sankalpas (selfish purposes), he is said to be advanced in yoga.

6.05

| उद्धरेदात्मनात्मानं नात्मानमवसादयेत् ।
आत्मैव ह्यात्मनो बन्धुरात्मैव रिपुरात्मनः ॥ | Uddharedaatmanaatmaanam naatmaanamavasaadayet;
Atmaiva hyaatmano bandhuraatmaiva ripuraatmanah. |

A person should raise himself by himself, and not lower himself. His own mind is his friend and his foe.

Commentary: Lord Krishna says that a human being can progress spiritually by his own efforts and not by others' efforts. We have trapped ourselves in samsara (cycle of birth and death) and only we can extricate ourselves from this trap. Nobody else can do it for us. Our own mind plays an important role in this regard. It can dispel our ignorance and raise us spiritually. Or it can delude us and drag us down spiritually. This is how our own mind can be both friend and enemy.

6.06

बन्धुरात्मात्मनस्तस्य येनात्मैवात्मना जितः । अनात्मनस्तु शत्रुत्वे वर्तेतात्मैव शत्रुवत् ॥	Bandhuraatmaa'tmanastasya yenaatmaivaatmanaa jitah; Anaatmanastu shatrutve vartetaatmaiva shatruvat.

If a person has conquered his mind, it is his best friend. If not, it is his worst foe.

6.07

जितात्मनः प्रशान्तस्य परमात्मा समाहितः । शीतोष्णसुखदुःखेषु तथा मानापमानयोः ॥	Jitaatmanah prashaantasya paramaatmaa samaahitah; Sheetoshna sukha duhkheshu tathaa maanaapamaanayoh.

The supreme Self of a self-disciplined and tranquil person remains steadfast in cold and heat, pleasure and pain, and honor and dishonor.

6.08

ज्ञानविज्ञानतृप्तात्मा कूटस्थो विजितेन्द्रियः । युक्त इत्युच्यते योगी समलोष्टाश्मकाञ्चनः ॥	Jnaana vijnaana triptaatmaa kootastho vijitendriyah; Yuktah ityuchyate yogee samaloshtaashmakaanchanah.

The person who is content with knowledge and wisdom, who is stable under all circumstances, who has controlled his senses and who looks upon a clump of mud, a stone, and a piece of gold alike, is said to be an accomplished yogi.

Commentary: This does not mean that the yogi is ignorant of the differences in qualities between mud, stone and gold. It means that because he is established in clarity and self-control, he sees them for what they truly are, and does not develop attachment towards them.

6.09

सुहृन्मित्रार्युदासीनमध्यस्थद्वेष्यबन्धुषु । साधुष्वपि च पापेषु समबुद्धिर्विशिष्यते ॥	Suhrinmitraary udaaseena madhyastha dveshya bandhushu; Saadhushwapi cha paapeshu samabuddhirvishishyate.

One who views well wishers, friends, enemies, the neutral, mediators, the hateful, relatives, saints and sinners all with a pure mind is an extraordinary person.

6.10

योगी युञ्जीत सततमात्मानं रहसि स्थितः । एकाकी यतचित्तात्मा निराशीरपरिग्रहः ॥	Yogee yunjeeta satatamaatmaanam rahasi sthitah; Ekaakee yatachittaatmaa niraasheeraparigrahah.

A yogi should constantly meditate, living alone in seclusion, with body and mind under full control, free from desire and without any possessions.

6.11

शुचौ देशे प्रतिष्ठाप्य स्थिरमासनमात्मनः । नात्युच्छ्रितं नातिनीचं चैलाजिनकुशोत्तरम् ॥	Shuchau deshe pratishthaapya sthiramaasanamaatmanah; Naatyucchritam naatineecham chailaajinakushottaram.

He should set up in a clean place a firm seat, neither too high nor too low, and cover it with Kusha grass, a deer skin, and a piece of cloth.

6.12

तत्रैकाग्रं मनः कृत्वा यतचित्तेन्द्रियक्रियः । उपविश्यासने युञ्ज्याद्योगमात्मविशुद्धये ॥	Tatraikaagram manah kritvaa yatachittendriyakriyah; Upavishyaasane yunjyaadyogamaatmavishuddhaye.

Sitting on that seat, with his mind focused on a single point and holding his thought and sense activity under control, he should practice yoga for self purification.

6.13-6.14

समं कायशिरोग्रीवं धारयन्नचलं स्थिरः । सम्प्रेक्ष्य नासिकाग्रं स्वं दिशश्चानवलोकयन् ॥ प्रशान्तात्मा विगतभीर्ब्रह्मचारिव्रते स्थितः । मनः संयम्य मच्चित्तो युक्त आसीत मत्परः ॥	Samam kaayashirogreevam dhaarayannachalam sthirah; Samprekshya naasikaagram swam dishashchaanavalokayan. Prashaantaatmaa vigatabheer brahmachaarivrate sthitah; Manah samyamya macchitto yukta aaseeta matparah.

He should keep his trunk, head and neck straight and still. He should gaze on the tip of his nose without looking in other directions. He should be calm, fearless, and practice strict celibacy. With his mind under full control and focused on Me, the yogi should sit still absorbed in Me alone.

6.15

युञ्जन्नेवं सदात्मानं योगी नियतमानसः । शान्तिं निर्वाणपरमां मत्संस्थामधिगच्छति ॥	Yunjannevam sadaa'tmaanam yogee niyatamaanasah; Shaantim nirvaanaparamaam matsamsthaamadhigacchati.

Thus constantly meditating on Me, the yogi of disciplined mind attains everlasting peace that culminates in the highest state of Nirvana which rests in Me.

6.16

नात्यश्नतस्तु योगोऽस्ति न चैकान्तमनश्नतः । न चातिस्वप्नशीलस्य जाग्रतो नैव चार्जुन ॥	Naatyashnatastu yogo'sti nachaikaantamanashnatah; Na chaatiswapnasheelasya jaagrato naiva chaarjuna.

Arjuna, yoga is not the path for a person who eats too much or too little, or who sleeps too much or too little.

6.17

युक्ताहारविहारस्य युक्तचेष्टस्य कर्मसु । युक्तस्वप्नावबोधस्य योगो भवति दुःखहा ॥	Yuktaahaaravihaarasya yuktacheshtasya karmasu; Yuktaswapnaavabodhasya yogo bhavati duhkhahaa.

Yoga practice removes the sorrow of those who are moderate in eating, recreation, work, sleeping and staying awake.

6.18

यदा विनियतं चित्तमात्मन्येवावतिष्ठते । निःस्पृहः सर्वकामेभ्यो युक्त इत्युच्यते तदा ॥	Yadaa viniyatam chittamaatmanyevaavatishthate; Nihsprihah sarvakaamebhyo yukta ityuchyate tadaa.

When the disciplined mind is completely absorbed in the Self, detached from all desires, it is said to be established in yoga.

6.19

यथा दीपो निवातस्थो नेङ्गते सोपमा स्मृता । योगिनो यतचित्तस्य युञ्जतो योगमात्मनः ॥	Yathaa deepo nivaatastho nengate sopamaa smritaa; Yogino yatachittasya yunjato yogamaatmanah.

Just like a lamp's flame does not flicker when protected from wind, a yogi whose mind is controlled and focused on the Self does not waver.

6.20

यत्रोपरमते चित्तं निरुद्धं योगसेवया । यत्र चैवात्मनात्मानं पश्यन्नात्मनि तुष्यति ॥	Yatroparamate chittam niruddham yogasevayaa; Yatra chaivaatmanaa'tmaanam pashyannaatmani tushyati.

When the mind disciplined by the practice of yoga becomes completely calm, one sees the Self through the self and rests in the Self, rejoicing. One sees nothing but the Self with Joy.

6.21

सुखमात्यन्तिकं यत्तद् बुद्धिग्राह्यमतीन्द्रियम् । वेत्ति यत्र न चैवायं स्थितश्चलति तत्त्वतः ॥	Sukhamaatyantikam yattad buddhi graahyamateendriyam; Vetti yatra na chaivaayam sthitashchalati tattvatah.

One experiences the supreme Joy through the intellect that is beyond the senses. Established in this state, the yogi does not deviate from the truth.

6.22

यं लब्ध्वा चापरं लाभं मन्यते नाधिकं ततः । यस्मिन्स्थितो न दुःखेन गुरुणापि विचाल्यते ॥	Yam labdhvaa chaaparam laabham manyate naadhikam tatah; Yasmin sthito na duhkhena gurunaapi vichaalyate.

Having attained this state, the yogi realizes that there is nothing more beyond this state. Established in this state, the yogi is not disturbed even by the gravest sorrow.

6.23

तं विद्याद् दुःखसंयोगवियोगं योगसंज्ञितम् । स निश्चयेन योक्तव्यो योगोऽनिर्विण्णचेतसा ॥	Tam vidyaad duhkhasamyogaviyogam yogasamjnitam; Sa nishchayena yoktavyo yogo'nirvinna chetasaa.

Let the severance of ties with sorrow be known by the name yoga. This yoga must be practiced with determination, perseverance, and with an undisturbed mind.

6.24-6.25

सङ्कल्पप्रभवान्कामांस्त्यक्त्वा सर्वानशेषतः । मनसैवेन्द्रियग्रामं विनियम्य समन्ततः ॥ शनैः शनैरुपरमेद् बुद्ध्या धृतिगृहीतया । आत्मसंस्थं मनः कृत्वा न किञ्चिदपि चिन्तयेत् ॥	Sankalpaprabhavaan kaamaan styaktvaa sarvaan asheshatah; Manasaivendriyagraamam viniyamya samantatah. Shanaih shanairuparamed buddhyaa dhritigriheetayaa; Aatmasamstham manah kritvaa na kinchidapi chintayet.

The yogi gradually attains tranquility of mind by completely renouncing all desires born of sankalpa (selfish purpose), by controlling the senses from all sides with the mind, by keeping the mind fully absorbed in the Self with the help of the well-trained intellect, and by not thinking about anything else.

6.26

यतो यतो निश्चरति मनश्चञ्चलमस्थिरम् । ततस्ततो नियम्यैतदात्मन्येव वशं नयेत् ॥	Yato yato nishcharati manashchanchalamasthiram; Tatastato niyamyaitad aatmanyeva vasham nayet.

Whenever the fickle and unstable mind wanders, the yogi should bring it back to concentrate on the Self.

6.27

प्रशान्तमनसं ह्येनं योगिनं सुखमुत्तमम् । उपैति शान्तरजसं ब्रह्मभूतमकल्मषम् ॥	Prashaantamanasam hyenam yoginam sukhamuttamam; Upaiti shaantarajasam brahmabhootamakalmasham.

The yogi whose mind is perfectly calm, who has no passions, who is free from sin and has become one with Brahman, attains supreme bliss.

6.28

| युञ्जन्नेवं सदात्मानं योगी विगतकल्मषः ।
सुखेन ब्रह्मसंस्पर्शमत्यन्तं सुखमश्नुते ॥ | Yunjannevam sadaa'tmaanam yogee vigatakalmashah;
Sukhena brahmasamsparsham atyantam sukham ashnute. |

The sinless yogi, who constantly keeps the mind focused on the Self, easily attains the supreme bliss of unity with Brahman.

6.29

| सर्वभूतस्थमात्मानं सर्वभूतानि चात्मनि ।
ईक्षते योगयुक्तात्मा सर्वत्र समदर्शनः ॥ | Sarvabhootasthamaatmaanam sarvabhootaani chaatmani;
Eekshate yogayuktaatmaa sarvatra samadarshanah. |

The yogi who has attained unity with Brahman sees the Self in all beings and all beings within the Self. He sees the same everywhere.

6.30

| यो मां पश्यति सर्वत्र सर्वं च मयि पश्यति ।
तस्याहं न प्रणश्यामि स च मे न प्रणश्यति ॥ | Yo maam pashyati sarvatra sarvam cha mayi pashyati;
Tasyaaham na pranashyaami sa cha me na pranashyati. |

For one who sees Me in everything and sees everything in Me, I am always with him and he is always with Me.

6.31

| सर्वभूतस्थितं यो मां भजत्येकत्वमास्थितः ।
सर्वथा वर्तमानोऽपि स योगी मयि वर्तते ॥ | Sarvabhootasthitam yo maam bhajatyekatvamaasthitah;
Sarvathaa vartamaano'pi sa yogee mayi vartate. |

The yogi who has attained unity with Me adores Me as the one in all beings, and abides in Me regardless of his mode of living.

6.32

आत्मौपम्येन सर्वत्र समं पश्यति योऽर्जुन । सुखं वा यदि वा दुःखं स योगी परमो मतः ॥	Aatmaupamyena sarvatra samam pashyati yo'rjuna; Sukham vaa yadi vaa duhkham sa yogee paramo matah.

Arjuna, one is regarded as a perfect yogi who thinks of everyone like himself, and who feels the joy and sorrow of others as his own.

6.33

अर्जुन उवाच । योऽयं योगस्त्वया प्रोक्तः साम्येन मधुसूदन । एतस्याहं न पश्यामि चञ्चलत्वात्स्थितिं स्थिराम् ॥	Arjuna uvaacha: Yo'yam yogastvayaa proktah saamyena madhusoodana; Etasyaaham na pashyaami chanchalatvaat sthitim sthiraam.

Arjuna said: O Madhusudana (Krishna), the yoga you have explained is based on calmness of mind. I do not know how this is possible because the mind is fickle.

6.34

चञ्चलं हि मनः कृष्ण प्रमाथि बलवद् दृढम् । तस्याहं निग्रहं मन्ये वायोरिव सुदुष्करम् ॥	Chanchalam hi manah krishna pramaathi balavad dridham; Tasyaaham nigraham manye vaayoriva sudushkaram.

The mind is unsteady, Krishna. It is turbulent, powerful and stubborn. I think controlling it is as difficult as controlling the wind.

6.35

श्रीभगवानुवाच । असंशयं महाबाहो मनो दुर्निग्रहं चलम् । अभ्यासेन तु कौन्तेय वैराग्येण च गृह्यते ॥	Sri Bhagavaan uvaacha: Asamshayam mahaabaaho mano durnigraham chalam; Abhyaasena tu kaunteya vairaagyena cha grihyate.

Bhagavan (Lord Krishna) said: There is no doubt, Arjuna, that the mind is restless and hard to control. But it can be controlled, Arjuna, through regular practice and non-attachment.

6.36

असंयतात्मना योगो दुष्प्राप इति मे मतिः । वश्यात्मना तु यतता शक्योऽवाप्तुमुपायतः ॥	Asamyataatmanaa yogo dushpraapa iti me matih; Vashyaatmanaa tu yatataa shakyo'vaaptumupaayatah.

I agree that yoga is difficult to attain without self-control. However, a person with self-control who strives properly can attain it.

6.37

अर्जुन उवाच । अयतिः श्रद्धयोपेतो योगाच्चलितमानसः । अप्राप्य योगसंसिद्धिं कां गतिं कृष्ण गच्छति ॥	Arjuna uvaacha: Ayatih shraddhayopeto yogaacchalitamaanasah; Apraapya yogasamsiddhim kaam gatim krishna gacchati.

Arjuna said: O Krishna, what happens to a person who has faith and cannot control his mind, who deviates from the path of yoga before attaining perfection?

6.38

कच्चिन्नोभयविभ्रष्टश्छिन्नाभ्रमिव नश्यति । अप्रतिष्ठो महाबाहो विमूढो ब्रह्मणः पथि ॥	Kacchinnobhayavibhrashtash cchinnaabhramiva nashyati; Apratishtho mahaabaaho vimoodho brahmanah pathi.

O Krishna, having lost both (material and spiritual success), does he not perish, supportless and deluded, in the path of Brahman like a torn piece of cloud?

6.39

एतन्मे संशयं कृष्ण छेत्तुमर्हस्यशेषतः । त्वदन्यः संशयस्यास्य छेत्ता न ह्युपपद्यते ॥	Etanme samshayam krishna cchettumarhasyasheshatah; Tvadanyah samshayasyaasya cchettaa na hyupapadyate.

O Krishna, this is my doubt. Please clear this doubt of mine. There is no one else for me but you who can do it.

6.40

| श्रीभगवानुवाच ।
पार्थ नैवेह नामुत्र विनाशस्तस्य विद्यते ।
न हि कल्याणकृत्कश्चिद् दुर्गतिं तात गच्छति ॥ | Sri Bhagavaan uvaacha:
Paartha naiveha naamutra vinaashas tasya vidyate;
Nahi kalyaanakrit kashchid durgatim taata gacchati. |

Bhagavan (Lord Krishna) said: Arjuna, my friend, he will not be lost either here or hereafter. No one who does good work will be ruined.

6.41

| प्राप्य पुण्यकृतां लोकानुषित्वा शाश्वतीः समाः ।
शुचीनां श्रीमतां गेहे योगभ्रष्टोऽभिजायते ॥ | Praapya punyakritaam lokaanushitvaa shaashvateeh samaah;
Shucheenaam shreemataam gehe yogabhrashto'bhijaayate. |

After death, yogis who have stumbled on the path of yoga go to the heavenly world of the righteous. They live there for a number of years and subsequently take birth on earth in the homes of the pure and prosperous.

6.42

| अथवा योगिनामेव कुले भवति धीमताम् ।
एतद्धि दुर्लभतरं लोके जन्म यदीदृशम् ॥ | Athavaa yoginaameva kule bhavati dheemataam;
Etaddhi durlabhataram loke janma yadeedrisham. |

A few of them will be born into a family of enlightened yogis, but such births are difficult to obtain.

6.43

| तत्र तं बुद्धिसंयोगं लभते पौर्वदेहिकम् ।
यतते च ततो भूयः संसिद्धौ कुरुनन्दन ॥ | Tatra tam buddhisamyogam labhate paurvadehikam;
Yatate cha tato bhooyah samsiddhau kurunandana. |

There, they regain the knowledge of their previous lives, Arjuna, and will strive even harder for perfection.

6.44

पूर्वाभ्यासेन तेनैव ह्रियते ह्यवशोऽपि सः । जिज्ञासुरपि योगस्य शब्दब्रह्मातिवर्तते ॥	Poorvaabhyaasena tenaiva hriyate hyavasho'pi sah; Jijnaasurapi yogasya shabdabrahmaativartate.

By virtue of their previous life's experience, they are drawn automatically to yoga. Even one who inquires about yoga rises above those who perform rituals.

6.45

प्रयत्नाद्यतमानस्तु योगी संशुद्धकिल्बिषः । अनेकजन्मसंसिद्धस्ततो याति परां गतिम् ॥	Prayatnaadyatamaanastu yogee samshuddhakilbishah; Anekajanmasamsiddhas tato yaati paraam gatim.

The yogi who constantly strives for perfection through many lifetimes cleanses himself of all sins and attains the supreme goal.

6.46

तपस्विभ्योऽधिको योगी ज्ञानिभ्योऽपि मतोऽधिकः । कर्मिभ्यश्चाधिको योगी तस्माद्योगी भवार्जुन ॥	Tapasvibhyo'dhiko yogee jnaanibhyo'pi mato'dhikah; Karmibhyashchaadhiko yogee tasmaad yogee bhavaarjuna.

The yogi is superior to the ascetic or the scholar or the performers of rituals. Therefore, be a yogi, Arjuna.

6.47

योगिनामपि सर्वेषां मद्गतेनान्तरात्मना । श्रद्धावान्भजते यो मां स मे युक्ततमो मतः ॥	Yoginaamapi sarveshaam madgatenaantaraatmanaa; Shraddhaavaan bhajate yo maam sa me yuktatamo matah.

Of all the yogis, the one who worships Me with full faith and is completely absorbed in Me is the best yogi.

ॐ तत्सदिति श्रीमद्भगवद्गीतासूपनिषत्सु ब्रह्मविद्यायां योगशास्त्रे श्रीकृष्णार्जुनसंवादे ध्यानायोगो नाम षष्ठोऽध्यायः	Om Tat Saditi Srimad Bhagavadgeetaasoopanishatsu Brahmavidyaayaam Yogashaastre Sri Krishnaarjunasamvaade Dhyanayogo Naama Shashtho'dhyaayah

Thus ends the sixth discourse entitled Dhyana Yoga in the Upanishad, the divine Bhagavad Gita, the knowledge of Brahman, the scripture on Yoga and the dialogue between Sri Krishna and Arjuna.

Chapter 7
Jnana Vijnana Yoga

7.01

| श्रीभगवानुवाच \|
 मय्यासक्तमनाः पार्थ योगं युञ्जन्मदाश्रयः \|
 असंशयं समग्रं मां यथा ज्ञास्यसि तच्छृणु \|\| | Sri Bhagavaan uvaacha:
 Mayyaasaktamanaah paartha yogam yunjanmadaashrayah;
 Asamshayam samagram maam yathaa jnaasyasi tacchrinu. |

Bhagavan (Lord Krishna) said: Listen now, Arjuna, to how you can get to know Me fully beyond any doubt, by practicing yoga with your mind totally absorbed in Me and by taking refuge in Me.

7.02

| ज्ञानं तेऽहं सविज्ञानमिदं वक्ष्याम्यशेषतः \|
 यज्ज्ञात्वा नेह भूयोऽन्यज्ज्ञातव्यमवशिष्यते \|\| | Jnaanam te'ham savijnaanam idam vakshyaamyasheshatah;
 Yajjnaatvaa neha bhooyo'nyaj jnaatavyamavashishyate. |

I will explain to you fully the theory and practice of this approach. When you know this, there is nothing more you need to know in this world.

7.03

| मनुष्याणां सहस्रेषु कश्चिद्यतति सिद्धये ।
यततामपि सिद्धानां कश्चिन्मां वेत्ति तत्त्वतः ॥ | Manushyaanaam sahasreshu kashchidyatati siddhaye;
Yatataamapi siddhaanaam kashchinmaam vetti tattvatah. |

Among thousands of persons, one person may seek perfection. Even among those who have achieved perfection, hardly one may truly get to know Me.

7.04

| भूमिरापोऽनलो वायुः खं मनो बुद्धिरेव च ।
अहंकार इतीयं मे भिन्ना प्रकृतिरष्टधा ॥ | Bhoomiraapo'nalo vaayuh kham mano buddhireva cha;
Ahamkaara iteeyam me bhinnaa prakritirashtadhaa. |

Earth, water, fire, air, space, mind, intellect and ego are eight aspects of my prakriti (physical nature).

7.05

| अपरेयमितस्त्वन्यां प्रकृतिं विद्धि मे पराम् ।
जीवभूतां महाबाहो ययेदं धार्यते जगत् ॥ | Apareyamitastvanyaam prakritim viddhi me paraam;
Jeevabhootaam mahaabaaho yayedam dhaaryate jagat. |

This is my lower physical nature. My higher nature, Arjuna, supports the whole universe and the life force of all living beings.

7.06

| एतद्योनीनि भूतानि सर्वाणीत्युपधारय ।
अहं कृत्स्नस्य जगतः प्रभवः प्रलयस्तथा ॥ | Etadyoneeni bhootaani sarvaaneetyupadhaaraya;
Aham kritsnasya jagatah prabhavah pralayastathaa. |

Arjuna, the combination of my lower and higher natures is the womb of all beings. The universe evolves from Me and dissolves in Me.

Jnana Vijnana Yoga

7.07

| मत्तः परतरं नान्यत्किञ्चिदस्ति धनञ्जय ।
मयि सर्वमिदं प्रोतं सूत्रे मणिगणा इव ॥ | Mattah parataram naanyat kinchidasti dhananjaya;
Mayi sarvamidam protam sootre maniganaa iva. |

There is nothing higher than Me, Arjuna. Everything is strung on Me like gems on a thread.

7.08

| रसोऽहमप्सु कौन्तेय प्रभास्मि शशिसूर्ययोः ।
प्रणवः सर्ववेदेषु शब्दः खे पौरुषं नृषु ॥ | Raso'hamapsu kaunteya prabhaasmi shashisooryayoh;
Pranavah sarvavedeshu shabdah khe paurusham nrishu. |

I am the fluidity in the water, Arjuna. I am the radiance of the Moon and the Sun. I am the sacred syllable OM in all the Vedas. I am the sound in space. I am the courage in human beings.

7.09

| पुण्यो गन्धः पृथिव्यां च तेजश्चास्मि विभावसौ ।
जीवनं सर्वभूतेषु तपश्चास्मि तपस्विषु ॥ | Punyo gandhah prithivyaam cha tejashchaasmi vibhaavasau;
Jeevanam sarvabhooteshu tapashchaasmi tapasvishu. |

I am the pure scent of the earth and the warmth in the fire. I am the life in all beings and the austerity in ascetics.

7.10

| बीजं मां सर्वभूतानां विद्धि पार्थ सनातनम् ।
बुद्धिर्बुद्धिमतामस्मि तेजस्तेजस्विनामहम् ॥ | Beejam maam sarvabhootaanaam viddhi paartha sanaatanam;
Buddhir buddhimataamasmi tejastejaswinaamaham. |

I am the primordial seed of all beings. I am the power of discrimination in those who are intelligent. I am the splendor of the splendid.

7.11

बलं बलवतां चाहं कामरागविवर्जितम् । धर्माविरुद्धो भूतेषु कामोऽस्मि भरतर्षभ ॥	Balam balavataam asmi kaamaraagavivarjitam; Dharmaaviruddho bhooteshu kaamo'smi bharatarshabha.

I am the strength of the strong. Free from passion and desire, I am desire itself if that desire is in harmony with dharma.

7.12

ये चैव सात्त्विका भावा राजसास्तामसाश्च ये । मत्त एवेति तान्विद्धि न त्वहं तेषु ते मयि ॥	Ye chaiva saattvikaa bhaavaa raajasaastaamasaashcha ye; Matta eveti taanviddhi na tvaham teshu te mayi.

The three gunas of material nature, Sattva (goodness), Rajas (activity) and Tamas (inertia) come from me. I am not in them. They are in Me.

7.13

त्रिभिर्गुणमयैर्भावैरेभिः सर्वमिदं जगत् । मोहितं नाभिजानाति मामेभ्यः परमव्ययम् ॥	Tribhirgunamayair bhaavairebhih sarvamidam jagat; Mohitam naabhijaanaati maamebhyah paramavyayam.

People are deluded by these gunas and fail to know Me, eternal and beyond them.

7.14

दैवी ह्येषा गुणमयी मम माया दुरत्यया । मामेव ये प्रपद्यन्ते मायामेतां तरन्ति ते ॥	Daivee hyeshaa gunamayee mama maayaa duratyayaa; Maameva ye prapadyante maayaametaam taranti te.

This wonderful illusion (Maya) of mine consisting of the three gunas is very difficult to overcome, but those who take refuge in Me cross over the maya.

7.15

| न मां दुष्कृतिनो मूढाः प्रपद्यन्ते नराधमाः ।
 माययापहृतज्ञाना आसुरं भावमाश्रिताः ॥ | Na maam dushkritino moodhaah prapadyante naraadhamaah;
 Maayayaapahritajnaanaa aasuram bhaavamaashritaah. |

The evildoers, the foolish and the wretched do not worship Me because their wisdom is clouded by maya. They take to devilish ways.

7.16

| चतुर्विधा भजन्ते मां जनाः सुकृतिनोऽर्जुन ।
 आर्तो जिज्ञासुरर्थार्थी ज्ञानी च भरतर्षभ ॥ | Chaturvidhaa bhajante maam janaah sukritino'rjuna;
 Aarto jijnaasurarthartheee jnaanee cha bharatarshabha. |

Arjuna, four types of good people worship Me. They are the afflicted, the seekers of wealth, the seekers of knowledge and the enlightened.

7.17

| तेषां ज्ञानी नित्ययुक्त एकभक्तिर्विशिष्यते ।
 प्रियो हि ज्ञानिनोऽत्यर्थमहं स च मम प्रियः ॥ | Teshaam jnaanee nityayukta eka bhaktirvishishyate;
 Priyo hi jnaanino'tyarthamaham sa cha mama priyah. |

Of these, the enlightened person who constantly meditates on Me, devoting himself only to Me, is the best. I am very dear to him and he is very dear to Me.

7.18

| उदाराः सर्व एवैते ज्ञानी त्वात्मैव मे मतम् ।
 आस्थितः स हि युक्तात्मा मामेवानुत्तमां गतिम् ॥ | Udaaraah sarva evaite jnaanee tvaatmaiva me matam;
 Aasthitah sa hi yuktaatmaa maamevaanuttamaam gatim. |

All of these four types are good. However, I consider the enlightened one like my own Self. The enlightened one makes Me his supreme goal.

7.19

| बहूनां जन्मनामन्ते ज्ञानवान्मां प्रपद्यते ।
 वासुदेवः सर्वमिति स महात्मा सुदुर्लभः ॥ | Bahoonaam janmanaamante jnaanavaanmaam prapadyate;
 Vaasudevah sarvamiti sa mahaatmaa sudurlabhah. |

After many births, these wise ones realize Me. They see Vasudeva (Brahman) in everything. Such great beings are rare.

7.20

| कामैस्तैस्तैर्हृतज्ञानाः प्रपद्यन्तेऽन्यदेवताः ।
 तं तं नियममास्थाय प्रकृत्या नियताः स्वया ॥ | Kaamaistaistairhritajnaanaah prapadyante'nyadevataah;
 Tam tam niyamamaasthaaya prakrityaa niyataah swayaa. |

Following their own nature, those whose discrimination has been overcome by various desires worship different devas with specific rites and rituals.

7.21

| यो यो यां यां तनुं भक्तः श्रद्धयार्चितुमिच्छति ।
 तस्य तस्याचलां श्रद्धां तामेव विदधाम्यहम् ॥ | Yo yo yaam yaam tanum bhaktah shraddhayaarchitum icchati;
 Tasya tasyaachalaam shraddhaam taameva vidadhaamyaham. |

Whatever deva a devotee chooses to worship in good faith, I will strengthen his faith.

7.22

| स तया श्रद्धया युक्तस्तस्याराधनमीहते ।
 लभते च ततः कामान्मयैव विहितान्हि तान् ॥ | Sa tayaa shraddhayaa yuktastasyaaraadhanameehate;
 Labhate cha tatah kaamaan mayaiva vihitaan hi taan. |

Endowed with strong faith, he worships his chosen deva and fulfills his desires. In reality, I fulfill his desires through that deva.

7.23

अन्तवत्तु फलं तेषां तद्भवत्यल्पमेधसाम् | देवान्देवयजो यान्ति मद्भक्ता यान्ति मामपि ||	Antavattu phalam teshaam tadbhavatyalpamedhasaam; Devaan devayajo yaanti madbhaktaa yaanti maamapi.

The rewards received by these devotees of insufficient knowledge are temporary. The worshipers of devas go to the devas, but my devotees attain Me.

7.24

अव्यक्तं व्यक्तिमापन्नं मन्यन्ते मामबुद्धयः | परं भावमजानन्तो ममाव्ययमनुत्तमम् ||	Avyaktam vyaktimaapannam manyante maamabuddhayah; Param bhaavamajaananto mamaavyayamanuttamam.

Those who lack real knowledge think that I, the unmanifest, have become manifest. They do not know my supreme, eternal and changeless nature.

7.25

नाहं प्रकाशः सर्वस्य योगमायासमावृतः | मूढोऽयं नाभिजानाति लोको मामजमव्ययम् ||	Naaham prakaashah sarvasya yogamaayaasamaavritah; Moodho'yam naabhijaanaati loko maamajamavyayam.

Covered by my yoga maya, I am not known by all. The deluded world does not know Me as the unborn and eternal.

7.26

वेदाहं समतीतानि वर्तमानानि चार्जुन | भविष्याणि च भूतानि मां तु वेद न कश्चन ||	Vedaaham samateetaani vartamaanaani chaarjuna; Bhavishyaani cha bhootani maam tu veda na kashchana.

Arjuna, I know the past, the present and the future beings, but nobody knows Me completely.

7.27

इच्छाद्वेषसमुत्थेन द्वन्द्वमोहेन भारत । सर्वभूतानि सम्मोहं सर्गे यान्ति परन्तप ॥	Icchaadveshasamutthena dvandvamohena bhaarata; Sarvabhootaani sammoham sarge yaanti parantapa.

Arjuna, all beings are subject to delusion at birth by the dualities born of likes and dislikes.

7.28

येषां त्वन्तगतं पापं जनानां पुण्यकर्मणाम् । ते द्वन्द्वमोहनिर्मुक्ता भजन्ते मां दृढव्रताः ॥	Yeshaam tvantagatam paapam janaanaam punyakarmanaam; Te dvandvamohanirmuktaa bhajante maam dridhavrataah.

Virtuous men, their sins cleansed, are free from duality and worship Me with complete devotion.

7.29

जरामरणमोक्षाय मामाश्रित्य यतन्ति ये । ते ब्रह्म तद्विदुः कृत्स्नमध्यात्मं कर्म चाखिलम् ॥	Jaraamaranamokshaaya maamaashritya yatanti ye; Te brahma tadviduh kritsnam adhyaatmam karma chaakhilam.

Those who seek refuge in Me, seeking liberation from old age and death, will know Brahman, the Self and all the secrets of karma.

7.30

साधिभूताधिदैवं मां साधियज्ञं च ये विदुः । प्रयाणकालेऽपि च मां ते विदुर्युक्तचेतसः ॥	Saadhibhootaadhidaivam maam saadhiyajnam cha ye viduh; Prayaanakaale'pi cha maam te vidur yuktachetasah.

Those who know Me as the Adhibhuta (principle of material manifestation), Adhidaiva (principle of divinity) and Adhiyajna (principle of sacrifice) are conscious of Me even at the time of death.

Jnana Vijnana Yoga

ॐ तत्सदिति श्रीमद्भगवद्गीतासूपनिषत्सु ब्रह्मविद्यायां योगशास्त्रे श्रीकृष्णार्जुनसंवादे ज्ञानविज्ञानयोगो नाम सप्तमोऽध्यायः	Om Tat Saditi Srimad Bhagavadgeetaasoopanishatsu Brahmavidyaayaam Yogashaastre Sri Krishnaarjunasamvaade Jnaanavijnaanayogo Naama Saptamo'dhyaayah

Thus ends the seventh discourse entitled Jnana Vijnana Yoga in the Upanishad, the divine Bhagavad Gita, the knowledge of Brahman, the scripture on Yoga and the dialogue between Sri Krishna and Arjuna.

Chapter 8
Akshara Brahma Yoga

8.01-8.02

अर्जुन उवाच |
किं तद् ब्रह्म किमध्यात्मं किं कर्म पुरुषोत्तम |
अधिभूतं च किं प्रोक्तमधिदैवं किमुच्यते ||
अधियज्ञः कथं कोऽत्र देहेऽस्मिन्मधुसूदन |
प्रयाणकाले च कथं ज्ञेयोऽसि नियतात्मभिः ||

Arjuna uvaacha:
Kim tadbrahma kim adhyaatmam kim karma purushottama;
Adhibhootam cha kim proktam adhidaivam kimuchyate.
Adhiyajnah katham ko'tra dehe'smin madhusoodana;
Prayaanakaale cha katham jneyo'si niyataatmabhih.

Arjuna said: What is that Brahman? What is that Adhyatma? What is Karma? What is Adhibhuta? What is Adhidaiva? And how and who is Adhiyagnya? How exactly can those of steadfast mind realize you at the time of death?

8.03

श्रीभगवानुवाच |
अक्षरं ब्रह्म परमं स्वभावोऽध्यात्ममुच्यते |
भूतभावोद्भवकरो विसर्गः कर्मसंज्ञितः ||

Sri Bhagavaan uvaacha:
Aksharam brahma paramam swabhaavo'dhyaatmamuchyate;
Bhootabhaavodbhavakaro visargah karmasamjnitah.

Bhagavan (Lord Krishna) said: Brahman is the indestructible supreme. The embodied self is the Adhyatma. The creative force that brings forth existence of beings is called Karma.

8.04

अधिभूतं क्षरो भावः पुरुषश्चाधिदैवतम् |
अधियज्ञोऽहमेवात्र देहे देहभृतां वर ||

Adhibhootam ksharo bhaavah
purushashchaadhidaivatam;
Adhiyajno'hamevaatra dehe
dehabhritaam vara.

Arjuna, the Adhibhuta is the perishable body. The Adhidaivata is the supreme divine agent (Purusha) that dwells in the body. I am Myself the Adhiyagnya (Lord of the Sacrifice), here in the body.

8.05

अन्तकाले च मामेव स्मरन्मुक्त्वा कलेवरम् |
यः प्रयाति स मद्भावं याति नास्त्यत्र संशयः ||

Antakaale cha maameva smaran
muktvaa kalevaram;
Yah prayaati sa madbhaavam yaati
naastyatra samshayah.

Whoever remembers only Me at the time of death will attain Me. There is no doubt about it.

8.06

यं यं वापि स्मरन्भावं त्यजत्यन्ते कलेवरम् |
तं तमेवैति कौन्तेय सदा तद्भावभावितः ||

Yam yam vaapi smaran bhaavam
tyajatyante kalevaram;
Tam tamevaiti kaunteya sadaa
tadbhaavabhaavitah.

After death, a person attains the thought that occupied his mind at the time of death. The last thoughts of a person are the same ones that he harbors constantly during his lifetime.

8.07

तस्मात्सर्वेषु कालेषु मामनुस्मर युध्य च |
मय्यर्पितमनोबुद्धिर्मामेवैष्यस्यसंशयः ||

Tasmaat sarveshu kaaleshu
maamanusmara yudhya cha;
Mayyarpitamanobuddhir
maamevaishyasyasamshayam.

Always think of Me and perform your duty. You will attain Me if you always focus on Me with your mind and intellect.

Akshara Brahma Yoga

8.08

अभ्यासयोगयुक्तेन चेतसा नान्यगामिना । परमं पुरुषं दिव्यं याति पार्थानुचिन्तयन् ।।	Abhyaasayogayuktena chetasaa naanyagaaminaa; Paramam purusham divyam yaati paarthaanuchintayan.

Arjuna, one who has made the mind steadfast by the practice of yoga and contemplates the supreme divine purusha with single-minded devotion attains Him.

8.09-8.10

कविं पुराणमनुशासितार-मणोरणीयंसमनुस्मरेद्यः । सर्वस्य धातारमचिन्त्यरूप-मादित्यवर्णं तमसः परस्तात् ।। प्रयाणकाले मनसाऽचलेन भक्त्या युक्तो योगबलेन चैव । भ्रुवोर्मध्ये प्राणमावेश्य सम्यक् स तं परं पुरुषमुपैति दिव्यम् ।।	Kavim puraanamanushaasitaaram Anoraneeyaamsam anusmaredyah; Sarvasya dhaataaram achintyaroopam Aadityavarnam tamasah parastaat. Prayaanakaale manasaachalena Bhaktyaa yukto yogabalena chaiva; Bhruvormadhye praanamaaveshya samyak Sa tam param purusham upaiti divyam.

One should meditate on the eternal Wise who is the Lord of all, smaller than the smallest, bright like the sun and beyond darkness. He should concentrate his life breath between the eyebrows through the power of yoga, and meditate upon Me with an unwavering mind at the hour of death. Such a person attains the supreme state.

8.11

यदक्षरं वेदविदो वदन्ति विशन्ति यद्यतयो वीतरागाः । यदिच्छन्तो ब्रह्मचर्यं चरन्ति तत्ते पदं संग्रहेण प्रवक्ष्ये ।।	Yadaksharam vedavido vadanti Vishanti yadyatayo veetaraagaah; Yadicchanto brahmacharyam charanti Tatte padam samgrahena pravakshye.

I shall briefly explain to you the process to attain that supreme state which the persons learned in the Vedas call imperishable. The ascetics who seek this state free themselves of attachment and practice Brahmacharya (celibacy).

8.12-8.13

सर्वद्वाराणि संयम्य मनो हृदि निरुध्य च । मूर्ध्न्याधायात्मनः प्राणमास्थितो योगधारणाम् ॥ ओमित्येकाक्षरं ब्रह्म व्याहरन्मामनुस्मरन् । यः प्रयाति त्यजन्देहं स याति परमां गतिम् ॥	Sarvadvaaraani samyamya mano hridi nirudhya cha; Moordhnyaadhaayaatmanah praanamaasthito yogadhaaranaam. Omityekaaksharam brahma vyaaharan maamanusmaran; Yah prayaati tyajan deham sa yaati paramaam gatim.

They should control all the senses, hold the mind in the heart and fix the life breath in the head. Then they should meditate on Me with full concentration and recite OM – which is Brahman in one syllable. Those who leave the body this way attain the supreme state.

8.14

अनन्यचेताः सततं यो मां स्मरति नित्यशः । तस्याहं सुलभः पार्थ नित्ययुक्तस्य योगिनः ॥	Ananyachetaah satatam yo maam smarati nityashah; Tasyaaham sulabhah paartha nityayuktasya yoginah.

Arjuna, the ever devout yogi can easily attain Me by constantly meditating on Me without other thoughts.

8.15

मामुपेत्य पुनर्जन्म दुःखालयमशाश्वतम् । नाप्नुवन्ति महात्मानः संसिद्धिं परमां गताः ॥	Maamupetya punarjanma duhkhaalayamashaashvatam; Naapnuvanti mahaatmaanah samsiddhim paramaam gataah.

Those perfect beings who have reached Me are no longer subject to rebirth in this transient place of suffering.

8.16

आब्रह्मभुवनाल्लोकाः पुनरावर्तिनोऽर्जुन । मामुपेत्य तु कौन्तेय पुनर्जन्म न विद्यते ॥	Aabrahmabhuvanaallokaah punaraavartino'rjuna; Maamupetya tu kaunteya punarjanma na vidyate.

Arjuna, everyone dwelling in Brahmaloka and other lokas (worlds) below is subject to rebirth. But there is no rebirth after reaching Me.

8.17

| सहस्रयुगपर्यन्तमहर्यद् ब्रह्मणो विदुः ।
 रात्रिं युगसहस्रान्तां तेऽहोरात्रविदो जनाः ॥ | Sahasrayugaparyantam aharyad brahmano viduh;
 Raatrim yugasahasraantaam te'horaatravido janaah. |

Brahma's day lasts a thousand yugas (about 4.3 billion years) and his night is of the same duration. Those who know this fact can appreciate the immensity of Brahma's night and day.

8.18

| अव्यक्ताद् व्यक्तयः सर्वाः प्रभवन्त्यहरागमे ।
 रात्र्यागमे प्रलीयन्ते तत्रैवाव्यक्तसंज्ञके ॥ | Avyaktaadvyaktayah sarvaah prabhavantyaharaagame;
 Raatryaagame praleeyante tatraivaavyaktasamjnake. |

At the dawn of Brahma's day, all manifestations emerge from the unmanifest, and at the beginning of Brahma's night, they are absorbed into the unmanifest.

8.19

| भूतग्रामः स एवायं भूत्वा भूत्वा प्रलीयते ।
 रात्र्यागमेऽवशः पार्थ प्रभवत्यहरागमे ॥ | Bhootagraamah sa evaayam bhootvaa bhootvaa praleeyate;
 Raatryaagame'vashah paartha prabhavatyaharaagame. |

Multitudes of beings come into existence again and again with the coming of Brahma's day and are reabsorbed into the unmanifest with the coming of Brahma's night.

8.20

| परस्तस्मात्तु भावोऽन्योऽव्यक्तोऽव्यक्तात्सनातनः ।
 यः स सर्वेषु भूतेषु नश्यत्सु न विनश्यति ॥ | Parastasmaat tu bhaavo'nyo'vyakto'vyaktaatsanaatanah;
 Yah sa sarveshu bhooteshu nashyatsu na vinashyati. |

Beyond this unmanifest, there is another unmanifest. This is eternal and not destroyed even when all things perish.

Commentary: Two types of avyaktas (umanifest) exist. One of them is primordial prakriti, from which all the manifestations occur during Brahma's day and are reabsorbed at the beginning of Brahma's night. Distinct from this, there is another unmanifest which remains unaffected forever. The first type of avyakta, although eternal, changes in a cyclical way with time, whereas the second is timeless.

8.21

| अव्यक्तोऽक्षर इत्युक्तस्तमाहुः परमां गतिम् ।
 यं प्राप्य न निवर्तन्ते तद्धाम परमं मम ॥ | Avyakto'kshara ityuktastamaahuh paramaam gatim;
 Yam praapya na nivartante taddhaama paramam mama. |

This imperishable unmanifest is the supreme goal. Those who reach it will never return. This is my supreme abode.

8.22

| पुरुषः स परः पार्थ भक्त्या लभ्यस्त्वनन्यया ।
 यस्यान्तःस्थानि भूतानि येन सर्वमिदं ततम् ॥ | Purushah sa parah paartha bhaktyaa labhyastvananyayaa;
 Yasyaantahsthaani bhootaani yena sarvamidam tatam. |

O Partha (Arjuna), the supreme Purusha (spirit) in whom all beings rest and by whom all existence is pervaded is attainable only by total devotion.

8.23

| यत्र काले त्वनावृत्तिमावृत्तिं चैव योगिनः ।
प्रयाता यान्ति तं कालं वक्ष्यामि भरतर्षभ ॥ | Yatra kaale tvanaavrittim aavrittim chaiva yoginah;
Prayaataa yaanti tam kaalam vakshyaami bharatarshabha. |

Now I will tell you, Arjuna, how the time of a yogi's death determines whether or not he is reborn.

8.24

| अग्निर्ज्योतिरहः शुक्लः षण्मासा उत्तरायणम् ।
तत्र प्रयाता गच्छन्ति ब्रह्म ब्रह्मविदो जनाः ॥ | Agnijyotirahah shuklah shanmaasaa uttaraayanam;
Tatra prayaataa gacchanti brahma brahmavido janaah. |

Yogis who are knowers of Brahman, who die in Shuklapaksha (bright half of the month) during the six month period of Uttarayana (northern course of the sun), and proceed on the path presided over by the deities of fire, light and day, are not reborn.

8.25

| धूमो रात्रिस्तथा कृष्णः षण्मासा दक्षिणायनम् ।
तत्र चान्द्रमसं ज्योतिर्योगी प्राप्य निवर्तते ॥ | Dhoomo raatristathaa krishnah shanmaasaa dakshinaayanam;
Tatra chaandramasam jyotir yogee praapya nivartate. |

Yogis who die in Krishnapaksha (dark half of the month) during the six month period of Dakshinayana (southern course of the sun), and proceed on the path presided over by the deities of smoke and night, attain the radiance of the moon and are reborn.

8.26

| शुक्लकृष्णे गती ह्येते जगतः शाश्वते मते ।
एकया यात्यनावृत्तिमन्ययावर्तते पुनः ॥ | Shuklakrishne gatee hyete jagatah shaashvate mate;
Ekayaa yaatyanaavrittim anyayaa'vartate punah. |

These two paths of light and darkness to depart from the mortal world are eternal. The yogi taking the path of light is not reborn, but the yogi who takes the dark path is reborn.

8.27

नैते सृती पार्थ जानन्योगी मुह्यति कश्चन । तस्मात्सर्वेषु कालेषु योगयुक्तो भवार्जुन ॥	Naite sritee paartha jaanan yogee muhyati kashchana; Tasmaat sarveshu kaaleshu yogayukto bhavaarjuna.

O Partna (Arjuna), a yogi who understands these paths is never deluded. Therefore, Arjuna, at all times be a yoga yukta (one who is steadfast in yoga).

8.28

वेदेषु यज्ञेषु तपःसु चैव दानेषु यत्पुण्यफलं प्रदिष्टम् । अत्येति तत्सर्वमिदं विदित्वा योगी परं स्थानमुपैति चाद्यम् ॥	Vedeshu yajneshu tapahsu chaiva Daaneshu yat punyaphalam pradishtam; Atyeti tatsarvam idam viditvaa Yogee param sthaanamupaiti chaadyam.

The yogi who understands this reaps the rewards that are beyond those obtained by reciting the Vedas and making sacrifices, austerities, gifts and charities. He attains the supreme, primal abode.

ॐ तत्सदिति श्रीमद्भगवद्गीतासूपनिषत्सु ब्रह्मविद्यायां योगशास्त्रे श्रीकृष्णार्जुनसंवादे अक्षरब्रह्मयोगो नामाष्टमोऽध्यायः	Om Tat Saditi Srimad Bhagavadgeetaasoopanishatsu Brahmavidyaayaam Yogashaastre Sri Krishnaarjunasamvaade Aksharabrahmayogo Naama Ashtamo'dhyaayah

Thus ends the eighth discourse entitled Akshara Brahma Yoga in the Upanishad, the divine Bhagavad Gita, the knowledge of Brahman, the scripture on Yoga and the dialogue between Sri Krishna and Arjuna.

Chapter 9
Rajavidya Rajaguhya Yoga

	9.01
श्रीभगवानुवाच । इदं तु ते गुह्यतमं प्रवक्ष्याम्यनसूयवे । ज्ञानं विज्ञानसहितं यज्ज्ञात्वा मोक्ष्यसेऽशुभात् ॥	Sri Bhagavaan uvaacha: Idam tu te guhyatamam pravakshyaamyanasooyave; Jnaanam vijnaanasahitam yajjnaatvaa mokshyase'shubhaat.

Bhagavan (Lord Krishna) said: Arjuna, because you are not cynical, I shall reveal to you the profound mystery of Self-knowledge and Self-realization. With this knowledge you will become free from the misery of worldly existence.

	9.02
राजविद्या राजगुह्यं पवित्रमिदमुत्तमम् । प्रत्यक्षावगमं धर्म्यं सुसुखं कर्तुमव्ययम् ॥	Raajavidyaa raajaguhyam pavitramidamuttamam; Pratyakshaavagamam dharmyam susukham kartumavyayam.

This is the King of Sciences and the King of Mysteries. It is the supreme purifier and is easily understandable. It is in harmony with dharma, easy to practice and to remember.

9.03

अश्रद्दधानाः पुरुषा धर्मस्यास्य परन्तप । अप्राप्य मां निवर्तन्ते मृत्युसंसारवर्त्मनि ॥	Ashraddhadhaanaah purushaa dharmasyaasya parantapa; Apraapya maam nivartante mrityusamsaaravartmani.

Arjuna, those who lack faith in this dharma will not reach Me. They stay in the cycle of birth and death.

9.04

मया ततमिदं सर्वं जगदव्यक्तमूर्तिना । मत्स्थानि सर्वभूतानि न चाहं तेष्ववस्थितः ॥	Mayaa tatamidam sarvam jagadavyaktamoortinaa; Matsthaani sarvabhootaani na chaaham teshvavasthitah.

I pervade the entire universe in my unmanifest form. All beings are in Me, but I do not exist in them.

Commentary: Lord Krishna's statement *"All beings are in me"* means that everything owes its existence to Lord Krishna and nothing can exist without Him. His statement *"I do not exist in them"* means that his existence does not depend on them. He continues to exist even when the manifest world ceases to exist. Although he pervades everything, he is not attached to or affected by anything. He does not exclusively belong to nor is confined by anyone or anything. He is omnipresent.

9.05

न च मत्स्थानि भूतानि पश्य मे योगमैश्वरम् । भूतभृन्न च भूतस्थो ममात्मा भूतभावनः ॥	Na cha matsthaani bhootaani pashya me yogamaishvaram; Bhootabhrinna cha bhootastho mamaatmaa bhootabhaavanah.

All beings appear to be in Me but in reality they are not in Me. Look at my divine yoga. I am the creator and sustainer of all beings, but I am not limited to them.

Commentary: Lord Krishna says in 9.04 that all beings exist in Him and in 9.05 he says that, in reality, they do not exist in Him. Although these statements appear to contradict one another on the surface, a deeper reading shows a consistent progression of thought. Right after his statement that all beings do not exist in Him, he instructs Arjuna to look at the supreme power of His yoga (maya). It is maya that creates and sustains the illusion of multitudes of beings. In reality, there are no distinct entities that can be "inside" or "outside" one other – there is only Brahman. Lord Krishna's explanation takes Arjuna a step further to Brahma Jnana, leading him to see through maya and realize the Self. For a Self-realized person, nothing exists but God.

9.06

यथाकाशस्थितो नित्यं वायुः सर्वत्रगो महान् । तथा सर्वाणि भूतानि मत्स्थानीत्युपधारय ॥	Yathaakaashasthito nityam vaayuh sarvatrago mahaan; Tathaa sarvaani bhootaani matsthaaneetyupadhaaraya.

Just as the mighty wind that moves everywhere is contained in the sky, all beings are contained in Me.

Commentary: The wind depends on space for its existence whereas space does not depend on the wind. Space can exist even in the absence of wind. Although space supports the wind, it is not affected by the wind. Similarly, all beings depend on God for their existence. For human beings operating at the relative level of awareness, it is a helpful reminder that all beings are contained in God.

9.07

सर्वभूतानि कौन्तेय प्रकृतिं यान्ति मामिकाम् । कल्पक्षये पुनस्तानि कल्पादौ विसृजाम्यहम् ॥	Sarvabhootaani kaunteya prakritim yaanti maamikaam; Kalpakshaye punastaani kalpaadau visrijaamyaham.

Arjuna, at the end of a kalpa (Brahma's day), all beings merge into my prakriti (unmanifested matter) and at the beginning of a kalpa, I create them again.

9.08

प्रकृतिं स्वामवष्टभ्य विसृजामि पुनः पुनः । भूतग्राममिमं कृत्स्नमवशं प्रकृतेर्वशात् ॥	Prakritim swaamavashtabhya visrijaami punah punah; Bhootagraamamimam kritsnamavasham prakritervashaat.

Using my prakriti, I create multitudes of beings and place them under the influence of my prakriti.

9.09

न च मां तानि कर्माणि निबध्नन्ति धनञ्जय । उदासीनवदासीनमसक्तं तेषु कर्मसु ॥	Na cha maam taani karmaani nibadhnanti dhananjaya; Udaaseenavadaaseenam asaktam teshu karmasu.

Arjuna, these actions do not bind Me because I remain indifferent and unattached.

9.10

मयाध्यक्षेण प्रकृतिः सूयते सचराचरम् । हेतुनानेन कौन्तेय जगद्विपरिवर्तते ॥	Mayaa'dhyakshena prakritih sooyate sacharaacharam; Hetunaa'nena kaunteya jagadviparivartate.

Arjuna, under my keen supervision, prakriti creates all animates and inanimates, and keeps the wheel of the universe revolving.

9.11

| अवजानन्ति मां मूढा मानुषीं तनुमाश्रितम् ।
परं भावमजानन्तो मम भूतमहेश्वरम् ॥ | Avajaananti maam moodhaah maanusheem tanumaashritam;
Param bhaavamajaananto mama bhootamaheshwaram. |

Simpletons disregard Me when I appear in the human form because they are unaware of my higher state, as the supreme Lord of all beings.

9.12

| मोघाशा मोघकर्माणो मोघज्ञाना विचेतसः ।
राक्षसीमासुरीं चैव प्रकृतिं मोहिनीं श्रिताः ॥ | Moghaashaa moghakarmaano moghajnaanaa vichetasah;
Raakshaseemaasureem chaiva prakritim mohineem shritaah. |

These thoughtless beings with false ideas, hollow knowledge and futile actions assume the behavior of savage beasts.

9.13

| महात्मानस्तु मां पार्थ दैवीं प्रकृतिमाश्रिताः ।
भजन्त्यनन्यमनसो ज्ञात्वा भूतादिमव्ययम् ॥ | Mahaatmaanastu maam paartha daiveem prakritimaashritaah;
Bhajantyananyamanaso jnaatvaa bhootaadimavyayam. |

Arjuna, the Mahatmas (great beings) seek my divine nature. They worship Me with total devotion as the imperishable source of all beings.

9.14

| सततं कीर्तयन्तो मां यतन्तश्च दृढव्रताः ।
नमस्यन्तश्च मां भक्त्या नित्ययुक्ता उपासते ॥ | Satatam keertayanto maam yatantashcha dridhavrataah;
Namasyantashcha maam bhaktyaa nityayuktaa upaasate. |

With firm resolve to attain Me, they worship Me by constantly singing my glories and bowing down to Me with devotion.

9.15

ज्ञानयज्ञेन चाप्यन्ये यजन्तो मामुपासते । एकत्वेन पृथक्त्वेन बहुधा विश्वतोमुखम् ॥	Jnaanayajnena chaapyanye yajanto maamupaasate; Ekatvena prithaktvena bahudhaa vishwatomukham.

Some approach Me with the offering of knowledge and worship Me as one or many manifested forms.

9.16

अहं क्रतुरहं यज्ञः स्वधाहमहमौषधम् । मन्त्रोऽहमहमेवाज्यमहमग्निरहं हुतम् ॥	Aham kraturaham yajnah swadhaa'hamahamaushadham; Mantro'hamahamevaajyam ahamagniraham hutam.

I am the Vedic ritual. I am the sacrifice. I am the offering. I am the medicinal herb. I am the mantra. I am the ghee. I am the sacred fire. I am also the act of offering oblations to the fire.

9.17

पिताहमस्य जगतो माता धाता पितामहः । वेद्यं पवित्रमोंकार ऋक्साम यजुरेव च ॥	Pitaahamasya jagato maataa dhaataa pitaamahah; Vedyam pavitram omkaara riksaama yajureva cha.

I am the supporter of the universe, its father, mother and grandfather. I am all that is to be known. I am the means of purification. I am the sacred syllable OM and also the Rig, the Yajur, and the Sama Vedas.

9.18

गतिर्भर्ता प्रभुः साक्षी निवासः शरणं सुहृत् । प्रभवः प्रलयः स्थानं निधानं बीजमव्ययम् ॥	Gatirbhartaa prabhuh saakshee nivaasah sharanam suhrit; Prabhavah pralayah sthaanam nidhaanam beejamavyayam.

I am the supporter, the Lord, the inner witness, the abode, the refuge, the friend, the origin and end, the storehouse and the eternal seed.

9.19

तपाम्यहमहं वर्षं निगृह्णाम्युत्सृजामि च । अमृतं चैव मृत्युश्च सदसच्चाहमर्जुन ॥	Tapaamyahamaham varsham nigrihnaamyutsrijaami cha; Amritam chaiva mrityushcha sadasacchaahamarjuna.

Arjuna, I radiate heat. I withhold the rain and release it. I am immortality and also death. I am being and also non-being.

9.20

त्रैविद्या मां सोमपाः पूतपापा यज्ञैरिष्ट्वा स्वर्गतिं प्रार्थयन्ते । ते पुण्यमासाद्य सुरेन्द्रलोक- मश्नन्ति दिव्यान्दिवि देवभोगान् ॥	Traividyaa maam somapaah pootapaapaa Yajnairishtvaa swargatim praarthayante; Te punyamaasaadya surendraloka- Mashnanti divyaan divi devabhogaan.

Those who perform rituals as prescribed in the Vedas and drink Soma juice are freed from sins. If they worship Me with sacrifices and pray for heaven, they go to heaven and enjoy heavenly pleasures.

9.21

ते तं भुक्त्वा स्वर्गलोकं विशालं क्षीणे पुण्ये मर्त्यलोकं विशन्ति । एवं त्रयीधर्ममनुप्रपन्ना गतागतं कामकामा लभन्ते ॥	Te tam bhuktvaa swargalokam vishaalam Ksheene punye martyalokam vishanti; Evam trayeedharmamanuprapannaa Gataagatam kaamakaamaa labhante.

After enjoying the heavenly pleasures, they return to the mortal world upon the exhaustion of their punya (merit). Thus following the Vedas to perform fruitive actions, they repeatedly come and go.

9.22

अनन्याश्चिन्तयन्तो मां ये जनाः पर्युपासते । तेषां नित्याभियुक्तानां योगक्षेमं वहाम्यहम् ॥	Ananyaashchintayanto maam ye janaah paryupaasate; Teshaam nityaabhiyuktaanaam yogakshemam vahaamyaham.

For those who worship Me with devotion and meditate on Me without distraction, I take care of their security and all other needs.

9.23

| येऽप्यन्यदेवता भक्ता यजन्ते श्रद्धयान्विताः ।
तेऽपि मामेव कौन्तेय यजन्त्यविधिपूर्वकम् ॥ | Ye'pyanyadevataa bhaktaa yajante shraddhayaa'nvitaah;
Te'pi maameva kaunteya yajantyavidhipoorvakam. |

Arjuna, even those devotees who worship other devas are really worshipping Me, indirectly.

9.24

| अहं हि सर्वयज्ञानां भोक्ता च प्रभुरेव च ।
न तु मामभिजानन्ति तत्त्वेनातश्च्यवन्ति ते ॥ | Aham hi sarvayajnaanaam bhoktaa cha prabhureva cha;
Na tu maamabhijaananti tattvenaatashchyavanti te. |

I am the only recipient and master of all sacrifices. Those who perform sacrifices without recognizing my true nature suffer rebirth.

9.25

| यान्ति देवव्रता देवान्पितॄन्यान्ति पितृव्रताः ।
भूतानि यान्ति भूतेज्या यान्ति मद्याजिनोऽपि माम् ॥ | Yaanti devavrataa devaan pitreen yaanti pitrivrataah;
Bhutaani yaanti bhutejyaa yaanti madyaajino'pi maam. |

Those who worship the devas go to the devas; those who worship the ancestors go to the ancestors; those who worship the spirits go to the spirits; but those who worship Me come to Me.

9.26

| पत्रं पुष्पं फलं तोयं यो मे भक्त्या प्रयच्छति ।
तदहं भक्त्युपहृतमश्नामि प्रयतात्मनः ॥ | Patram pushpam phalam toyam yo me bhaktyaa prayacchati;
Tadaham bhaktyupahritamashnaami prayataatmanah. |

I accept with joy whatever is offered with pure mind and devotion – a leaf, a flower, a fruit or water.

9.27

| यत्करोषि यदश्नासि यज्जुहोषि ददासि यत् ।
 यत्तपस्यसि कौन्तेय तत्कुरुष्व मदर्पणम् ॥ | Yatkaroshi yadashnaasi yajjuhoshi dadaasi yat;
 Yattapasyasi kaunteya tatkurushva madarpanam. |

Arjuna, whatever you do, whatever you eat, whatever sacrifice you perform, whatever you give in charity, whatever austerity you perform, do it all as an offering to Me.

9.28

| शुभाशुभफलैरेवं मोक्ष्यसे कर्मबन्धनैः ।
 संन्यासयोगयुक्तात्मा विमुक्तो मामुपैष्यसि ॥ | Shubhaashubhaphalairevam mokshyase karmabandhanaih;
 Sannyaasayogayuktaatmaa vimukto maamupaishyasi. |

This frees you from the bondage of karma and its good or bad consequences. Thus, your mind firmly established in the yoga of renunciation, you will come to Me.

9.29

| समोऽहं सर्वभूतेषु न मे द्वेष्योऽस्ति न प्रियः ।
 ये भजन्ति तु मां भक्त्या मयि ते तेषु चाप्यहम् ॥ | Samo'ham sarvabhooteshu na me dveshyo'sti na priyah;
 Ye bhajanti tu maam bhaktyaa mayi te teshu chaapyaham. |

All beings are the same to Me, Arjuna. I see none as friend or foe. Those who are my devotional worshipers are in Me and I am in them.

Commentary: Lord Krishna is emphasizing here, and in the next few verses, that he is not *partial* to anyone. He is the Self in everyone. Anyone who worships him with devotion realizes that there is nothing else but God. This is what he means by *"my devotional worshipers are in Me and I am in them."*

9.30

| अपि चेत्सुदुराचारो भजते मामनन्यभाक् \|
साधुरेव स मन्तव्यः सम्यग्व्यवसितो हि सः \|\| | Api chet suduraachaaro bhajate maamananyabhaak;
Saadhureva sa mantavyah samyagvyavasito hi sah. |

Even the worst person, if he worships Me wholeheartedly, shall be considered saintly because he has started to go in the right path.

9.31

| क्षिप्रं भवति धर्मात्मा शश्वच्छान्तिं निगच्छति \|
कौन्तेय प्रतिजानीहि न मे भक्तः प्रणश्यति \|\| | Kshipram bhavati dharmaatmaa shashwacchaantim nigacchati;
Kaunteya pratijaaneehi na me bhaktah pranashyati. |

Soon he will become virtuous and achieve everlasting peace. I promise you, Arjuna, that no worshiper of mine is ever lost.

9.32

| मां हि पार्थ व्यपाश्रित्य येऽपि स्युः पापयोनयः \|
स्त्रियो वैश्यास्तथा शूद्रास्तेऽपि यान्ति परां गतिम् \|\| | Maam hi paartha vyapaashritya ye'pi syuh paapayonayah;
Striyo vaishyaastathaa shoodraaste'pi yaanti paraam gatim. |

Arjuna, by taking refuge in Me, even those who are born into unfortunate circumstances, women, Vaishyas and Shudras reach the supreme goal.

Commentary: Historically, Brahmin and Kshatriya males had ready access to spiritual training, whereas others did not. Lord Krishna is making it abundantly clear that he cares for everyone regardless of birth, sex and social status. He is emphasizing that even those who are discriminated against by society and who are deprived of formal spiritual training need not give up hope of reaching God. All have access to God via bhakti. Anyone who seeks refuge in Him and worships Him with a pure heart attains Him.

9.33

| किं पुनर्ब्राह्मणाः पुण्या भक्ता राजर्षयस्तथा । अनित्यमसुखं लोकमिमं प्राप्य भजस्व माम् ॥ | Kim punarbraahmanaah punyaa bhaktaa raajarshayastathaa; Anityamasukham lokam imam praapya bhajaswa maam. |

It is no wonder that pious Brahmins and royal sages come to Me. Having come to this impermanent and suffering world, they worship Me with devotion.

9.34

| मन्मना भव मद्भक्तो मद्याजी मां नमस्कुरु । मामेवैष्यसि युक्त्वैवमात्मानं मत्परायणः ॥ | Manmanaa bhava madbhakto madyaajee maam namaskuru; Maamevaishyasi yuktvaivamaatmaanam matparaayanah. |

Fix your mind on Me, be devoted to Me, offer sacrifices to Me, pay homage to Me, consider Me as the highest goal. Then you shall come to Me.

| ॐ तत्सदिति श्रीमद्भगवद्गीतासूपनिषत्सु ब्रह्मविद्यायां योगशास्त्रे श्रीकृष्णार्जुनसंवादे राजविद्याराजगुह्ययोगो नाम नवमोऽध्यायः । | Om Tat Saditi Srimad Bhagavadgeetaasoopanishatsu Brahmavidyaayaam Yogashaastre Sri Krishnaarjunasamvaade Raajavidyaa-raajaguhyayogo Naama Navamo'dhyaayah |

Thus ends the ninth discourse entitled Rajavidya Rajaguhya Yoga in the Upanishad, the divine Bhagavad Gita, the knowledge of Brahman, the scripture on Yoga and the dialogue between Sri Krishna and Arjuna.

Chapter 10
Vibhuti Yoga

10.01

श्रीभगवानुवाच |
भूय एव महाबाहो शृणु मे परमं वचः |
यत्तेऽहं प्रीयमाणाय वक्ष्यामि हितकाम्यया ||

Sri Bhagavaan uvaacha:
Bhooya eva mahaabaaho shrinu me paramam vachah;
Yatte'ham preeyamaanaaya vakshyaami hitakaamyayaa.

Bhagavan (Lord Krishna) said: Arjuna, since you are dear to Me, I will tell you my supreme word. Listen carefully, it benefits you.

10.02

न मे विदुः सुरगणाः प्रभवं न महर्षयः |
अहमादिर्हि देवानां महर्षीणां च सर्वशः ||

Na me viduh suraganaah prabhavam na maharshayah;
Ahamaadirhi devaanaam maharsheenaam cha sarvashah.

Neither the gods nor the seers know my beginning, because I am their origin also.

10.03

यो मामजमनादिं च वेत्ति लोकमहेश्वरम् |
असम्मूढः स मर्त्येषु सर्वपापैः प्रमुच्यते ||

Yo maamajamanaadim cha vetti lokamaheshwaram;
Asammoodhah sa martyeshu sarvapaapaih pramuchyate.

That person among mortals who knows that I am the supreme Lord of the universe, unborn and without beginning, is free from delusions and is released of all sins.

10.04-10.05

| बुद्धिर्ज्ञानमसम्मोहः क्षमा सत्यं दमः शमः ।
 सुखं दुःखं भवोऽभावो भयं चाभयमेव च ॥
 अहिंसा समता तुष्टिस्तपो दानं यशोऽयशः ।
 भवन्ति भावा भूतानां मत्त एव पृथग्विधाः ॥ | Buddhir jnaanamasammohah kshamaa satyam damah shamah;
 Sukham duhkham bhavo'bhaavo bhayam chaabhayameva cha.
 Ahimsaa samataa tushtistapo daanam yasho'yashah;
 Bhavanti bhaavaa bhootaanaam matta eva prithagvidhaah. |

Intelligence, knowledge, non-delusion, forgiveness, truthfulness, self-restraint, happiness and sorrow, birth and death, fear and courage, nonviolence, equanimity, contentment, austerity, charity, fame and infamy – all these different states arise from Me alone.

10.06

| महर्षयः सप्त पूर्वे चत्वारो मनवस्तथा ।
 मद्भावा मानसा जाता येषां लोक इमाः प्रजाः ॥ | Maharshayah sapta poorve chatvaaro manavastathaa;
 Madbhaavaa maanasaa jaataa yeshaam loka imaah prajaah. |

The seven great seers, the four earliest sages, and the Manus (world administrators) were born from my mind. All the creations of the world were born from them.

10.07

| एतां विभूतिं योगं च मम यो वेत्ति तत्त्वतः ।
 सोऽविकम्पेन योगेन युज्यते नात्र संशयः ॥ | Etaam vibhootim yogam cha mama yo vetti tattvatah; So'vikampena yogena yujyate naatra samshayah. |

One who truly understands my power gets united with Me through unswerving devotion. There is no doubt about it.

10.08

| अहं सर्वस्य प्रभवो मत्तः सर्वं प्रवर्तते ।
 इति मत्वा भजन्ते मां बुधा भावसमन्विताः ॥ | Aham sarvasya prabhavo mattah sarvam pravartate; Iti matvaa bhajante maam budhaa bhaavasamanvitaah. |

I am the source of all and everything evolves from Me. Having realized this, the wise worship Me with total devotion.

Vibhuti Yoga

10.09

मच्चित्ता मद्गतप्राणा बोधयन्तः परस्परम् । कथयन्तश्च मां नित्यं तुष्यन्ति च रमन्ति च ॥	Macchittaa madgatapraanaa bodhayantah parasparam; Kathayantashcha maam nityam tushyanti cha ramanti cha.

They think always of Me, dedicate their lives to Me and enlighten each other about my glory. They speak about Me always and ever remain content and happy.

10.10

तेषां सततयुक्तानां भजतां प्रीतिपूर्वकम् । ददामि बुद्धियोगं तं येन मामुपयान्ति ते ॥	Teshaam satatayuktaanaam bhajataam preetipoorvakam; Dadaami buddhiyogam tam yena maamupayaanti te.

To those who are steadfast and who worship Me with love, I grant Buddhi Yoga, through which they come to Me.

10.11

तेषामेवानुकम्पार्थमहमज्ञानजं तमः । नाशयाम्यात्मभावस्थो ज्ञानदीपेन भास्वता ॥	Teshaam evaanukampaartham aham ajnaanajam tamah; Naashayaamyaatmabhaavastho jnaanadeepena bhaasvataa.

Out of compassion for them, I dwell in their hearts and remove the darkness of ignorance by shining the light of knowledge.

10.12

अर्जुन उवाच । परं ब्रह्म परं धाम पवित्रं परमं भवान् । पुरुषं शाश्वतं दिव्यमादिदेवमजं विभुम् ॥	Arjuna uvaacha: Param brahma param dhaama pavitram paramam bhavaan; Purusham shaashvatam divyam aadidevamajam vibhum.

Arjuna said: You are the supreme Brahman, the supreme shelter, the supreme purifier, the eternal divine being, the primordial God, the unborn and all pervading.

10.13

| आहुस्त्वामृषयः सर्वे देवर्षिर्नारदस्तथा ।
असितो देवलो व्यासः स्वयं चैव ब्रवीषि मे ॥ | Aahustvaam rishayah sarve devarshirnaaradastathaa;
Asito devalo vyaasah swayam chaiva braveeshi me. |

This is how the divine sage Narada, the sages Asita, Devala and Vyasa have described you. Now you have told me this yourself.

10.14

| सर्वमेतदृतं मन्ये यन्मां वदसि केशव ।
न हि ते भगवन्व्यक्तिं विदुर्देवा न दानवाः ॥ | Sarvametadritam manye yanmaam vadasi keshava;
Na hi te bhagavan vyaktim vidurdevaa na daanavaah. |

Now Krishna, I believe that everything you have told Me is the truth. O Lord, neither the gods nor the demons know your manifestations.

10.15

| स्वयमेवात्मनात्मानं वेत्थ त्वं पुरुषोत्तम ।
भूतभावन भूतेश देवदेव जगत्पते ॥ | Swayamevaatmanaatmaanam vettha tvam purushottama;
Bhootabhaavana bhootesha devadeva jagatpate. |

O creator and Lord of all beings, O God of gods, Master of the Universe, O supreme Purusha (being), you alone know yourself.

10.16

| वक्तुमर्हस्यशेषेण दिव्या ह्यात्मविभूतयः ।
याभिर्विभूतिभिर्लोकानिमांस्त्वं व्याप्य तिष्ठसि ॥ | Vaktum arhasyasheshena divyaa hyaatmavibhootayah;
Yaabhir vibhootibhir lokaanimaamstvam vyaapya tishthasi. |

Please fully describe to Me your divine manifestations and glories which fill the entire universe.

10.17

| कथं विद्यामहं योगिंस्त्वां सदा परिचिन्तयन् ।
केषु केषु च भावेषु चिन्त्योऽसि भगवन्मया ॥ | Katham vidyaamaham yogimstvaam sadaa parichintayan;
Keshu keshu cha bhaaveshu chintyo'si bhagavanmayaa. |

O supreme yogi, how am I to know you through constant meditation? O Lord, in what forms am I to meditate upon you?

10.18

| विस्तरेणात्मनो योगं विभूतिं च जनार्दन ।
भूयः कथय तृप्तिर्हि शृण्वतो नास्ति मेऽमृतम् ॥ | Vistarenaatmano yogam vibhootim cha janaardana;
Bhooyah kathaya triptirhi shrinvato naasti me'mritam. |

O Janardana, describe again your power of yoga and your glories. I can never feel that I have heard enough of your nectar-like words.

10.19

| श्रीभगवानुवाच ।
हन्त ते कथयिष्यामि दिव्या ह्यात्मविभूतयः ।
प्राधान्यतः कुरुश्रेष्ठ नास्त्यन्तो विस्तरस्य मे ॥ | Sri Bhagavaan uvaacha:
Hanta te kathayishyaami divyaa hyaatmavibhootayah;
Praadhaanyatah kurushreshtha naastyanto vistarasya me. |

Bhagavan (Lord Krishna) said: Arjuna, I will tell you of my divine manifestations, but only the prominent ones because they are unlimited.

10.20

| अहमात्मा गुडाकेश सर्वभूताशयस्थितः ।
अहमादिश्च मध्यं च भूतानामन्त एव च ॥ | Ahamaatmaa gudaakesha sarvabhootaashayasthitah;
Ahamaadishcha madhyam cha bhootaanaamanta eva cha. |

Arjuna, I am the Self in the hearts of all beings. I am the beginning, the middle and also the end of all beings.

10.21

आदित्यानामहं विष्णुर्ज्योतिषां रविरंशुमान् ‌। मरीचिर्मरुतामस्मि नक्षत्राणामहं शशी ‌॥	Aadityaanaamaham vishnur jyotishaam raviramshumaan; Mareechirmarutaamasmi nakshatraanaamaham shashee.

I am the Sun among the luminaries. Among the adityas (the twelve names of the Sun), I am Vishnu (the name for the January Sun). I am Marichi among the wind gods and the moon among the stars.

10.22

वेदानां सामवेदोऽस्मि देवानामस्मि वासवः ‌। इन्द्रियाणां मनश्चास्मि भूतानामस्मि चेतना ‌॥	Vedaanaam saamavedo'smi devaanaam asmi vaasavah; Indriyaanaam manashchaasmi bhootaanaamasmi chetanaa.

I am Sama Veda among the Vedas. I am Indra among the devas. I am the mind among the senses, and the consciousness in living beings.

10.23

रुद्राणां शङ्करश्चास्मि वित्तेशो यक्षरक्षसाम् ‌। वसूनां पावकश्चास्मि मेरुः शिखरिणामहम् ‌॥	Rudraanaam shankarashchaasmi vittesho yaksharakshasaam; Vasoonaam paavakashchaasmi meruh shikharinaamaham.

Of the Rudras (gods of destruction), I am Shankara. Of the Yakshas and Rakshasas, I am the Lord of wealth (Kubera). Of the Vasus (the eight atmospheric lords), I am the fire god and of the peaks I am Meru (the golden mountain at the center of the cosmos).

10.24

पुरोधसां च मुख्यं मां विद्धि पार्थ बृहस्पतिम् ‌। सेनानीनामहं स्कन्दः सरसामस्मि सागरः ‌॥	Purodhasaam cha mukhyam maam viddhipaartha brihaspatim; Senaaneenaamaham skandah sarasaamasmi saagarah.

Arjuna, among the priests I am the chief priest of the devas, Brihaspati. I am Skanda (Kartikeya) among the generals and I am the ocean among bodies of water.

10.25

महर्षीणां भृगुरहं गिरामस्म्येकमक्षरम् |
यज्ञानां जपयज्ञोऽस्मि स्थावराणां हिमालयः ||

Maharsheenaam bhriguraham giraamasmyekamaksharam;
Yajnaanaam japayajno'smi sthaavaraanaam himaalayah.

Of the great seers, I am Bhrigu. I am the sacred monosyllable OM among words. I am the sacrifice consisting of japa (silently uttering a mantra) and I am the Himalayas among the mountains.

10.26

अश्वत्थः सर्ववृक्षाणां देवर्षीणां च नारदः |
गन्धर्वाणां चित्ररथः सिद्धानां कपिलो मुनिः ||

Ashwatthah sarvavrikshaanaam devarsheenaam cha naaradah;
Gandharvaanaam chitrarathah siddhaanaam kapilo munih.

Of the trees, I am Ashvatta (Peepal). Of the divine seers I am Narada. Of the Gandharvas (celestial singers and musicians) I am Chitraratha, and of all the siddhas (perfect beings) I am Kapila.

10.27

उच्चैःश्रवसमश्वानां विद्धि माममृतोद्भवम् |
ऐरावतं गजेन्द्राणां नराणां च नराधिपम् ||

Ucchaihshravasamashwaanaam viddhi maamamritodbhavam;
Airaavatam gajendraanaam naraanaam cha naraadhipam.

Among horses, I am Uchchaishrava (the horse that emerged along with nectar during the churning of the ocean). Among the mighty elephants I am Airavata (Indra's elephant) and among men I am King.

10.28

आयुधानामहं वज्रं धेनूनामस्मि कामधुक् |
प्रजनश्चास्मि कन्दर्पः सर्पाणामस्मि वासुकिः ||

Aayudhaanaamaham vajram dhenoonaamasmi kaamadhuk;
Prajanashchaasmi kandarpah sarpaanaamasmi vaasukih.

Among the weapons, I am the Vajra (thunderbolt). Of the cows I am Kamadhenu (the cow that grants all desires). I am Kandarpa (Cupid) among the procreators, and of the serpents I am Vasuki (Lord of serpents).

10.29

| अनन्तश्चास्मि नागानां वरुणो यादसामहम् ।
पितॄणामर्यमा चास्मि यमः संयमतामहम् ॥ | Anantashchaasmi naagaanaam varuno yaadasaamaham;
Pitreenaamaryamaa chaasmi yamah samyamataamaham. |

Of the Nagas (celestial serpents) I am Ananta (serpent on whom Vishnu rests). Of the aquatic beings I am Varuna (god of water). Of the ancestors I am Aryama, and of the controllers I am Yama (god of death).

10.30

| प्रह्लादश्चास्मि दैत्यानां कालः कलयतामहम् ।
मृगाणां च मृगेन्द्रोऽहं वैनतेयश्च पक्षिणाम् ॥ | Prahlaadashchaasmi daityaanaam kaalah kalayataamaham;
Mrigaanaam cha mrigendro'ham vainateyashcha pakshinaam. |

Among the Daityas (demons) I am Prahlada (great devotee of Vishnu). Among the measures, I am time. Among the beasts I am the king of beasts (Lion), and among the birds I am Garuda (Vishnu's vehicle).

10.31

| पवनः पवतामस्मि रामः शस्त्रभृतामहम् ।
झषाणां मकरश्चास्मि स्रोतसामस्मि जाह्नवी ॥ | Pavanah pavataamasmi raamah shastrabhritaamaham;
Jhashaanaam makarashchaasmi srotasaamasmi jaahnavee. |

Of the purifiers, I am the wind. Among the wielders of weapons, I am Rama. Among the fishes, I am the shark, and among the rivers, I am the Ganges.

10.32

| सर्गाणामादिरन्तश्च मध्यं चैवाहमर्जुन ।
अध्यात्मविद्या विद्यानां वादः प्रवदतामहम् ॥ | Sargaanaamaadirantashcha madhyam chaivaaham arjuna;
Adhyaatmavidyaa vidyaanaam vaadah pravadataamaham. |

Arjuna, I am the beginning, the middle and the end of all creation. Among the sciences, I am the science of Self. I am the logic in debates.

10.33

अक्षराणामकारोऽस्मि द्वन्द्वः सामासिकस्य च । अहमेवाक्षयः कालो धाताहं विश्वतोमुखः ॥	Aksharaanaamakaaro'smi dvandvah saamaasikasya cha; Ahamevaakshayah kaalo dhaataaham vishwatomukhah.

I am the first letter among the alphabets. Among the different kinds of compounds in grammar, I am dvandva (dual compound). I am the endless time and the sustainer who is seen everywhere.

10.34

मृत्युः सर्वहरश्चाहमुद्भवश्च भविष्यताम् । कीर्तिः श्रीर्वाक्च नारीणां स्मृतिर्मेधा धृतिः क्षमा ॥	Mrityuh sarvaharashchaaham udbhavashcha bhavishyataam; Keertih shreervaakcha naareenaam smritirmedhaadhritih kshamaa.

I am the death that destroys all and the source of all beings to be born. Among the feminine qualities I am fame, prosperity, speech, memory, intelligence, stability and forgiveness.

10.35

बृहत्साम तथा साम्नां गायत्री छन्दसामहम् । मासानां मार्गशीर्षोऽहमृतूनां कुसुमाकरः ॥	Brihatsaama tathaa saamnaam gaayatree cchandasaamaham; Maasaanaam maargasheersho'hamritoonaam kusumaakarah.

Among the hymns of the Sama Veda, I am Brihatsama. Among the mantras, I am Gayatri. Among the twelve (lunar) months I am Margashirsha (November-December), and among the seasons the Spring.

10.36

द्यूतं छलयतामस्मि तेजस्तेजस्विनामहम् । जयोऽस्मि व्यवसायोऽस्मि सत्त्वं सत्त्ववतामहम् ॥	Dyootam cchalayataamasmi tejastejaswinaamaham; Jayo'smi vyavasaayo'smi sattvam sattvavataamaham.

Among the practices of fraud, I am gambling. I am the splendor of the splendid and the victory of the victorious. I am the resolution of the resolute and the goodness of the good-natured.

	10.37
वृष्णीनां वासुदेवोऽस्मि पाण्डवानां धनञ्जयः । मुनीनामप्यहं व्यासः कवीनामुशना कविः ॥	Vrishneenaam vaasudevo'smi paandavaanaam dhananjayah; Muneenaamapyaham vyaasah kaveenaamushanaa kavih.

Among the members of the Vrishni clan I am Krishna. Among the Pandavas I am Arjuna. Among sages I am Vyasa, and among poets I am Shukra.

	10.38
दण्डो दमयतामस्मि नीतिरस्मि जिगीषताम् । मौनं चैवास्मि गुह्यानां ज्ञानं ज्ञानवतामहम् ॥	Dando damayataamasmi neetirasmi jigeeshataam; Maunam chaivaasmi guhyaanaam jnaanam jnaanavataamaham.

I am the scepter of the punishers. I am the strategy of those seeking victory. I am the silence of secrets and the wisdom of the wise.

	10.39
यच्चापि सर्वभूतानां बीजं तदहमर्जुन । न तदस्ति विना यत्स्यान्मया भूतं चराचरम् ॥	Yachchaapi sarvabhootaanaam beejam tadahamarjuna; Na tadasti vinaa yatsyaanmayaa bhootam charaacharam.

Arjuna, I am the seed in every being. Nothing in this world, movable or immovable, can exist without Me.

	10.40
नान्तोऽस्ति मम दिव्यानां विभूतीनां परन्तप । एष तूद्देशतः प्रोक्तो विभूतेर्विस्तरो मया ॥	Naanto'sti mama divyaanaam vibhooteenaam parantapa; Esha tooddeshatah prokto vibhootervistaro mayaa.

Arjuna, there is no end to my divine manifestations. I have described to you the extent of my powers with a few examples.

Vibhuti Yoga

10.41

| यद्यद्विभूतिमत्सत्त्वं श्रीमदूर्जितमेव वा ।
तत्तदेवावगच्छ त्वं मम तेजोंऽशसम्भवम् ॥ | Yadyad vibhootimat sattvam shreemadoorjitameva vaa;
Tattadevaavagaccha tvam mama tejom'shasambhavam. |

Whatever is glorious, beautiful and powerful in this world has come from just a small portion of my power.

10.42

| अथवा बहुनैतेन किं ज्ञातेन तवार्जुन ।
विष्टभ्याहमिदं कृत्स्नमेकांशेन स्थितो जगत् ॥ | Athavaa bahunaitena kim jnaatena tavaarjuna;
Vishtabhyaahamidam kritsnamekaamshena sthito jagat. |

Arjuna, what do you gain by knowing all of this? It's enough to know that I support the entire universe with a small portion of myself.

| ॐ तत्सदिति श्रीमद्भगवद्गीतासूपनिषत्सु ब्रह्मविद्यायां योगशास्त्रे श्रीकृष्णार्जुनसंवादे विभूतियोगो नाम दशमोऽध्यायः | Om Tat Saditi Srimad Bhagavadgeetaasoopanishatsu Brahmavidyaayaam Yogashaastre Sri Krishnaarjunasamvaade Vibhootiyogo Naama Dashamo'dhyaayah |

Thus ends the tenth discourse entitled Vibhuti Yoga in the Upanishad, the divine Bhagavad Gita, the knowledge of Brahman, the scripture on Yoga and the dialogue between Sri Krishna and Arjuna.

Chapter 11
Vishvaroopa Sandarshana Yoga

11.01	
अर्जुन उवाच | मदनुग्रहाय परमं गुह्यमध्यात्मसंज्ञितम् | यत्त्वयोक्तं वचस्तेन मोहोऽयं विगतो मम ||	Arjuna uvaacha: Madanugrahaaya paramam guhyamadhyaatmasamjnitam; Yattvayoktam vachastena moho'yam vigato mama.

Arjuna said: Out of compassion, you have revealed to me the supreme spiritual wisdom. It has cleared my delusion.

11.02	
भवाप्ययौ हि भूतानां श्रुतौ विस्तरशो मया | त्वत्तः कमलपत्राक्ष माहात्म्यमपि चाव्ययम् ||	Bhavaapyayau hi bhootaanaam shrutau vistarasho mayaa; Tvattah kamalapatraaksha maahaatmyamapi chaavyayam.

O lotus-eyed Lord, I have heard from you the beginning and end of all beings, and also your infinite glory.

11.03

एवमेतद्यथात्थ त्वमात्मानं परमेश्वर | द्रष्टुमिच्छामि ते रूपमैश्वरं पुरुषोत्तम ||	Evametadyathaattha tvamaatmaanam parameshwara; Drashtumicchaami te roopamaishvaram purushottama.

O Parameshwara (Great Lord), you are exactly what you have said. However, I would very much like to see your divine form, Purushottama (Krishna).

11.04

मन्यसे यदि तच्छक्यं मया द्रष्टुमिति प्रभो | योगेश्वर ततो मे त्वं दर्शयात्मानमव्ययम् ||	Manyase yadi tacchakyam mayaa drashtumiti prabho; Yogeshwara tato me tvam darshayaatmaanamavyayam.

O Lord, master of yoga, if you think I am capable of looking at your imperishable form, reveal it to me.

11.05

श्रीभगवानुवाच | पश्य मे पार्थ रूपाणि शतशोऽथ सहस्रशः | नानाविधानि दिव्यानि नानावर्णाकृतीनि च ||	Sri Bhagavaan uvaacha: Pashya me paartha roopaani shatasho'tha sahasrashah; Naanaavidhaani divyaani naanaavarnaakriteeni cha.

Bhagavan (Lord Krishna) said: Look, Arjuna, at my divine forms by the hundreds and thousands, of various colors and shapes.

11.06

पश्यादित्यान्वसून्रुद्रानश्विनौ मरुतस्तथा | बहून्यदृष्टपूर्वाणि पश्याश्चर्याणि भारत ||	Pashyaadityaan vasoon rudraan ashwinau marutastathaa; Bahoonyadrishtapoorvaani pashyaashcharyaani bhaarata.

See, Arjuna, the Adityas, the Vasus, the Rudras, the Ashvins and the Maruts. See the many wonders never seen before.

11.07

| इहैकस्थं जगत्कृत्स्नं पश्याद्य सचराचरम् ।
मम देहे गुडाकेश यच्चान्यद् द्रष्टुमिच्छसि ॥ | Ihaikastham jagatkritsnam pashyaadya sacharaacharam;
Mama dehe gudaakesha yachchaanyad drashtumicchasi. |

O Arjuna, see in my body the entire universe including the movables and the immovables, and everything else you like to see.

11.08

| न तु मां शक्यसे द्रष्टुमनेनैव स्वचक्षुषा ।
दिव्यं ददामि ते चक्षुः पश्य मे योगमैश्वरम् ॥ | Na tu maam shakyase drashtum anenaiva swachakshushaa;
Divyam dadaami te chakshuh pashya me yogamaishvaram. |

You cannot see Me with your human eye. Therefore, I give you divine sight to see my divine power of yoga.

11.09

| सञ्जय उवाच ।
एवमुक्त्वा ततो राजन्महायोगेश्वरो हरिः ।
दर्शयामास पार्थाय परमं रूपमैश्वरम् ॥ | Sanjaya uvaacha:
Evamuktvaa tato raajan mahaayogeshwaro harih;
Darshayaamaasa paarthaaya paramam roopamaishvaram. |

Sanjaya said: O King (Dhritarashtra), with these words, Hari (Krishna), the great master of yoga, revealed to Arjuna his supreme divine form.

11.10-11.11

अनेकवक्त्रनयनमनेकाद्भुतदर्शनम् । अनेकदिव्याभरणं दिव्यानेकोद्यतायुधम् ॥ दिव्यमाल्याम्बरधरं दिव्यगन्धानुलेपनम् । सर्वाश्चर्यमयं देवमनन्तं विश्वतोमुखम् ॥	Anekavaktra nayanam anekaadbhuta darshanam; Anekadivyaabharanam divyaanekodyataayudham. Divyamaalyaambaradharam divyagandhaanulepanam; Sarvaashcharyamayam devam anantam vishwatomukham.

Arjuna saw the divine form consisting of countless eyes and mouths, appearing in various forms, decorated with several beautiful ornaments, holding many divine weapons, wearing divine garlands and robes, anointed with divine perfumes, the all-wonderful, infinite God with faces on all sides.

11.12

दिवि सूर्यसहस्रस्य भवेद्युगपदुत्थिता । यदि भाः सदृशी सा स्याद्भासस्तस्य महात्मनः ॥	Divi sooryasahasrasya bhavedyugapadutthitaa; Yadi bhaah sadrishee saa syaadbhaasastasya mahaatmanah.

If a thousand suns were to shine in the sky simultaneously, the brightness would not be equal to the splendor of the supreme Lord.

11.13

तत्रैकस्थं जगत्कृत्स्नं प्रविभक्तमनेकधा । अपश्यद्देवदेवस्य शरीरे पाण्डवस्तदा ॥	Tatraikastham jagatkritsnam pravibhaktamanekadhaa; Apashyaddevadevasya shareere paandavastadaa.

Arjuna then saw the entire universe with its manifold divisions united as one in the body of the God of gods.

11.14-11.15

ततः स विस्मयाविष्टो हृष्टरोमा धनञ्जयः | प्रणम्य शिरसा देवं कृताञ्जलिरभाषत || अर्जुन उवाच | पश्यामि देवांस्तव देव देहे सर्वांस्तथा भूतविशेषसङ्घान् | ब्रह्माणमीशं कमलासनस्थ- मृषींश्च सर्वानुरगांश्च दिव्यान् ||	Tatah sa vismayaavishto hrishtaromaa dhananjayah; Pranamya shirasaa devam kritaanjalirabhaashata. Arjuna uvaacha: Pashyaami devaamstava deva dehe Sarvaamstathaa bhootavisheshasanghaan; Brahmaanameesham kamalaasanastha- Mrisheemshcha sarvaanuragaamshcha divyaan.

Then Arjuna, full of astonishment and with his hair standing on end, bowed his head to the Lord with folded hands and said: O Lord, I see in your body all gods, different kinds of creatures, the lord Brahma seated on the lotus, all of the sages and the celestial serpents.

11.16

अनेकबाहूदरवक्त्रनेत्रं पश्यामि त्वां सर्वतोऽनन्तरूपम् | नान्तं न मध्यं न पुनस्तवादिं पश्यामि विश्वेश्वर विश्वरूप ||	Anekabaahoodaravaktranetram Pashyaami tvaam sarvato'nantaroopam; Naantam na madhyam na punastavaadim Pashyaami vishveshwara vishvaroopa.

O Lord of the universe, I see your infinite form everywhere with countless arms, stomachs, faces and eyes. I do not see your beginning, middle, or end, O Lord of the universe.

11.17

किरीटिनं गदिनं चक्रिणं च तेजोराशिं सर्वतो दीप्तिमन्तम् | पश्यामि त्वां दुर्निरीक्ष्यं समन्ताद् दीप्तानलार्कद्युतिमप्रमेयम् ||	Kireetinam gadinam chakrinam cha, Tejoraashim sarvato deeptimantam; Pashyaami tvaam durnireekshyam samantaad Deeptaanalaarkadyutimaprameyam.

I see you with your crown, mace and discus. I see you full of effulgence shining everywhere. It is difficult to see you because you are dazzling like the blazing fire of a Sun with immeasurable intensity on all sides.

11.18

त्वमक्षरं परमं वेदितव्यं त्वमस्य विश्वस्य परं निधानम् । त्वमव्ययः शाश्वतधर्मगोप्ता सनातनस्त्वं पुरुषो मतो मे ॥	Tvamaksharam paramam veditavyam Tvamasya vishwasya param nidhaanam; Tvamavyayah shaashvatadharmagoptaa Sanaatanastvam purusho mato me.

You are the supreme, imperishable being worth knowing. You are the ultimate refuge of the universe. You are the eternal protector of this eternal Dharma. I understand that you are the eternal being.

11.19

अनादिमध्यान्तमनन्तवीर्य- मनन्तबाहुं शशिसूर्यनेत्रम् । पश्यामि त्वां दीप्तहुताशवक्त्रं स्वतेजसा विश्वमिदं तपन्तम् ॥	Anaadimadhyaantamanantaveeryam Anantabaahum shashisooryanetram; Pashyaami tvaam deeptahutaashavaktram Swatejasaa vishwamidam tapantam.

I see you without beginning, middle or end. You have unlimited power. The Sun and the moon are your eyes and blazing fire is your mouth. Your radiance heats up the entire universe.

11.20

द्यावापृथिव्योरिदमन्तरं हि व्याप्तं त्वयैकेन दिशश्च सर्वाः । दृष्ट्वाद्भुतं रूपमुग्रं तवेदं लोकत्रयं प्रव्यथितं महात्मन् ॥	Dyaavaaprithivyoridamantaram hi Vyaaptam tvayaikena dishashcha sarvaah; Drishtvaa'dbhutam roopamugram tavedam Lokatrayam pravyathitam mahaatman.

You alone fill the entire space between heaven and earth, and in all directions. All the three worlds tremble at the sight of this unusual and fierce body, O Lord.

11.21

अमी हि त्वां सुरसङ्घा विशन्ति केचिद्भीताः प्राञ्जलयो गृणन्ति । स्वस्तीत्युक्त्वा महर्षिसिद्धसङ्घाः स्तुवन्ति त्वां स्तुतिभिः पुष्कलाभिः ॥	Amee hi tvaam surasanghaah vishanti Kechid bheetaah praanjalayo grinanti; Swasteetyuktvaa maharshisiddhasanghaah Stuvanti tvaam stutibhih pushkalaabhih.

Hordes of gods are entering you. Some, out of fear, are singing your glory. Multitudes of maharishis (great seers) and siddhas (perfect beings) are saying "let there be peace" and are chanting hymns of prayer to you.

Vishvaroopa Sandarshana Yoga

11.22

| रुद्रादित्या वसवो ये च साध्या
विश्वेऽश्विनौ मरुतश्चोष्मपाश्च ।
गन्धर्वयक्षासुरसिद्धसङ्घा
वीक्षन्ते त्वां विस्मिताश्चैव सर्वे ॥ | Rudraadityaa vasavo ye cha saadhyaa
Vishve'shvinau marutashchoshmapaashcha;
Gandharvayakshaasurasiddhasanghaa
Veekshante tvaam vismitaashchaiva sarve. |

The Rudras, Adityas, Vasus, Sadhyas, Vishvadevas, Ashvins, Maruts, ancestors and numerous Gandharvas, Yakshas, Asuras and Siddhas are all looking at you in awe and wonder.

11.23

| रूपं महत्ते बहुवक्त्रनेत्रं
महाबाहो बहुबाहूरुपादम् ।
बहूदरं बहुदंष्ट्राकरालं
दृष्ट्वा लोकाः प्रव्यथितास्तथाहम् ॥ | Roopam mahat te bahuvaktranetram
Mahaabaaho bahubaahoorupaadam;
Bahoodaram bahudamshtraakaraalam
Drishtvaa lokaah pravyathitaastathaa'ham. |

O Lord, looking at your colossal figure with many mouths, eyes, arms, thighs, feet, stomach and fierce teeth, the worlds are terrified and I am too.

11.24

| नभःस्पृशं दीप्तमनेकवर्णं
व्यात्ताननं दीप्तविशालनेत्रम् ।
दृष्ट्वा हि त्वां प्रव्यथितान्तरात्मा
धृतिं न विन्दामि शमं च विष्णो ॥ | Nabhahsprisham deeptamanekavarnam
Vyaattaananam deeptavishaalanetram;
Drishtvaa hi tvaam pravyathitaantaraatmaa
Dhritim na vindaami shamam cha vishno. |

O Vishnu, seeing you touching the sky, glittering in many colors, with mouths wide open and with brilliant eyes, I am terrified at heart. I have lost stability and tranquility.

11.25

| दंष्ट्राकरालानि च ते मुखानि
दृष्ट्वैव कालानलसन्निभानि ।
दिशो न जाने न लभे च शर्म
प्रसीद देवेश जगन्निवास ॥ | Damshtraakaraalaani cha te mukhaani
Drishtvaiva kaalaanalasannibhaani;
Disho na jaane na labhe cha sharma
Praseeda devesha jagannivaasa. |

As I see your mouth with fierce teeth resembling the fire at the end of time, I lose all sense of direction and have no place to go. O Lord of gods and refuge of the universe, be kind, be merciful.

11.26-11.27

अमी च त्वां धृतराष्ट्रस्य पुत्राः सर्वे सहैवावनिपालसङ्घैः | भीष्मो द्रोणः सूतपुत्रस्तथासौ सहास्मदीयैरपि योधमुख्यैः || वक्त्राणि ते त्वरमाणा विशन्ति दंष्ट्राकरालानि भयानकानि | केचिद्विलग्ना दशनान्तरेषु सन्दृश्यन्ते चूर्णितैरुत्तमाङ्गैः ||	Amee cha tvaam dhritaraashtrasya putraah Sarve sahaivaavanipaalasanghaih; Bheeshmo dronah sootaputrastathaa'sau Sahaasmadeeyairapi yodhamukhyaih. Vaktraani te tvaramaanaa vishanti Damshtraakaraalaani bhayaanakaani; Kechidvilagnaa dashanaantareshu Sandrishyante choornitairuttamaangaih.

All the sons of Dhritarashtra along with a number of Kings, Bhishma, Drona, Karna, and our chief warriors are rushing into your dreadful jaws. Some are caught between your teeth and their heads are being crushed to powder.

11.28

यथा नदीनां बहवोऽम्बुवेगाः समुद्रमेवाभिमुखा द्रवन्ति | तथा तवामी नरलोकवीरा विशन्ति वक्त्राण्यभिविज्वलन्ति ||	Yathaa nadeenaam bahavo'mbuvegaah Samudramevaabhimukhaah dravanti; Tathaa tavaamee naralokaveeraah Vishanti vaktraanyabhivijwalanti.

As the rivers flow towards the ocean, all the warriors of the world rush into your flaming mouths.

11.29

यथा प्रदीप्तं ज्वलनं पतङ्गा विशन्ति नाशाय समृद्धवेगाः | तथैव नाशाय विशन्ति लोकास्- तवापि वक्त्राणि समृद्धवेगाः ||	Yathaa pradeeptam jwalanam patangaa Vishanti naashaaya samriddhavegaah; Tathaiva naashaaya vishanti lokaas Tavaapi vaktraani samriddhavegaah.

As moths furiously rush into a blazing fire only to die, so do these warriors rush into your mouth only to die.

11.30

लेलिह्यसे ग्रसमानः समन्ताल्- लोकान्समग्रान्वदनैर्ज्वलद्भिः | तेजोभिरापूर्य जगत्समग्रं भासस्तवोग्राः प्रतपन्ति विष्णो ||	Lelihyase grasamaanah samantaal Lokaan samagraan vadanair jwaladbhih; Tejobhiraapoorya jagatsamagram Bhaasastavograah pratapanti vishno.

O Vishnu, you lick up all the worlds and swallow them through your burning mouth. Your dreadful rays are filling the entire universe and burning it to ashes.

11.31

आख्याहि मे को भवानुग्ररूपो नमोऽस्तु ते देववर प्रसीद | विज्ञातुमिच्छामि भवन्तमाद्यं न हि प्रजानामि तव प्रवृत्तिम् ||	Aakhyaahi me ko bhavaanugraroopo Namo'stu te devavara praseeda; Vijnaatumicchaami bhavantamaadyam Na hi prajaanaami tava pravrittim.

Tell me, who are you in this ferocious form? My obeisance to you, O supreme God. Have mercy. I wish to know you, the primeval one. I do not understand your purpose.

11.32

श्रीभगवानुवाच | कालोऽस्मि लोकक्षयकृत्प्रवृद्धो लोकान्समाहर्तुमिह प्रवृत्तः | ऋतेऽपि त्वां न भविष्यन्ति सर्वे येऽवस्थिताः प्रत्यनीकेषु योधाः ||	Sri Bhagavaan uvaacha: Kaalo'smi lokakshayakrit pravriddho Lokaan samaahartumiha pravrittah; Rite'pi tvaam na bhavishyanti sarve Ye'vasthitaah pratyaneekeshu yodhaah.

Bhagavan (Lord Krishna) said: I am time, the destroyer of the world. I am here now to destroy these people. Even without you, all the warriors assembled here will die.

11.33

तस्मात्त्वमुत्तिष्ठ यशो लभस्व जित्वा शत्रून् भुङ्क्ष्व राज्यं समृद्धम् । मयैवैते निहताः पूर्वमेव निमित्तमात्रं भव सव्यसाचिन् ॥	Tasmaat tvam uttishtha yasho labhaswa Jitvaa shatroon bhungkshwa raajyam samriddham; Mayaivaite nihataah poorvameva Nimittamaatram bhava savyasaachin.

Therefore, stand up and win fame, conquer your enemies, and enjoy a prosperous kingdom. I have already killed the warriors assembled here. You shall only be the instrument, Savyasachi (Arjuna), by which this happens.

11.34

द्रोणं च भीष्मं च जयद्रथं च कर्णं तथान्यानपि योधवीरान् । मया हतांस्त्वं जहि मा व्यथिष्ठा युध्यस्व जेतासि रणे सपत्नान् ॥	Dronam cha bheeshmam cha jayadratham cha Karnam tathaa'nyaanapi yodhaveeraan; Mayaa hataamstvam jahi maa vyathishthaa Yudhyasva jetaasi rane sapatnaan.

Drona, Bhishma, Jayadratha, Karna and other warriors are doomed to die. Do not be afraid, fight and you shall conquer your enemies.

11.35

सञ्जय उवाच । एतच्छ्रुत्वा वचनं केशवस्य कृताञ्जलिर्वेपमानः किरीटी । नमस्कृत्वा भूय एवाह कृष्णं सगद्गदं भीतभीतः प्रणम्य ॥	Sanjaya uvaacha: Etacchrutvaa vachanam keshavasya Kritaanjalirvepamaanah kireetee; Namaskritvaa bhooya evaaha krishnam Sagadgadam bheetabheetah pranamya.

Sanjaya said: Having heard the words of Keshava (Krishna), Arjuna trembled with fear. He folded his hands, bowed to Krishna, and addressed him in a faltering voice.

11.36

अर्जुन उवाच । स्थाने हृषीकेश तव प्रकीर्त्या जगत्प्रहृष्यत्यनुरज्यते च । रक्षांसि भीतानि दिशो द्रवन्ति सर्वे नमस्यन्ति च सिद्धसङ्घाः ॥	Arjuna uvaacha: Sthaane hrisheekesha tava prakeertyaa Jagat prahrishyatyanurajyate cha; Rakshaamsi bheetaani disho dravanti Sarve namasyanti cha siddhasanghaah.

Arjuna said: Hrishikesha (Krishna), it is only proper that the world delights and rejoices in praising you. Fearing you, demons run in all directions. All the Siddhas (perfected ones) are bowing to you.

11.37

कस्माच्च ते न नमेरन्महात्मन् गरीयसे ब्रह्मणोऽप्यादिकर्त्रे । अनन्त देवेश जगन्निवास त्वमक्षरं सदसत्तत्परं यत् ॥	Kasmaachcha te na nameran mahaatman Gareeyase brahmano'pyaadikartre; Ananta devesha jagannivaasa Tvamaksharam sadasattatparam yat.

O Mahatma (great person), why should they not worship you? You are the creator of Brahma himself and the greatest among the great, O Lord of the gods and abode of the universe. You are the imperishable, the existing and non existing, and are beyond both.

11.38

त्वमादिदेवः पुरुषः पुराणस्- त्वमस्य विश्वस्य परं निधानम् । वेत्तासि वेद्यं च परं च धाम त्वया ततं विश्वमनन्तरूप ॥	Tvamaadidevah purushah puraanas Tvamasya vishwasya param nidhaanam; Vettaasi vedyam cha param cha dhaama Tvayaa tatam vishwamanantaroopa.

You are the primal God and most ancient being. You are the ultimate refuge of this universe. You are the knower and the known. You are the supreme goal of all seekers. You have pervaded the entire universe with your infinite forms.

11.39

वायुर्यमोऽग्निर्वरुणः शशाङ्कः प्रजापतिस्त्वं प्रपितामहश्च । नमो नमस्तेऽस्तु सहस्रकृत्वः पुनश्च भूयोऽपि नमो नमस्ते ॥	Vaayuryamo'gnirvarunah shashaankah Prajaapatistvam prapitaamahashcha; Namo namaste'stu sahasrakritvah Punashcha bhooyo'pi namo namaste.

You are Vayu (wind god), Yama (god of death), Agni (fire god), Varuna (water god), Shashanka (moon god), Prajapati (Brahma) and Prapitamaha (great grandfather). I bow to you a thousand times.

11.40

नमः पुरस्तादथ पृष्ठतस्ते नमोऽस्तु ते सर्वत एव सर्व । अनन्तवीर्यामितविक्रमस्त्वं सर्वं समाप्नोषि ततोऽसि सर्वः ॥	Namah purastaadatha prishthataste Namo'stu te sarvata eva sarva; Anantaveeryaamitavikramastvam Sarvam samaapnoshi tato'si sarvah.

I bow before you and behind you. I bow from all sides. Your prowess is infinite and your might is immeasurable. You pervade all and you are all.

11.41

सखेति मत्वा प्रसभं यदुक्तं हे कृष्ण हे यादव हे सखेति । अजानता महिमानं तवेदं मया प्रमादात्प्रणयेन वापि ॥	Sakheti matvaa prasabham yaduktam He krishna he yaadava he sakheti; Ajaanataa mahimaanam tavedam Mayaa pramaadaat pranayena vaapi.

Unaware of your greatness and thinking you merely as a friend, I addressed you either out of thoughtlessness or affection as O Krishna, O Yadava, and O friend.

11.42

यच्चावहासार्थमसत्कृतोऽसि विहारशय्यासनभोजनेषु । एकोऽथवाप्यच्युत तत्समक्षं तत्क्षामये त्वामहमप्रमेयम् ॥	Yachchaavahaasaartham asatkrito'si Vihaarashayyaasanabhojaneshu; Eko'thavaapyachyuta tatsamaksham Tatkshaamaye tvaamaham aprameyam.

If I have ever insulted you while joking, while playing, at rest-time or at mealtime while alone or in company, O Achyuta (Krishna), I beg your forgiveness, O immeasurable one.

11.43

| पितासि लोकस्य चराचरस्य
त्वमस्य पूज्यश्च गुरुर्गरीयान् ।
न त्वत्समोऽस्त्यभ्यधिकः कुतोऽन्यो
लोकत्रयेऽप्यप्रतिमप्रभाव ॥ | Pitaasi lokasya charaacharasya
Tvamasya poojyashcha gururgareeyaan;
Na tvatsamo'styabhyadhikah kuto'nyo
Lokatraye'pyapratimaprabhaava. |

You are the father of all moving and nonmoving in this world. You are the most revered and the greatest Guru. There is no one equal to you in all the three worlds. How can there be anyone greater than you, O being of incomparable power?

11.44

| तस्मात्प्रणम्य प्रणिधाय कायं
प्रसादये त्वामहमीशमीड्यम् ।
पितेव पुत्रस्य सखेव सख्युः
प्रियः प्रियायार्हसि देव सोढुम् ॥ | Tasmaatpranamya pranidhaaya kaayam
Prasaadaye tvaamahameeshameedyam;
Piteva putrasya sakheva sakhyuh
Priyah priyaayaarhasi deva sodhum. |

O most adorable Lord, I prostrate myself before you and seek your forgiveness. Please forgive me, just as a father forgives his son, a friend his friend, and a loving husband his wife.

11.45

| अदृष्टपूर्वं हृषितोऽस्मि दृष्ट्वा
भयेन च प्रव्यथितं मनो मे ।
तदेव मे दर्शय देव रूपं
प्रसीद देवेश जगन्निवास ॥ | Adrishtapoorvam hrishito'smi drishtvaa
Bhayena cha pravyathitam mano me;
Tadeva me darshaya deva roopam
Praseeda devesha jagannivaasa. |

I am delighted to have seen the sight that has never been seen before, but my mind is afflicted with fear. O Lord of gods, O refuge of the universe, please be gracious and resume your original form.

11.46

| किरीटिनं गदिनं चक्रहस्तं
इच्छामि त्वां द्रष्टुमहं तथैव ।
तेनैव रूपेण चतुर्भुजेन
सहस्रबाहो भव विश्वमूर्ते ॥ | Kireetinam gadinam chakrahastam
Icchaami tvaam drashtumaham tathaiva;
Tenaiva roopena chaturbhujena
Sahasrabaaho bhava vishwamoorte. |

I wish to see you as you were before, with a crown on your head and the mace and discus in your hands. O thousand-armed Lord, O Lord of universal form, please resume your four-armed form.

11.47

| श्रीभगवानुवाच \|
 मया प्रसन्नेन तवार्जुनेदं
 रूपं परं दर्शितमात्मयोगात् \|
 तेजोमयं विश्वमनन्तमाद्यं
 यन्मे त्वदन्येन न दृष्टपूर्वम् \|\| | Sri Bhagavaan uvaacha:
 Mayaa prasannena tavaarjunedam
 Roopam param darshitamaatmayogaat;
 Tejomayam vishwamanantamaadyam
 Yanme tvadanyena na drishtapoorvam. |

Bhagavan (Lord Krishna) said: Arjuna, being pleased with you I have shown you by my yoga power this supreme, shining, primal, infinite and universal form which none but you have seen till now.

11.48

| न वेदयज्ञाध्ययनैर्न दानैर्-
 न च क्रियाभिर्न तपोभिरुग्रैः \|
 एवंरूपः शक्य अहं नृलोके
 द्रष्टुं त्वदन्येन कुरुप्रवीर \|\| | Na vedayajnaadhyayanairna daanair
 Na cha kriyaabhirna tapobhirugraih;
 Evam roopah shakya aham nriloke
 Drashtum tvadanyena karupraveera. |

Arjuna, I cannot be seen in this form by anyone but you, whether by the study of Vedas, by performing sacrifices, giving charity, conducting rituals or undergoing severe austerities.

11.49

| मा ते व्यथा मा च विमूढभावो
 दृष्ट्वा रूपं घोरमीदृङ्ममेदम् \|
 व्यपेतभीः प्रीतमनाः पुनस्त्वं
 तदेव मे रूपमिदं प्रपश्य \|\| | Maa te vyathaa maa cha vimoodhabhaavo
 Drishtvaa roopam ghorameedringmamedam;
 Vyapetabheeh preetamanaah punastvam
 Tadeva me roopamidam prapashya. |

Do not be afraid and confused on seeing this dreadful form of mine. Without fear and with joy in your heart, look at my previous form.

11.50

| सञ्जय उवाच ।
इत्यर्जुनं वासुदेवस्तथोक्त्वा
स्वकं रूपं दर्शयामास भूयः ।
आश्वासयामास च भीतमेनं
भूत्वा पुनः सौम्यवपुर्महात्मा ॥ | Sanjaya uvaacha:
Ityarjunam vaasudevastathoktvaa
Swakam roopam darshayaamaasa bhooyah;
Aashwaasayaamaasa cha bheetamenam
Bhootvaa punah saumyavapurmahaatmaa. |

Sanjaya said: Having thus spoken to Arjuna, Vasudeva (Krishna) showed his familiar form. Assuming his gentle human form, the Mahatma (Krishna) comforted the terrified Arjuna.

11.51

| अर्जुन उवाच ।
दृष्ट्वेदं मानुषं रूपं तव सौम्यं जनार्दन ।
इदानीमस्मि संवृत्तः सचेताः प्रकृतिं गतः ॥ | Arjuna uvaacha:
Drishtvedam maanusham roopam
tava saumyam janaardana;
Idaaneemasmi samvrittah
sachetaah prakritim gatah. |

Arjuna said: O Janardana (Krishna), seeing this human form again, I have regained my composure. I am my normal self again.

11.52

| श्रीभगवानुवाच ।
सुदुर्दर्शमिदं रूपं दृष्टवानसि यन्मम ।
देवा अप्यस्य रूपस्य नित्यं दर्शनकाङ्क्षिणः ॥ | Sri Bhagavaan uvaacha:
Sudurdarshamidam roopam
drishtavaanasi yanmama;
Devaa apyasya roopasya nityam
darshanakaangkshinah. |

Bhagavan (Lord Krishna) said: This form of mine which you have just seen is very difficult to see. Even the gods are ever longing to see this form.

11.53

| नाहं वेदैर्न तपसा न दानेन न चेज्यया ।
शक्य एवंविधो द्रष्टुं दृष्टवानसि मां यथा ॥ | Naa ham vedairna tapasaa na daanena na chejyayaa;
Shakya evamvidho drashtum drishtavaanasi maam yathaa. |

It is not possible to see Me as you have done even by the study of the Vedas, undergoing austerities, giving charity or conducting rituals.

11.54

भक्त्या त्वनन्यया शक्य अहमेवंविधोऽर्जुन । ज्ञातुं द्रष्टुं च तत्त्वेन प्रवेष्टुं च परन्तप ॥	Bhaktyaa tvananyayaa shakyam aham evamvidho'rjuna; Jnaatum drashtum cha tattvena praveshtum cha parantapa.

Arjuna, only through single-minded devotion can I be seen in this form, known fully and even also entered into.

11.55

मत्कर्मकृन्मत्परमो मद्भक्तः सङ्गवर्जितः । निर्वैरः सर्वभूतेषु यः स मामेति पाण्डव ॥	Matkarmakrinmatparamo madbhaktah sangavarjitah; Nirvairah sarvabhooteshu yah sa maameti paandava.

Arjuna, one who performs all actions for my sake, who makes Me his exclusive goal, who devotes himself to Me, who is free from attachment and who has no hatred for any creature, comes to Me.

ॐ तत्सदिति श्रीमद्भगवद्गीतासूपनिषत्सु ब्रह्मविद्यायां योगशास्त्रे श्रीकृष्णार्जुनसंवादे विश्वरूपदर्शनयोगो नामैकादशोऽध्यायः।	Om Tat Saditi Srimad Bhagavadgeetaasoopanishatsu Brahmavidyaayaam Yogashaastre Sri Krishnaarjunasamvaade Vishwaroopa Darshanayogo Naama Ekaadasho'dhyaayah

Thus ends the eleventh discourse entitled Vishvaroopa Sandarshana Yoga in the Upanishad, the divine Bhagavad Gita, the knowledge of Brahman, the scripture on Yoga and the dialogue between Sri Krishna and Arjuna.

Chapter 12
Bhakti Yoga

12.01	
अर्जुन उवाच | एवं सततयुक्ता ये भक्तास्त्वां पर्युपासते | ये चाप्यक्षरमव्यक्तं तेषां के योगवित्तमाः ||	Arjuna uvaacha: Evam satatayuktaa ye bhaktaastvaam paryupaasate; Ye chaapyaksharamavyaktam teshaam ke yogavittamaah.
Arjuna said: Some devotees worship you by fixing their mind on a specific form of you with attributes (Saguna Brahman). Others only worship the formless and imperishable (Nirguna Brahman). Which of these has better knowledge of yoga?	
12.02	
श्रीभगवानुवाच | मय्यावेश्य मनो ये मां नित्ययुक्ता उपासते | श्रद्धया परयोपेताः ते मे युक्ततमा मताः ||	Sri Bhagavaan uvaacha: Mayyaaveshya mano ye maam nityayuktaa upaasate; Shraddhayaa parayopetaaste me yuktatamaa mataah.
Bhagavan (Lord Krishna) said: I regard as best yogis those who worship Me with full faith and single-minded devotion.	

12.03-12.04

| ये त्वक्षरमनिर्देश्यमव्यक्तं पर्युपासते ।
सर्वत्रगमचिन्त्यञ्च कूटस्थमचलन्ध्रुवम् ॥
सन्नियम्येन्द्रियग्रामं सर्वत्र समबुद्धयः ।
ते प्राप्नुवन्ति मामेव सर्वभूतहिते रताः ॥ | Ye tvaksharamanirdeshyamavyaktam paryupaasate;
Sarvatragamachintyam cha kootasthamachalam dhruvam.
Samniyamyendriyagraamam sarvatra samabuddhayah;
Te praapnuvanti maameva sarvabhootahite rataah. |

Those who worship the imperishable, the indefinable, the unmanifest, the omnipresent, the unthinkable, the changeless, immovable and eternal with senses under control, even-mindedness, and total commitment for the welfare of all, also come to Me.

12.05

| क्लेशोऽधिकतरस्तेषामव्यक्तासक्तचेतसाम् ।
अव्यक्ता हि गतिर्दुःखं देहवद्भिरवाप्यते ॥ | Klesho'dhikatarasteshaam avyaktaasaktachetasaam;
Avyaktaa hi gatirduhkham dehavadbhiravaapyate. |

Self-realization is harder for those who worship the unmanifest. It is pretty challenging for a person in the physical form to fully comprehend the formless.

12.06-12.07

| ये तु सर्वाणि कर्माणि मयि संन्यस्य मत्परः ।
अनन्येनैव योगेन मां ध्यायन्त उपासते ॥
तेषामहं समुद्धर्ता मृत्युसंसारसागरात् ।
भवामि नचिरात्पार्थ मय्यावेशितचेतसाम् ॥ | Ye tu sarvaani karmaani mayi sannyasya matparaah;
Ananyenaiva yogena maam dhyaayanta upaasate.
Teshaamaham samuddhartaa mrityusamsaarasaagaraat;
Bhavaami nachiraat paartha mayyaaveshitachetasaam. |

Arjuna, I rescue from the cycle of birth and death those who accept Me as their supreme goal, offer all actions to Me, devote themselves to Me and constantly meditate on Me with single-minded devotion.

Bhakti Yoga

12.08

| मय्येव मन आधत्स्व मयि बुद्धिं निवेशय ।
निवसिष्यसि मय्येव अत ऊर्ध्वं न संशयः ॥ | Mayyeva mana aadhatsva mayi buddhim niveshaya;
Nivasishyasi mayyeva ata oordhvam na samshayah. |

Fix your mind only on Me. Let your intellect understand Me. Then you shall no doubt live in Me only.

12.09

| अथ चित्तं समाधातुं न शक्नोषि मयि स्थिरम् ।
अभ्यासयोगेन ततो मामिच्छाप्तुं धनञ्जय ॥ | Atha chittam samaadhaatum na shaknoshi mayi sthiram;
Abhyaasayogena tato maamicchaaptum dhananjaya. |

If you are unable to fix your mind steadily on Me, Arjuna, then seek to attain Me by constant practice of concentration.

12.10

| अभ्यासेऽप्यसमर्थोऽसि मत्कर्मपरमो भव ।
मदर्थमपि कर्माणि कुर्वन्सिद्धिमवाप्स्यसि ॥ | Abhyaase'pyasamartho'si matkarmaparamo bhava;
Madarthamapi karmaani kurvansiddhimavaapsyasi. |

If you are unable to practice concentration, engage yourself in action for my sake. Even by performing actions for my sake, you can attain perfection.

12.11

| अथैतदप्यशक्तोऽसि कर्तुं मद्योगमाश्रितः ।
सर्वकर्मफलत्यागं ततः कुरु यतात्मवान् ॥ | Athaitadapyashakto'si kartum madyogamaashritah;
Sarvakarmaphalatyaagam tatah kuru yataatmavaan. |

If you are unable to do even this, then seek refuge in Me with subdued mind and give up the fruits of all actions.

12.12

श्रेयो हि ज्ञानमभ्यासाज्ज्ञानाद्ध्यानं विशिष्यते । ध्यानात्कर्मफलत्यागस्त्यागाच्छान्तिरनन्तरम् ॥	Shreyo hi jnaanamabhyaasaat jnaanaaddhyaanam vishishyate; Dhyaanaat karmaphalatyaagas tyaagaacchaantir anantaram.

Knowledge is better than blind action. Meditation is superior to knowledge. Renunciation of the fruits of action excels even meditation. Peace immediately follows renunciation.

12.13-12.14

अद्वेष्टा सर्वभूतानां मैत्रः करुण एव च । निर्ममो निरहङ्कारः समदुःखसुखः क्षमी ॥ सन्तुष्टः सततं योगी यतात्मा दृढनिश्चयः । मय्यर्पितमनोबुद्धिर्यो मद्भक्तः स मे प्रियः ॥	Adveshtaa sarvabhootaanaam maitrah karuna eva cha; Nirmamo nirahankaarah samaduhkhasukhah kshamee. Santushtah satatam yogee yataatmaa dridhanishchayah; Mayyarpitamanobuddhiryo madbhaktah sa me priyah.

One who has no hatred for any being, who is kind and compassionate, who has no sense of "I" and "mine", who treats pleasure and pain alike, who is forgiving, who is ever content, who is steady in meditation, who is firm in faith, who is self-controlled and whose mind and intellect are focused on Me, such a yogi is dear to Me.

12.15

यस्मान्नोद्विजते लोको लोकान्नोद्विजते च यः । हर्षामर्षभयोद्वेगैर्मुक्तो यः स च मे प्रियः ॥	Yasmaannodvijate loko lokaannodvijate cha yah; Harshaamarshabhayodvegairmukto yah sa cha me priyah.

One who neither disturbs the world nor is disturbed by the world, who is free from excitement, envy, fear and anxiety – he is dear to Me.

12.16

| अनपेक्षः शुचिर्दक्ष उदासीनो गतव्यथः ।
 सर्वारम्भपरित्यागी यो मद्भक्तः स मे प्रियः ॥ | Anapekshah shuchirdaksha udaaseeno gatavyathah;
 Sarvaarambhaparityaagee yo madbhaktah sa me priyah. |

One who is free from desires, fear and anxiety, who is pure, wise, and impartial, who has renounced the feeling of doership in all undertakings and who is devoted to Me, such a person is dear to Me.

12.17

| यो न हृष्यति न द्वेष्टि न शोचति न काङ्क्षति ।
 शुभाशुभपरित्यागी भक्तिमान्यः स मे प्रियः ॥ | Yona hrishyati na dveshti na shochati na kaangkshati;
 Shubhaashubhaparityaagee bhaktimaan yah sa me priyah. |

One who neither rejoices nor laments, likes nor dislikes, to whom good and bad fortunes are alike and who is full of devotion to Me is dear to Me.

12.18-12.19

| समः शत्रौ च मित्रे च तथा मानापमानयोः ।
 शीतोष्णसुखदुःखेषु समः सङ्गविवर्जितः ॥
 तुल्यनिन्दास्तुतिर्मौनी सन्तुष्टो येन केनचित् ।
 अनिकेतः स्थिरमतिर्भक्तिमान्मे प्रियो नरः ॥ | Samah shatrau cha mitre cha tathaa maanaapamaanayoh;
 Sheetoshnasukhaduhkheshu samah sangavivarjitah.
 Tulyanindaastutirmaunee santushto yena kenachit;
 Aniketah sthiramatir bhaktimaan me priyo narah. |

One who treats alike friend and foe, honor and disgrace, heat and cold, pleasure and pain, praise and censure, who is restrained in speech, content with whatever comes, steady in mind and full of devotion to Me, that person is dear to Me.

12.20

ये तु धर्म्यामृतमिदं यथोक्तं पर्युपासते । श्रद्दधाना मत्परमा भक्तास्तेऽतीव मे प्रियाः ॥	Ye tu dharmyaamritamidam yathoktam paryupaasate; Shraddhadhaanaah matparamaa bhaktaaste'teeva me priyaah.

Those who follow this immortal dharma faithfully, who keep Me as their goal and who are solely devoted to Me, they are very dear to Me.

Commentary for 12.13-12.20: Here, *"dear to Me"* is also synonymous with *"close to Me"*. Those who follow the practices outlined in these verses are closer to Self-realization.

ॐ तत्सदिति श्रीमद्भगवद्गीतासूपनिषत्सु ब्रह्मविद्यायां योगशास्त्रे श्रीकृष्णार्जुनसंवादे भक्तियोगो नाम द्वादशोऽध्यायः	Om Tat Saditi Srimad Bhagavadgeetaasoopanishatsu Brahmavidyaayaam Yogashaastre Sri Krishnaarjunasamvaade Bhaktiyogo Naama Dwaadasho'dhyaayah

Thus ends the twelfth discourse entitled Bhakti Yoga in the Upanishad, the divine Bhagavad Gita, the knowledge of Brahman, the scripture on Yoga and the dialogue between Sri Krishna and Arjuna.

Chapter 13
Kshetra Kshetrajna Vibhaga Yoga

13.01

अर्जुन उवाच l प्रकृतिं पुरुषं चैव क्षेत्रं क्षेत्रज्ञमेव च l एतद्वेदितुमिच्छामि ज्ञानं ज्ञेयं च केशव ll	Arjuna uvaacha: Prakritim purusham chaiva kshetram kshetrajnameva cha; Etadveditumicchaami jnaanam jneyam cha keshava.

Arjuna said: O Keshava (Krishna), I would like to know about prakriti (primordial nature), purusha (spirit), the kshetra (field), kshetrajna (knower of the field), knowledge, and the object of knowledge.

13.02

श्रीभगवानुवाच | इदं शरीरं कौन्तेय क्षेत्रमित्यभिधीयते | एतद्यो वेत्ति तं प्राहुः क्षेत्रज्ञ इति तद्विदः ||	Sri Bhagavaan uvaacha: Idam shareeram kaunteya kshetramityabhidheeyate; Etadyo vetti tam praahuh kshetrajna iti tadvidah.

Bhagavan (Lord Krishna) said: Arjuna, this body is called the kshetra (field) and one who realizes it is called a kshetrajna (knower of the field).

Commentary: The body is referred to as the ksetra (field). Just as seeds sown in a field produce crops in due course of time, the seeds of karma sown in the body produce karmic results at the appropriate time.

13.03

क्षेत्रज्ञं चापि मां विद्धि सर्वक्षेत्रेषु भारत | क्षेत्रक्षेत्रज्ञयोर्ज्ञानं यत्तज्ज्ञानं मतं मम ||	Kshetrajnam chaapi maam viddhi sarvakshetreshu bhaarata; Kshetrakshetrajnayor jnaanam yattat jnaanam matam mama.

Arjuna, I am the kshetrajna in all kshetras. The knowledge of kshetra and kshetrajna is true knowledge.

Commentary: Lord Krishna is emphasizing the unity between himself and the ksetrajnas in different kshetras. He is the one and the same kshetrajna in all the innumerable kshetras. The kshetra is perishable, changeable, finite and inert, whereas the kshetrajna is imperishable, changeless, infinite and fully aware. Not to understand the difference between the two is ignorance, which causes bondage. The knowledge that enables one to realize the difference between the two is true knowledge.

Kshetra Kshetrajna Vibhaga Yoga

13.04

तत्क्षेत्रं यच्च यादृक्च यद्विकारि यतश्च यत् । स च यो यत्प्रभावश्च तत्समासेन मे शृणु ॥	Tat kshetram yaccha yaadrik cha yadvikaari yatashcha yat; Sa cha yo yatprabhaavashcha tatsamaasena me shrinu.

What is the kshetra? What is its nature? How does it change? Where is it from? Who is kshetrajna? What are his powers? I will briefly tell you about all these.

13.05

ऋषिभिर्बहुधा गीतं छन्दोभिर्विविधैः पृथक् । ब्रह्मसूत्रपदैश्चैव हेतुमद्भिर्विनिश्चितैः ॥	Rishibhirbahudhaa geetam cchandobhirvividhaih prithak; Brahmasootrapadaishchaiva hetumadbhirvinishchitaih.

These have been sung by seers in several ways, in various types of sacred hymns. It is also dealt with in the logical and conclusive Brahma Sutra.

13.06-13.07

महाभूतान्यहंकारो बुद्धिरव्यक्तमेव च । इन्द्रियाणि दशैकं च पञ्च चेन्द्रियगोचराः ॥ इच्छा द्वेषः सुखं दुःखं संघातश्चेतना धृतिः । एतत्क्षेत्रं समासेन सविकारमुदाहृतम् ॥	Mahaabhootaanyahankaaro buddhiravyaktameva cha; Indriyaani dashaikam cha pancha chendriyagocharaah. Icchaa dveshah sukham duhkham sanghaatashchetanaa dhritih; Etat kshetram samaasena savikaaramudaahritam.

Arjuna, the field consists of the following: the great elements, the ego, the intellect, the unmanifest, the ten sense organs, the mind, and the five sensory objects. Desire and aversion, pleasure and pain, the body, consciousness and fortitude arise in the field.

Commentary: In these verses, Lord Krishna lists the factors that constitute the kshetra. They are the following:
1. The Mahabhutas (great elements): Earth, Water, Fire, Air, Space
2. Ahamkara (ego): This is the sense of I and mine
3. Buddhi (intellect): The power of discrimination that enables one to decide right from wrong, good from bad, etc.
4. Avyakta (unmanifest): Primordial nature that contains the latent potential capable of manifesting at a later time.
5. Ten sense organs
    a. Five organs of perception: eyes, ears, nose, tongue, skin
    b. Five organs of action: hands, legs, anus, genitals, vocal organ
6. The mind
7. The five sensory objects: sight, sound, touch, taste, smell

13.08-13.12

अमानित्वमदम्भित्वमहिंसा क्षान्तिरार्जवम् । आचार्योपासनं शौचं स्थैर्यमात्मविनिग्रहः ॥ इन्द्रियार्थेषु वैराग्यमनहंकार एव च । जन्ममृत्युजराव्याधिदुःखदोषानुदर्शनम् ॥ असक्तिरनभिष्वङ्गः पुत्रदारगृहादिषु । नित्यं च समचित्तत्वमिष्टानिष्टोपपत्तिषु ॥ मयि चानन्ययोगेन भक्तिरव्यभिचारिणी । विविक्तदेशसेवित्वमरतिर्जनसंसदि ॥ अध्यात्मज्ञाननित्यत्वं तत्त्वज्ञानार्थदर्शनम् । एतज्ज्ञानमिति प्रोक्तमज्ञानं यदतोऽन्यथा ॥	Amaanitvam adambhitvam ahimsaa kshaantiraarjavam; Aachaaryopaasanam shaucham sthairyamaatmavinigrahah. Indriyaartheshu vairaagyamanahankaara eva cha; Janmamrityujaraavyaadhi duhkhadoshaanu darshanam. Asaktiranabhishwangah putradaaragrihaadishu; Nityam cha samachittatvam ishtaanishtopapattishu. Mayi chaananyayogena bhaktiravyabhichaarinee; Viviktadesha sevitvam aratir janasamsadi. Adhyaatma jnaana nityatvam tattva jnaanaartha darshanam; Etajjnaanamiti proktam ajnaanam yadato'nyathaa.

Humility, absence of deceit, nonviolence, forgiveness, uprightness, service to the guru, purity, stability, self control; Absence of attachment for sensory objects, absence of egoism, perception of the misfortune that comes with birth, death, old age, disease and sorrow; Absence of attachment, absence of excessive entanglements with son, wife, home, etc, even-mindedness in favorable and unfavorable circumstances; Unwavering love to Me by constantly thinking of Me only, preference for solitude and disinterest in social life; Constant longing for Self-knowledge and the perception of the goal of true knowledge – I declare all these to be knowledge, and the opposite is ignorance.

	13.13
ज्ञेयं यत्तत्प्रवक्ष्यामि यज्ज्ञात्वामृतमश्नुते । अनादिमत्परं ब्रह्म न सत्तन्नासदुच्यते ।।	Jneyam yattat pravakshyaami yajjnaatvaa'mritamashnute; Anaadimatparam brahma na sattannaasaduchyate.

I shall now explain to you that which has to be known. Knowing this, one attains immortality. It is the supreme Brahman without beginning. It is said to be neither sat (being) nor asat (non-being).

	13.14
सर्वतः पाणिपादं तत्सर्वतोऽक्षिशिरोमुखम् । सर्वतः श्रुतिमल्लोके सर्वमावृत्य तिष्ठति ।।	Sarvatah paanipaadam tat sarvato'kshishiromukham; Sarvatah shrutimalloke sarvamaavritya tishthati.

It has hands and feet everywhere, eyes, heads and mouths everywhere. It pervades all.

	13.15
सर्वेन्द्रियगुणाभासं सर्वेन्द्रियविवर्जितम् । असक्तं सर्वभृच्चैव निर्गुणं गुणभोक्तृ च ।।	Sarvendriyagunaabhaasam sarvendriyavivarjitam; Asaktam sarvabhricchaiva nirgunam gunabhoktru cha.

It shines by the function of the senses, yet it is beyond the senses. It is unattached, yet it supports all. It is free from the qualities and yet it experiences them.

	13.16
बहिरन्तश्च भूतानामचरं चरमेव च । सूक्ष्मत्वात्तदविज्ञेयं दूरस्थं चान्तिके च तत् ।।	Bahirantashcha bhootaanaam acharam charameva cha; Sookshmatvaat tadavijneyam doorastham chaantike cha tat.

It is outside and yet at the same time it is inside all beings. It moves and yet it does not move. It is hard to perceive because it is too subtle. It is far and yet it is near.

Kshetra Kshetrajna Vibhaga Yoga

13.17

अविभक्तं च भूतेषु विभक्तमिव च स्थितम् । भूतभर्तृ च तज्ज्ञेयं ग्रसिष्णु प्रभविष्णु च ॥	Avibhaktam cha bhooteshu vibhaktamiva cha sthitam; Bhootabhartru cha tajjneyam grasishnu prabhavishnu cha.

It is undivided and yet it appears to be divided into numerous beings. It is known to be the sustainer of all, and yet it is their destroyer and creator.

13.18

ज्योतिषामपि तज्ज्योतिस्तमसः परमुच्यते । ज्ञानं ज्ञेयं ज्ञानगम्यं हृदि सर्वस्य विष्ठितम् ॥	Jyotishaamapi tajjyotistamasah paramuchyate; Jnaanam jneyam jnaanagamyam hridi sarvasya vishthitam.

It is the light of all lights. It is said to be beyond darkness. It is knowledge, the object of knowledge and the goal of knowledge. It is present in everyone's heart.

13.19

इति क्षेत्रं तथा ज्ञानं ज्ञेयं चोक्तं समासतः । मद्भक्त एतद्विज्ञाय मद्भावायोपपद्यते ॥	Iti kshetram tathaa jnaanam jneyam choktam samaasatah; Madbhakta etadvijnaaya madbhaavaayopapadyate.

I have explained briefly the kshetra, as well as knowledge and the goal of that knowledge. Knowing this, my devotee becomes fit to enter into my being.

13.20

प्रकृतिं पुरुषं चैव विद्ध्यनादी उभावपि । विकारांश्च गुणांश्चैव विद्धि प्रकृतिसम्भवान् ॥	Prakritim purusham chaiva viddhyaanaadee ubhaavapi; Vikaaraamshcha gunaamshchaiva viddhi prakritisambhavaan.

Know that prakriti (primordial nature) and purusha (spirit) are both without beginning. Know also that the qualities and transformations are born of prakriti.

13.21

कार्यकारणकर्तृत्वे हेतुः प्रकृतिरुच्यते । पुरुषः सुखदुःखानां भोक्तृत्वे हेतुरुच्यते ॥	Kaaryakaaranakartrutve hetuh prakritiruchyate; Purushah sukhaduhkhaanaam bhoktritve heturuchyate.

Prakriti is said to be the cause of the body and the organs, while the purusha is the cause of the experience of pleasure and pain.

13.22

पुरुषः प्रकृतिस्थो हि भुङ्क्ते प्रकृतिजान्गुणान् । कारणं गुणसङ्गोऽस्य सदसद्योनिजन्मसु ॥	Purushah prakritistho hi bhungkte prakritijaan gunaan; Kaaranam gunasango'sya sadasadyoni janmasu.

The purusha rests in prakriti and experiences the qualities born of prakriti. Attachment to these qualities is the cause of its birth in either superior or inferior wombs.

13.23

उपद्रष्टानुमन्ता च भर्ता भोक्ता महेश्वरः । परमात्मेति चाप्युक्तो देहेऽस्मिन्पुरुषः परः ॥	Upadrashtaanumantaa cha bhartaa bhoktaa maheshwarah; Paramaatmeti chaapyukto dehe'smin purushah parah.

The supreme purusha in the body is called the observer, the approver, the sustainer, experiencer, the supreme Lord and the supreme Self.

13.24

य एवं वेत्ति पुरुषं प्रकृतिं च गुणैः सह । सर्वथा वर्तमानोऽपि न स भूयोऽभिजायते ॥	Ya evam vetti purusham prakritim cha gunaih saha; Sarvathaa vartamaano'pi na sa bhooyo'bhijaayate.

One who realizes the true nature of purusha and prakriti with its three gunas is not born again, regardless of his condition.

Commentary for 13.20-13.24: Prakriti (primordial nature) and purusha (spirit) are two aspects of creation that have no beginning. The three gunas (sattva, rajas and tamas) and everything material originate from prakriti. The human body with its various organs is caused by prakriti, whereas the experience of pleasure and pain is caused by purusha. Without purusha, there is no feeling of pleasure or pain. When purusha gets entangled with a body, he identifies with that body and experiences the qualities of prakriti manifesting as pleasure and pain, delusion, etc. The type of attachment one develops as a result of this experience determines the kind of rebirth one gets after death. The interaction of purusha and prakriti causes samsara. The purusha not entangled with the body is called the supreme purusha who functions as an onlooker, approver, experiencer, supporter, and supreme Lord. He is the absolute Self. Anyone who realizes the true nature of purusha and prakriti with its gunas transcends samsara, regardless of his station in life and the activities in which he is engaged.

13.25

ध्यानेनात्मनि पश्यन्ति केचिदात्मानमात्मना । अन्ये साङ्ख्येन योगेन कर्मयोगेन चापरे ॥	Dhyaanenaatmani pashyanti kechidaatmaanamaatmanaa; Anye saankhyena yogena karmayogena chaapare.

Some realize the Self in the self by means of meditation (dhyana yoga), others by means of wisdom (sankhya yoga), and yet others by selfless service (karma yoga).

13.26

अन्ये त्वेवमजानन्तः श्रुत्वान्येभ्य उपासते। तेऽपि चातितरन्त्येव मृत्युं श्रुतिपरायणाः॥	Anye tvevamajaanantah shrutvaanyebhya upaasate; Te'pi chaatitarantyeva mrityum shrutiparaayanaah.

Still others, having no knowledge of these paths, worship following the instructions received from others; they too go beyond death.

13.27

यावत्सञ्जायते किञ्चित्सत्त्वं स्थावरजङ्गमम्। क्षेत्रक्षेत्रज्ञसंयोगात्तद्विद्धि भरतर्षभ॥	Yaavat sanjaayate kinchit sattvam sthaavarajangamam; Kshetrakshetrajnasamyogaat tadviddhi bharatarshabha.

Arjuna, whatever is born, moving or nonmoving, is a result of the union of kshetra and kshetrajna.

13.28

समं सर्वेषु भूतेषु तिष्ठन्तं परमेश्वरम्। विनश्यत्स्वविनश्यन्तं यः पश्यति स पश्यति॥	Samam sarveshu bhooteshu tishthantam parameshwaram; Vinashyatswavinashyantam yah pashyati sa pashyati.

One who sees the presence of the supreme Lord equally in all beings, deathless in death, that person sees truly.

13.29

समं पश्यन्हि सर्वत्र समवस्थितमीश्वरम्। न हिनस्त्यात्मनात्मानं ततो याति परां गतिम्॥	Samam pashyan hi sarvatra samavasthitameeshwaram; Na hinastyaatmanaa'tmaanam tato yaati paraam gatim.

Seeing the same Lord in everything equally, he does not hurt himself or others and attains the supreme state.

13.30

| प्रकृत्यैव च कर्माणि क्रियमाणानि सर्वशः ।
 यः पश्यति तथात्मानमकर्तारं स पश्यति ॥ | Prakrityaiva cha karmaani kriyamaanaani sarvashah;
 Yah pashyati tathaa'tmaanam akartaaram sa pashyati. |

One who understands that all actions are performed by prakriti only and that the Self is not the doer, understands the truth.

13.31

| यदा भूतपृथग्भावमेकस्थमनुपश्यति ।
 तत एव च विस्तारं ब्रह्म सम्पद्यते तदा ॥ | Yadaa bhootaprithagbhaavam ekastham anupashyati;
 Tata eva cha vistaaram brahma sampadyate tadaa. |

He who sees the diversity of beings resting in one and coming from that one, attains Brahman.

13.32

| अनादित्वान्निर्गुणत्वात्परमात्मायमव्ययः ।
 शरीरस्थोऽपि कौन्तेय न करोति न लिप्यते ॥ | Anaaditvaan nirgunatvaat paramaatmaayam avyayah;
 Shareerastho'pi kaunteya na karoti na lipyate. |

Arjuna, the supreme Self is without beginning, without qualities and is imperishable. Although it exists in the body, it does not act or get tainted by action.

13.33

| यथा सर्वगतं सौक्ष्म्यादाकाशं नोपलिप्यते ।
 सर्वत्रावस्थितो देहे तथात्मा नोपलिप्यते ॥ | Yathaa sarvagatam saukshmyaadaakaasham nopalipyate;
 Sarvatraavasthito dehe tathaatmaa nopalipyate. |

Just as all-pervasive space retains its purity due to its subtle nature, the Self is not tainted, though present in all beings.

13.34

यथा प्रकाशयत्येकः कृत्स्नं लोकमिमं रविः । क्षेत्रं क्षेत्री तथा कृत्स्नं प्रकाशयति भारत ॥	Yathaa prakaashayatyekah kritsnam lokamimam ravih; Kshetram kshetree tathaa kritsnam prakaashayati bhaarata.

Arjuna, just as the Sun illuminates the whole world, so too he who dwells in the kshetra illuminates the entire kshetra.

13.35

क्षेत्रक्षेत्रज्ञयोरेवमन्तरं ज्ञानचक्षुषा । भूतप्रकृतिमोक्षं च ये विदुर्यान्ति ते परम् ॥	Kshetrakshetrajnayor evam antaram jnaanachakshushaa; Bhootaprakritimoksham cha ye vidur yaanti te param.

Those who see the difference between kshetra and kshetrajna with the eyes of knowledge, and know the way to free themselves from prakriti, attain the supreme.

ॐ तत्सदिति श्रीमद्भगवद्गीतासूपनिषत्सु ब्रह्मविद्यायां योगशास्त्रे श्रीकृष्णार्जुनसंवादे क्षेत्रक्षेत्रज्ञविभागयोगो नाम त्रयोदशोऽध्यायः ।	Om Tat Saditi Srimad Bhagavadgeetaasoopanishatsu Brahmavidyaayaam Yogashaastre Sri Krishnaarjunasamvaade Kshetrakshetrajnavibhaagayogo Naama Trayodasho'dhyaayah

Thus ends the thirteenth discourse entitled Kshetra Kshetrajna Vibhaga Yoga in the Upanishad, the divine Bhagavad Gita, the knowledge of Brahman, the scripture on Yoga and the dialogue between Sri Krishna and Arjuna.

Chapter 14
Gunatraya Vibhaga Yoga

14.01

श्रीभगवानुवाच |
परं भूयः प्रवक्ष्यामि ज्ञानानां ज्ञानमुत्तमम् |
यज्ज्ञात्वा मुनयः सर्वे परां सिद्धिमितो गताः ||

Sri Bhagavaan uvaacha:
Param bhooyah pravakshyaami jnaanaanaam jnaanamuttamam;
Yajjnaatvaa munayah sarve paraam siddhimito gataah.

Bhagavan (Lord Krishna) said: I shall impart to you the supreme knowledge, the ultimate knowledge, by which all sages have attained perfection.

14.02

इदं ज्ञानमुपाश्रित्य मम साधर्म्यमागताः |
सर्गेऽपि नोपजायन्ते प्रलये न व्यथन्ति च ||

Idam jnaanam upaashritya mama saadharmyam aagataah;
Sarge'pi nopajaayante pralaye na vyathanti cha.

Those who live according to this wisdom become one with Me. They are not reborn at the time of creation nor do they die at the time of dissolution.

14.03

मम योनिर्महद् ब्रह्म तस्मिन्गर्भं दधाम्यहम् । सम्भवः सर्वभूतानां ततो भवति भारत ॥	Mama yonirmahadbrahma tasmin garbham dadhaamyaham; Sambhavah sarvabhootaanaam tato bhavati bhaarata.

Arjuna, my material nature is the womb of all creation. In this womb I place the seed of consciousness. This is the way all created things are born.

14.04

सर्वयोनिषु कौन्तेय मूर्तयः सम्भवन्ति याः । तासां ब्रह्म महद्योनिरहं बीजप्रदः पिता ॥	Sarvayonishu kaunteya moortayah sambhavanti yaah; Taasaam brahma mahadyonir aham beejapradah pitaa.

Arjuna, whatever bodies are formed in any womb, the great prakriti is their mother and I am the seed-giving father.

14.05

सत्त्वं रजस्तम इति गुणाः प्रकृतिसम्भवाः । निबध्नन्ति महाबाहो देहे देहिनमव्ययम् ॥	Sattvam rajastama iti gunaah prakriti sambhavaah; Nibadhnanti mahaabaaho dehe dehinam avyayam.

The Gunas – sattva (goodness), rajas (passion) and tamas (ignorance), O Arjuna, bind the embodied self to the body.

14.06

तत्र सत्त्वं निर्मलत्वात्प्रकाशकमनामयम् । सुखसङ्गेन बध्नाति ज्ञानसङ्गेन चानघ ॥	Tatra sattvam nirmalatvaat prakaashakam anaamayam; Sukhasangena badhnaati jnaanasangena chaanagha.

Arjuna, of these, sattva, being pure, is illuminating and flawless. It binds the embodied self through attachment to happiness and knowledge.

14.07

| रजो रागात्मकं विद्धि तृष्णासङ्गसमुद्भवम् ।
 तन्निबध्नाति कौन्तेय कर्मसङ्गेन देहिनम् ॥ | Rajo raagaatmakam viddhi trishnaasangasamudbhavam;
 Tannibadhnaati kaunteya karmasangena dehinam. |

Arjuna, rajas is passion arising from the thirst for pleasure and attachment. It binds the embodied self by attachment to action.

14.08

| तमस्त्वज्ञानजं विद्धि मोहनं सर्वदेहिनाम् ।
 प्रमादालस्यनिद्राभिस्तन्निबध्नाति भारत ॥ | Tamastvajnaanajam viddhi mohanam sarvadehinaam;
 Pramaadaalasyanidraabhis tannibadhnaati bhaarata. |

Arjuna, tamas, born of ignorance, deludes all beings. It binds the embodied self through carelessness, indolence and sleep.

14.09

| सत्त्वं सुखे सञ्जयति रजः कर्मणि भारत ।
 ज्ञानमावृत्य तु तमः प्रमादे सञ्जयत्युत ॥ | Sattvam sukhe sanjayati rajah karmani bhaarata;
 Jnaanamaavritya tu tamah pramaade sanjayatyuta. |

Sattva causes attachment to happiness, rajas to action and tamas clouds understanding and causes attachment to negligence.

14.10

| रजस्तमश्चाभिभूय सत्त्वं भवति भारत ।
 रजः सत्त्वं तमश्चैव तमः सत्त्वं रजस्तथा ॥ | Rajastamashchaabhibhooya sattvam bhavati bhaarata;
 Rajah sattvam tamashchaiva tamah sattvam rajastathaa. |

Arjuna, sometimes sattva becomes prominent by overcoming rajas and tamas. Other times rajas becomes prominent by overcoming sattva and tamas. Yet other times tamas becomes prominent by overcoming sattva and rajas.

14.11

| सर्वद्वारेषु देहेऽस्मिन्प्रकाश उपजायते ।
 ज्ञानं यदा तदा विद्याद्विवृद्धं सत्त्वमित्युत ॥ | Sarvadvaareshu dehe'smin prakaasha upajaayate;
 Jnaanam yadaa tadaa vidyaa dvivriddham sattvamityuta. |

When the light of knowledge is felt by the entire body, then sattva is predominant.

14.12

| लोभः प्रवृत्तिरारम्भः कर्मणामशमः स्पृहा ।
 रजस्येतानि जायन्ते विवृद्धे भरतर्षभ ॥ | Lobhah pravrittir aarambhah karmanaam ashamah sprihaa;
 Rajasyetaani jaayante vivriddhe bharatarshabha. |

Arjuna, when rajas becomes prominent, greed, excessive activity, the undertaking of fruitive actions, and restlessness manifest.

14.13

| अप्रकाशोऽप्रवृत्तिश्च प्रमादो मोह एव च ।
 तमस्येतानि जायन्ते विवृद्धे कुरुनन्दन ॥ | Aprakaasho'pravrittishcha pramaado moha eva cha;
 Tamasyetaani jaayante vivriddhe kurunandana. |

Arjuna, when tamas dominates, ignorance, dullness, negligence of duty and delusion manifest.

14.14

| यदा सत्त्वे प्रवृद्धे तु प्रलयं याति देहभृत् ।
 तदोत्तमविदां लोकानमलान्प्रतिपद्यते ॥ | Yadaa sattve pravriddhe tu pralayam yaati dehabhrit;
 Tadottamavidaam lokaan amalaan pratipadyate. |

If a person dies when sattva is dominant, then he attains the pure world of the knowers of the supreme.

14.15

रजसि प्रलयं गत्वा कर्मसङ्गिषु जायते । तथा प्रलीनस्तमसि मूढयोनिषु जायते ॥	Rajasi pralayam gatvaa karmasangishu jaayate; Tathaa praleenastamasi moodhayonishu jaayate.

If a person dies when rajas is dominant, then he will be reborn among workaholics; and the one who dies when tamas is dominant will be born in the wombs of the ignorant.

14.16

कर्मणः सुकृतस्याहुः सात्त्विकं निर्मलं फलम् । रजसस्तु फलं दुःखमज्ञानं तमसः फलम् ॥	Karmanah sukritasyaahuh saattvikam nirmalam phalam; Rajasastu phalam duhkham ajnaanam tamasah phalam.

The fruits of good action are pure and sattvic. The fruit of rajas is sorrow, and the fruit of tamas is laziness.

14.17

सत्त्वात्सञ्जायते ज्ञानं रजसो लोभ एव च । प्रमादमोहौ तमसो भवतोऽज्ञानमेव च ॥	Sattvaat sanjaayate jnaanam rajaso lobha eva cha; Pramaadamohau tamaso bhavato'jnaanameva cha.

Sattva produces knowledge; greed is produced by rajas; and negligence, delusion and ignorance arise from tamas.

14.18

ऊर्ध्वं गच्छन्ति सत्त्वस्था मध्ये तिष्ठन्ति राजसाः । जघन्यगुणवृत्तिस्था अधो गच्छन्ति तामसाः ॥	Oordhvam gacchanti sattvasthaa madhye tishthanti raajasaah; Jaghanyagunavrittisthaa adho gacchanti taamasaah.

Those established in sattva move upwards, those in rajas stay in the middle, and those in tamas sink downwards.

14.19

| नान्यं गुणेभ्यः कर्तारं यदा द्रष्टानुपश्यति ।
गुणेभ्यश्च परं वेत्ति मद्भावं सोऽधिगच्छति ॥ | Naanyam gunebhyah kartaaram yadaa drashtaanupashyati;
Gunebhyashcha param vetti madbhaavam so'dhigacchati. |

When the seer understands that there are no other agents besides the gunas and realizes That which is above the gunas, he attains to my being.

14.20

| गुणानेतानतीत्य त्रीन्देही देहसमुद्भवान् ।
जन्ममृत्युजरादुःखैर्विमुक्तोऽमृतमश्नुते ॥ | Gunaanetaanateetya treen dehee dehasamudbhavaan;
Janmamrityujaraaduhkhair vimukto'mritamashnute. |

One who transcends the three gunas associated with the physical body is liberated from rebirth, death, old age and sorrow, and becomes immortal.

14.21

| अर्जुन उवाच ।
कैर्लिङ्गैस्त्रीन्गुणानेतानतीतो भवति प्रभो ।
किमाचारः कथं चैतांस्त्रीन्गुणानतिवर्तते ॥ | Arjuna uvaacha:
Kairlingais treen gunaanetaan ateeto bhavati prabho;
Kimaachaarah katham chaitaam streen gunaan ativartate. |

Arjuna said: O Lord, what are the characteristics of the person who has transcended the three gunas? How does he behave? How does one transcend these three gunas?

14.22

| श्रीभगवानुवाच ।
प्रकाशं च प्रवृत्तिं च मोहमेव च पाण्डव ।
न द्वेष्टि सम्प्रवृत्तानि न निवृत्तानि काङ्क्षति ॥ | Sri Bhagavaan uvaacha:
Prakaasham cha pravrittim cha mohameva cha paandava;
Na dveshti sampravrittaani na nivrittaani kaangkshati. |

Bhagavan (Lord Krishna) said: Arjuna, he does not dislike illumination, activity or even delusion when they are present and at the same time he does not miss them when they are absent.

14.23

| उदासीनवदासीनो गुणैर्यो न विचाल्यते ।
गुणा वर्तन्त इत्येवं योऽवतिष्ठति नेङ्गते ॥ | Udaaseenavadaaseeno gunairyo na vichaalyate;
Gunaa vartanta ityeva yo'vatishthati nengate. |

He remains unconcerned, unaffected by the gunas, understands that it is just the gunas acting and remains steadfastly absorbed in the Self.

14.24

| समदुःखसुखः स्वस्थः समलोष्टाश्मकाञ्चनः ।
तुल्यप्रियाप्रियो धीरस्तुल्यनिन्दात्मसंस्तुतिः ॥ | Samaduhkhasukhah swasthah samaloshtaashmakaanchanah;
Tulyapriyaapriyo dheeras tulyanindaatma samstutih. |

He is indifferent to pleasure and pain, ever absorbed in the Self, considers a clump of mud, a stone and gold alike, is not affected by pleasant or unpleasant happenings, is resolute and treats blame and praise alike.

14.25

| मानापमानयोस्तुल्यस्तुल्यो मित्रारिपक्षयोः ।
सर्वारम्भपरित्यागी गुणातीतः स उच्यते ॥ | Maanaapamaanayostulyas tulyo mitraaripakshayoh;
Sarvaarambhaparityaagee gunaateetah sa uchyate. |

He is indifferent to honor and to dishonor, is the same with friend and foe, is unattached to action, and is said to have transcended the gunas.

14.26

| मां च योऽव्यभिचारेण भक्तियोगेन सेवते ।
स गुणान्समतीत्यैतान्ब्रह्मभूयाय कल्पते ॥ | Maam cha yo'vyabhichaarena bhaktiyogena sevate;
Sa gunaan samateetyaitaan brahmabhooyaaya kalpate. |

One who worships Me with single-minded devotion (Bhakti Yoga) shall transcend these gunas and is worthy to become one with Brahman.

14.27

ब्रह्मणो हि प्रतिष्ठाहममृतस्याव्ययस्य च । शाश्वतस्य च धर्मस्य सुखस्यैकान्तिकस्य च ॥	Brahmano hi pratishthaa'ham amritasyaavyayasya cha; Shaashvatasya cha dharmasya sukhasyaikaantikasya cha.

I am the abode of Brahman, the immortal and immutable, the eternal Dharma and the everlasting bliss.

ॐ तत्सदिति श्रीमद्भगवद्गीतासूपनिषत्सु ब्रह्मविद्यायां योगशास्त्रे श्रीकृष्णार्जुनसंवादे गुणत्रयविभागयोगो नाम चतुर्दशोऽध्यायः	Om Tat Saditi Srimad Bhagavadgeetaasoopanishatsu Brahmavidyaayaam Yogashaastre Sri Krishnaarjunasamvaade Gunatrayavibhaagayogo Naama Chaturdasho'dhyaayah

Thus ends the fourteenth discourse entitled Gunatraya Vibhaga Yoga in the Upanishad, the divine Bhagavad Gita, the knowledge of Brahman, the scripture on Yoga and the dialogue between Sri Krishna and Arjuna.

Chapter 15
Purushottama Yoga

15.01	
श्रीभगवानुवाच । ऊर्ध्वमूलमधःशाखमश्वत्थं प्राहुरव्ययम् । छन्दांसि यस्य पर्णानि यस्तं वेद स वेदवित् ॥	Sri Bhagavaan uvaacha: Oordhvamoolam adhahshaakham ashwattham praahuravyayam; Cchandaamsi yasya parnaani yastam veda sa vedavit.

Bhagavan (Lord Krishna) said: They speak of an eternal Ashvattha (Peepal) tree that has its roots above and branches below, and whose leaves are the Vedas. One who knows this tree knows the Vedas.

15.02	
अधश्चोर्ध्वं प्रसृतास्तस्य शाखा गुणप्रवृद्धा विषयप्रवालाः । अधश्च मूलान्यनुसन्ततानि कर्मानुबन्धीनि मनुष्यलोके ॥	Adhashchordhvam prasritaastasya shaakhaah Gunapravriddhaa vishayapravaalaah; Adhashcha moolaanyanusantataani Karmaanubandheeni manushyaloke.

The branches of this tree extend up and down, and they are nourished by the gunas. Its buds are the sensory objects. The tree also has roots stretched downwards in the mortal world, which gives birth to karmic bondage.

15.03

न रूपमस्येह तथोपलभ्यते
नान्तो न चादिर्न च सम्प्रतिष्ठा |
अश्वत्थमेनं सुविरूढमूलं
असङ्गशस्त्रेण दृढेन छित्त्वा ||

Na roopamasyeha tathopalabhyate
Naanto na chaadirna cha sampratishthaa;
Ashwatthamenam suviroodhamoolam
Asangashastrena dridhena cchittvaa.

The real form of this tree, its beginning, its end and its foundation, are not perceptible in this world. Cut down this strongly rooted tree with the sharp axe of detachment.

15.04

ततः पदं तत्परिमार्गितव्यं
यस्मिन्गता न निवर्तन्ति भूयः |
तमेव चाद्यं पुरुषं प्रपद्ये |
यतः प्रवृत्तिः प्रसृता पुराणी ||

Tatah padam tat parimaargitavyam
Yasmin gataa na nivartanti bhooyah;
Tameva chaadyam purusham prapadye
Yatah pravrittih prasritaa puraanee.

Then seek the supreme state. Having reached it, there is no return. Take refuge in that primal being from whom has sprung this ancient world of action.

15.05

निर्मानमोहा जितसङ्गदोषा
अध्यात्मनित्या विनिवृत्तकामाः |
द्वन्द्वैर्विमुक्ताः सुखदुःखसंज्ञैर्-
गच्छन्त्यमूढाः पदमव्ययं तत् ||

Nirmaanamohaa jitasangadoshaa
Adhyaatmanityaa vinivrittakaamaah;
Dvandvairvimuktaah sukhaduhkhasamjnair
Gacchantyamoodhaah padamavyayam tat.

Those who are free from arrogance and delusion, who are free from the weakness of attachment, who are absorbed constantly in the supreme Self, whose desires have died, and who are beyond the duality of pleasure and pain, attain the imperishable goal.

15.06

न तद्भासयते सूर्यो न शशाङ्को न पावकः |
यद्गत्वा न निवर्तन्ते तद्धाम परमं मम ||

Na tadbhaasayate sooryo na shashaangko na paavakah;
Yadgatvaa na nivartante taddhaama paramam mama.

Neither the Sun nor the moon nor fire illuminates it. This is my supreme abode and, having reached it, there is no return.

15.07

ममैवांशो जीवलोके जीवभूतः सनातनः ।
मनःषष्ठानीन्द्रियाणि प्रकृतिस्थानि कर्षति ॥

Mamaivaamsho jeevaloke jeevabhootah sanaatanah;
Manah shashthaaneendriyaani prakritisthaani karshati.

An eternal part of Me becomes the jivatma (embodied self). It draws to itself the five senses and the mind, which are made of prakriti.

15.08

शरीरं यदवाप्नोति यच्चाप्युत्क्रामतीश्वरः ।
गृहीत्वैतानि संयाति वायुर्गन्धानिवाशयात् ॥

Shareeram yadavaapnoti yacchaapyutkraamateeshwarah;
Griheetvaitaani samyaati vaayurgandhaanivaashayaat.

Just as the wind transports scent from one place to the other, so does the jivatma carry these (the senses and the mind) from the body it has discarded into another body it obtains.

15.09

श्रोत्रं चक्षुः स्पर्शनं च रसनं घ्राणमेव च ।
अधिष्ठाय मनश्चायं विषयानुपसेवते ॥

Shrotram chakshuh sparshanam cha rasanam ghraanameva cha;
Adhishthaaya manashchaayam vishayaanupasevate.

Using the mind, ears, eyes, nose and the senses of taste and touch, the jivatma experiences the sensory objects.

15.10

उत्क्रामन्तं स्थितं वापि भुञ्जानं वा गुणान्वितम् ।
विमूढा नानुपश्यन्ति पश्यन्ति ज्ञानचक्षुषः ॥

Utkraamantam sthitam vaapi bhunjaanam vaa gunaanvitam;
Vimoodhaa naanupashyanti pashyanti jnaanachakshushah.

The deluded do not see the embodied self when it leaves the body or when it dwells in the body. They do not see that the embodied self experiences the sensory objects or that it is connected to the three gunas. Only those with wisdom realize this.

15.11

| यतन्तो योगिनश्चैनं पश्यन्त्यात्मन्यवस्थितम् ।
यतन्तोऽप्यकृतात्मानो नैनं पश्यन्त्यचेतसः ॥ | Yatanto yoginashchainam pashyantyaatmanyavasthitam;
Yatanto'pyakritaatmaano nainam pashyantyachetasah. |

The yogis who strive resolutely realize the Self dwelling in their heart. The ignorant, although striving, do not perceive the Self because their heart is not purified.

15.12

| यदादित्यगतं तेजो जगद्भासयतेऽखिलम् ।
यच्चन्द्रमसि यच्चाग्नौ तत्तेजो विद्धि मामकम् ॥ | Yadaadityagatam tejo jagad bhaasayate'khilam;
Yacchandramasi yacchaagnau tattejo viddhi maamakam. |

The light radiated by the Sun which illuminates the entire world, which is in the moon as well as in fire, is mine.

15.13

| गामाविश्य च भूतानि धारयाम्यहमोजसा ।
पुष्णामि चौषधीः सर्वाः सोमो भूत्वा रसात्मकः ॥ | Gaam aavishya cha bhootaani dhaarayaamyaham ojasaa;
Pushnaami chaushadheeh sarvaah somo bhootvaa rasaatmakah. |

Entering the earth, I sustain all beings by my power. Becoming the moon, the essence of all sap, I nourish all the vegetation.

15.14

| अहं वैश्वानरो भूत्वा प्राणिनां देहमाश्रितः ।
प्राणापानसमायुक्तः पचाम्यन्नं चतुर्विधम् ॥ | Aham vaishvaanaro bhootvaa praaninaam dehamaashritah;
Praanaapaana samaayuktah pachaamyannam chaturvidham. |

Dwelling in the bodies of living beings as Vaishvanara (digestive fire) and working with the prana and apana breaths, I digest the four kinds of food.

15.15

| सर्वस्य चाहं हृदि सन्निविष्टो
मत्तः स्मृतिर्ज्ञानमपोहनञ्च ।
वेदैश्च सर्वैरहमेव वेद्यो
वेदान्तकृद्वेदविदेव चाहम् ॥ | Sarvasya chaaham hridi sannivishto
Mattah smritir jnaanam apohanam cha;
Vedaischa sarvairahameva vedyo
Vedaantakrid vedavid eva chaaham. |

I am in the hearts of all. I am the cause of memory and knowledge, as well as their loss. I am the goal of the Vedas, the author of Vedanta, and the knower of the Vedas.

15.16

| द्वाविमौ पुरुषौ लोके क्षरश्चाक्षर एव च ।
क्षरः सर्वाणि भूतानि कूटस्थोऽक्षर उच्यते ॥ | Dvaavimau purushau loke
ksharashchaakshara eva cha;
Ksharah sarvaani bhootaani
kootastho'kshara uchyate. |

Two kinds of purushas (entities), kshara (perishable) and akshara (imperishable), exist in the world. The bodies of all beings are perishable and the embodied self is imperishable.

15.17

| उत्तमः पुरुषस्त्वन्यः परमात्मेत्युधाहृतः ।
यो लोकत्रयमाविश्य बिभर्त्यव्यय ईश्वरः ॥ | Uttamah purushastvanyah
paramaatmetyudaahritah;
Yo lokatrayamaavishya
bibhartyavyaya ishvarah. |

There is another besides these. The supreme purusha called the Supreme Self, the indestructible Lord, permeates and sustains the three worlds.

15.18

| यस्मात्क्षरमतीतोऽहमक्षरादपि चोत्तमः ।
अतोऽस्मि लोके वेदे च प्रथितः पुरुषोत्तमः ॥ | Yasmaat ksharam
ateeto'hamaksharaadapi chottamah;
Ato'smi loke vede cha prathitah
purushottamah. |

I transcend the perishable (kshara) and am also higher than the imperishable (akshara). I am known in the world and also in the Vedas as purushottama (supreme being).

15.19

यो मामेवमसम्मूढो जानाति पुरुषोत्तमम् । स सर्वविद्भजति मां सर्वभावेन भारत ॥	Yo maamevam asammoodho jaanaati purushottamam; Sa sarvavidbhajati maam sarvabhaavena bhaarata.

Arjuna, the undeluded person who knows Me as purushottama knows the truth. He worships Me with his whole being.

15.20

इति गुह्यतमं शास्त्रमिदमुक्तं मयानघ । एतद्बुद्ध्वा बुद्धिमान्स्यात्कृतकृत्यश्च भारत ॥	Iti guhyatamam shaastram idamuktam mayaa'nagha; Etadbuddhvaa buddhimaan syaat kritakrityashcha bhaarata.

Arjuna, I have taught you the most mysterious subject. One who understands this will attain wisdom and has nothing more to do.

ॐ तत्सदिति श्रीमद्भगवद्गीतासूपनिषत्सु ब्रह्मविद्यायां योगशास्त्रे श्रीकृष्णार्जुन संवादे पुरुषोत्तमयोगो नाम पञ्चदशोऽध्यायः	Om Tat Saditi Srimad Bhagavadgeetaasoopanishatsu Brahmavidyaayaam Yogashaastre Sri Krishnaarjunasamvaade Purushottamayogo Naama Panchadasho'dhyaayah

Thus ends the fifteenth discourse entitled Purushottama Yoga in the Upanishad, the divine Bhagavad Gita, the knowledge of Brahman, the scripture on Yoga and the dialogue between Sri Krishna and Arjuna.

Chapter 16
Daivasura Sampadvibhaga Yoga

16.01-16.03

श्रीभगवानुवाच | अभयं सत्त्वसंशुद्धिर्ज्ञानयोगव्यवस्थितिः | दानं दमश्च यज्ञश्च स्वाध्यायस्तप आर्जवम् || अहिंसा सत्यमक्रोधस्त्यागः शान्तिरपैशुनम् | दया भूतेष्वलोलुप्त्वं मार्दवं ह्रीरचापलम् || तेजः क्षमा धृतिः शौचमद्रोहो नातिमानिता | भवन्ति सम्पदं दैवीमभिजातस्य भारत ||	Sri Bhagavaan uvaacha: Abhayam sattvasamshuddhih jnaanayogavyavasthitih; Daanam damashcha yajnashcha swaadhyaayastapa aarjavam. Ahimsaa satyamakrodhas tyaagah shaantirapaishunam; Dayaa bhooteshvaloluptvam maardavam hreerachaapalam. Tejah kshamaa dhritih shauchamadroho naatimaanitaa; Bhavanti sampadam daiveem abhijaatasya bhaarata.

Bhagavan (Lord Krishna) said: Arjuna, a person born with the divine nature has the following qualities: he has no fear, has a pure heart, has unwavering devotion to acquire knowledge of the Self, is charitable, has self-restraint, performs sacrifice, studies the Vedas, practices austerity, is straightforward, is nonviolent, is truthful, is free from anger, practices renunciation, is serene, does not slander, is compassionate, does not covet, is gentle, is modest, is not fickle, is vigorous, is patient, has fortitude, bears enmity to none, and does not have vanity.

16.04

दम्भो दर्पोऽभिमानश्च क्रोधः पारुष्यमेव च । अज्ञानं चाभिजातस्य पार्थ सम्पदमासुरीम् ॥	Dambho darpo'bhimaanashcha krodhah paarushyameva cha; Ajnaanam chaabhijaatasya paartha sampadamaasureem.

Arjuna, a person born with demoniac nature has the following qualities: hypocrisy, arrogance, pride, anger and ignorance.

16.05

दैवी सम्पद्विमोक्षाय निबन्धायासुरी मता । मा शुचः सम्पदं दैवीमभिजातोऽसि पाण्डव ॥	Daivee sampadvimokshaaya nibandhaayaasuree mataa; Maa shuchah sampadam daiveem abhijaato'si paandava.

Arjuna, a person with divine nature will make progress towards liberation and a person with demoniac nature will be trapped in bondage. Do not worry – you are born with divine nature.

16.06

द्वौ भूतसर्गौ लोकेऽस्मिन्दैव आसुर एव च । दैवो विस्तरशः प्रोक्त आसुरं पार्थ मे शृणु ॥	Dvau bhootasargau loke'smin daiva aasura eva cha; Daivo vistarashah proktah aasuram paartha me shrinu.

There are two kinds of beings in this world, divine and demoniac. I have spoken about the beings of divine nature at length. Now listen, Arjuna, I will describe the demoniac being in detail.

16.07

प्रवृत्तिं च निवृत्तिं च जना न विदुरासुराः । न शौचं नापि चाचारो न सत्यं तेषु विद्यते ॥	Pravrittim cha nivrittim cha janaa na viduraasuraah; Na shaucham naapi chaachaaro na satyam teshu vidyate.

Demoniac beings do not know what to do and what not to do. They have neither purity nor good conduct nor truth.

16.08

असत्यमप्रतिष्ठं ते जगदाहुरनीश्वरम् । अपरस्परसम्भूतं किमन्यत्कामहैतुकम् ॥	Asatyamapratishtham te jagadaahuraneeshwaram; Aparasparasambhootam kimanyat kaamahaitukam.

They say that there is no truth in the world. It has no moral foundation and there is no God in charge. The world is the result of lust. What else is there?

16.09

एतां दृष्टिमवष्टभ्य नष्टात्मानोऽल्पबुद्धयः । प्रभवन्त्युग्रकर्माणः क्षयाय जगतोऽहिताः ॥	Etaam drishtimavashtabhya nashtaatmaano'lpabuddhayah; Prabhavantyugrakarmaanah kshayaaya jagato'hitaah.

Holding on to such views, these lost folks of little knowledge resort to cruelty and become enemies of the world.

16.10

काममाश्रित्य दुष्पूरं दम्भमानमदान्विताः । मोहाद्गृहीत्वासद्ग्राहान्प्रवर्तन्तेऽशुचिव्रताः ॥	Kaamamaashritya dushpooram dambhamaanamadaanvitaah; Mohaadgriheetvaasadgraahaan pravartante'shuchivrataah.

Deluded by lust beyond satisfaction, hypocrisy, conceit and arrogance, they act with evil intentions.

16.11

चिन्तामपरिमेयां च प्रलयान्तामुपाश्रिताः । कामोपभोगपरमा एतावदिति निश्चिताः ॥	Chintaamaparimeyaam cha pralayaantaamupaashritaah; Kaamopabhogaparamaa etaavaditi nishchitaah.

Although ridden with anxiety till the end of life, they keep the gratification of the senses as the highest goal and that is all.

16.12

आशापाशशतैर्बद्धाः कामक्रोधपरायणाः । ईहन्ते कामभोगार्थमन्यायेनार्थसञ्चयान् ॥	Aashaapaashashatairbaddhaah kaamakrodhaparaayanaah; Eehante kaamabhogaartha manyaayenaarthasanchayaan.

Filled with endless desires, taken over by lust and anger, they try to accumulate wealth by unjust means.

16.13

इदमद्य मया लब्धमिमं प्राप्स्ये मनोरथम् । इदमस्तीदमपि मे भविष्यति पुनर्धनम् ॥	Idamadya mayaa labdham imam praapsye manoratham; Idamasteedamapi me bhavishyati punardhanam.

I have acquired this today and I will also acquire that. This wealth is mine and that too will be mine.

16.14

असौ मया हतः शत्रुर्हनिष्ये चापरानपि । ईश्वरोऽहमहं भोगी सिद्धोऽहं बलवान्सुखी ॥	Asau mayaa hatah shatrur hanishye chaaparaanapi; Eeshwaro'hamaham bhogee siddho'ham balavaan sukhee.

I have killed this enemy today and I will also kill others. I am the Lord and the enjoyer. I am perfect, strong and happy.

16.15

आढ्योऽभिजनवानस्मि कोऽन्योऽस्ति सदृशो मया । यक्ष्ये दास्यामि मोदिष्य इत्यज्ञानविमोहिताः ॥	Aadhyo'bhijanavaanasmi ko'nyosti sadrisho mayaa; Yakshye daasyaami modishye ityajnaanavimohitaah.

I am rich and born in a noble family. Who is equal to me? I shall perform sacrifice. I shall give to charity. I shall enjoy. Thinking along these lines, they become deluded.

16.16

अनेकचित्तविभ्रान्ता मोहजालसमावृताः । प्रसक्ताः कामभोगेषु पतन्ति नरकेऽशुचौ ॥	Anekachittavibhraantaah mohajaalasamaavritaah; Prasaktaah kaamabhogeshu patanti narake'shuchau.

Haunted by random thoughts, they are trapped in the web of delusion. Obsessed with the gratification of lust, they drown in a stinking hell.

16.17

आत्मसम्भाविताः स्तब्धा धनमानमदान्विताः । यजन्ते नामयज्ञैस्ते दम्भेनाविधिपूर्वकम् ॥	Aatmasambhaavitaah stabdhaa dhanamaanamadaanvitaah; Yajante naamayajnaiste dambhenaavidhipoorvakam.

They are conceited, stubborn and intoxicated with the arrogance of affluence, and perform sacrifices only for outward show, without regard to scriptural rules.

16.18

अहंकारं बलं दर्पं कामं क्रोधं च संश्रिताः । मामात्मपरदेहेषु प्रद्विषन्तोऽभ्यसूयकाः ॥	Ahankaaram balam darpam kaamam krodham cha samshritaah; Maamaatmaparadeheshu pradvishanto'bhyasooyakaah.

Conditioned by egoism, violence, arrogance and lust, these spiteful people hate Me although I am present in them and others.

16.19

तानहं द्विषतः क्रूरान्संसारेषु नराधमान् । क्षिपाम्यजस्रमशुभानासुरीष्वेव योनिषु ॥	Taanaham dvishatah krooraan samsaareshu naraadhamaan; Kshipaamyajasram ashubhaan aasureeshweva yonishu.

Again and again I throw these malicious, evil, vile and cruel scums into the wombs of demons.

16.20

| आसुरीं योनिमापन्ना मूढा जन्मनि जन्मनि ।
 मामप्राप्यैव कौन्तेय ततो यान्त्यधमां गतिम् ॥ | Aasureem yonimaapannaa moodhaa janmani janmani;
 Maamapraapyaiva kaunteya tato yaantyadhamaam gatim. |

Arjuna, entering into the demonic wombs and deluded life after life, without ever attaining Me, they sink lower and lower.

16.21

| त्रिविधं नरकस्येदं द्वारं नाशनमात्मनः ।
 कामः क्रोधस्तथा लोभस्तस्मादेतत्त्रयं त्यजेत् ॥ | Trividham narakasyedam dvaaram naashanamaatmanah;
 Kaamah krodhastathaa lobhas tasmaadetat trayam tyajet. |

There are three gates to the hell of self destruction. These are lust, wrath and avarice, and therefore one should abandon them.

16.22

| एतैर्विमुक्तः कौन्तेय तमोद्वारैस्त्रिभिर्नरः ।
 आचरत्यात्मनः श्रेयस्ततो याति परां गतिम् ॥ | Etairvimuktah kaunteya tamodvaaraistribhirnarah;
 Aacharatyaatmanah shreyas tato yaati paraam gatim. |

Arjuna, a person who avoids these three gates to darkness and does what is right will attain the highest goal.

16.23

| यः शास्त्रविधिमुत्सृज्य वर्तते कामकारतः ।
 न स सिद्धिमवाप्नोति न सुखं न परां गतिम् ॥ | Yah shaastravidhimutsrijya vartate kaamakaaratah;
 Na sa siddhimavaapnoti na sukham na paraam gatim. |

One who ignores the spiritual ordinances and acts impulsively out of selfish desires will not attain perfection, happiness or the highest goal.

16.24

| तस्माच्छास्त्रं प्रमाणं ते कार्याकार्यव्यवस्थितौ । ज्ञात्वा शास्त्रविधानोक्तं कर्म कर्तुमिहार्हसि ॥ | Tasmaat shaastram pramaanam te kaaryaakaaryavyavasthitau; Jnaatvaa shaastravidhaanoktam karma kartumihaarhasi. |

Therefore, let scriptures be your authority to guide you as to what you should do and what you should not do. Understand the scriptures and act accordingly.

| ॐ तत्सदिति श्रीमद्भगवद्गीतासूपनिषत्सु ब्रह्मविद्यायां योगशास्त्रे श्रीकृष्णार्जुनसंवादे दैवासुरसम्पद्विभागयोगो नाम षोडशोऽध्यायः | Om Tat Saditi Srimad Bhagavadgeetaasoopanishatsu Brahmavidyaayaam Yogashaastre Sri Krishnaarjunasamvaade Daivaasurasampadvibhaagayogo Naama Shodasho'dhyaayah |

Thus ends the sixteenth discourse entitled Daivasura Sampadvibhaga Yoga in the Upanishad, the divine Bhagavad Gita, the knowledge of Brahman, the scripture on Yoga and the dialogue between Sri Krishna and Arjuna.

Chapter 17
Shraddha Thraya Vibhaga Yoga

17.01

अर्जुन उवाच |
ये शास्त्रविधिमुत्सृज्य यजन्ते श्रद्धयान्विताः |
तेषां निष्ठा तु का कृष्ण सत्त्वमाहो रजस्तमः ||

Arjuna uvaacha:
Ye shaastravidhimutsrijya yajante shraddhayaanvitaah;
Teshaam nishthaa tu kaa krishna sattvamaaho rajastamah.

Arjuna said: O Krishna, those who perform sacrifice with faith but not according to scriptures, what type of guna are they associated with, sattva, rajas, or tamas?

17.02

श्रीभगवानुवाच |
त्रिविधा भवति श्रद्धा देहिनां सा स्वभावजा |
सात्त्विकी राजसी चैव तामसी चेति तां शृणु ||

Sri Bhagavaan uvaacha:
Trividhaa bhavati shraddhaa dehinaam saa swabhaavajaa;
Saattvikee raajasee chaiva taamasee cheti taam shrinu.

Bhagavan (Lord Krishna) said: The faith of the living beings that is inherent in their nature is of three kinds: sattvic, rajasic and tamasic.

17.03

| सत्त्वानुरूपा सर्वस्य श्रद्धा भवति भारत ।
श्रद्धामयोऽयं पुरुषो यो यच्छ्रद्धः स एव सः ॥ | Sattvaanuroopaa sarvasya shraddhaa bhavati bhaarata;
Shraddhaamayo'yam purusho yo yacchraddhah sa eva sah. |

The faith of each person evolves from one's own inherent nature. Arjuna, the person is a reflection of his faith. Faith is a person's core.

17.04

| यजन्ते सात्त्विका देवान्यक्षरक्षांसि राजसाः ।
प्रेतान्भूतगणांश्चान्ये यजन्ते तामसा जनाः ॥ | Yajante saattvikaa devaan yaksharakshaamsi raajasaah;
Pretaan bhootaganaamshchaanye yajante taamasaa janaah. |

Those with sattvic guna worship gods, rajasics worship yakshas and rakshasas, and the tamasics worship the spirits of the dead and harmful deities.

17.05-17.06

| अशास्त्रविहितं घोरं तप्यन्ते ये तपो जनाः ।
दम्भाहंकारसंयुक्ताः कामरागबलान्विताः ॥
कर्षयन्तः शरीरस्थं भूतग्राममचेतसः ।
मां चैवान्तःशरीरस्थं तान्विद्ध्यासुरनिश्चयान् ॥ | Ashaastravihitam ghoram tapyante ye tapo janaah;
Dambhaahamkaarasamyuktaah kaamaraagabalaanvitaah.
Karshayantah shareerastham bhootagraamamachetasah;
Maam chaivaantahshareerastham taanviddhyaasuranishchayaan. |

Those who undertake severe penance not approved by the scriptures, who are full of hypocrisy and egoism, who are driven by lust, hatred and attachment and who stupidly torture the body and also Me who dwells in their body have demonic intentions.

17.07

| आहारस्त्वपि सर्वस्य त्रिविधो भवति प्रियः ।
 यज्ञस्तपस्तथा दानं तेषां भेदमिमं शृणु ॥ | Aahaarastvapi sarvasya trividho bhavati priyah;
 Yajnastapastathaa daanam teshaam bhedamimam shrinu. |

Even the foods people prefer to eat are of three types. Likewise, the sacrifice they perform, the penance they practice and the gifts they give are each of the three types. Now listen to the differences between them.

17.08

| आयुःसत्त्वबलारोग्यसुखप्रीतिविवर्धनाः ।
 रस्याः स्निग्धाः स्थिरा हृद्या
 आहाराः सात्त्विकप्रियाः ॥ | Aayuh sattvabalaaroyga sukha preetivi vardhanaah;
 Rasyaah snigdhaah sthiraa hridyaa aahaaraah saattvikapriyaah. |

People with sattva guna prefer food that promotes longevity, purity, strength, health, happiness and satisfaction, foods which are juicy, smooth, nutritious and hearty.

17.09

| कट्वम्ललवणात्युष्णतीक्ष्णरूक्षविदाहिनः ।
 आहारा राजसस्येष्टा दुःखशोकामयप्रदाः ॥ | Katvamlalavanaatyushna teekshna rooksha vidaahinah;
 Aahaaraah raajasasyeshtaa duhkhashokaamayapradaah. |

People with rajo guna like foods that are bitter, sour, salty, very hot, pungent, dry and burning. These foods cause discomfort, grief and illness.

17.10

| यातयामं गतरसं पूति पर्युषितं च यत् ।
 उच्छिष्टमपि चामेध्यं भोजनं तामसप्रियम् ॥ | Yaatayaamam gatarasam pooti paryushitam cha yat;
 Ucchishtamapi chaamedhyam bhojanam taamasapriyam. |

People with tamo guna enjoy foods that are not properly cooked, stale, tasteless, putrid, rotten, discarded and dirty.

17.11

अफलाकाङ्क्षिभिर्यज्ञो विधिदृष्टो य इज्यते । यष्टव्यमेवेति मनः समाधाय स सात्त्विकः ॥	Aphalaakaangkshibhiryajno vidhidrishto ya ijyate; Yashtavyameveti manah samaadhaaya sa saattvikah.

A sacrifice is sattvic when it is performed according to scriptures as a duty without any desire for its fruits.

17.12

अभिसन्धाय तु फलं दम्भार्थमपि चैव यत् । इज्यते भरतश्रेष्ठ तं यज्ञं विद्धि राजसम् ॥	Abhisandhaaya tu phalam dambhaarthamapi chaiva yat; Ijyate bharatashreshtha tam yajnam viddhi raajasam.

Arjuna, a sacrifice is rajasic when it is performed with a desire for fruits and for show.

17.13

विधिहीनमसृष्टान्नं मन्त्रहीनमदक्षिणम् । श्रद्धाविरहितं यज्ञं तामसं परिचक्षते ॥	Vidhiheenam asrishtaannam mantraheenam adakshinam; Shraddhaavirahitam yajnam taamasam parichakshate.

A sacrifice is tamasic when it is performed without any regard to scriptures, without offering food, without reciting mantras, without faith and without giving proper gifts.

17.14

देवद्विजगुरुप्राज्ञपूजनं शौचमार्जवम् । ब्रह्मचर्यमहिंसा च शारीरं तप उच्यते ॥	Devadvijagurupraajna poojanam shauchamaarjavam; Brahmacharyamahimsaa cha shaareeram tapa uchyate.

Worship of gods, brahmanas, teachers and the wise and being clean, simple, celibate, and nonviolent constitute the bodily austerities.

17.15

अनुद्वेगकरं वाक्यं सत्यं प्रियहितं च यत् । स्वाध्यायाभ्यसनं चैव वाङ्मयं तप उच्यते ॥	Anudvegakaram vaakyam satyam priyahitam cha yat; Swaadhyaayaabhyasanam chaiva vaangmayam tapa uchyate.

Speech that does not upset others, that is truthful, pleasant and helpful, and that is also used in the recitation of scriptures, constitutes the austerity of speech.

17.16

मनः प्रसादः सौम्यत्वं मौनमात्मविनिग्रहः । भावसंशुद्धिरित्येतत्तपो मानसमुच्यते ॥	Manahprasaadah saumyatvam maunamaatmavinigrahah; Bhaavasamshuddhirityetat tapo maanasamuchyate.

Calmness, gentleness, self-restraint and purity constitute the austerity of mind.

17.17

श्रद्धया परया तप्तं तपस्तत्त्रिविधं नरैः । अफलाकाङ्क्षिभिर्युक्तैः सात्त्विकं परिचक्षते ॥	Shraddhayaa parayaa taptam tapastattrividham naraih; Aphalaakaangkshibhiryuktaih saattvikam parichakshate.

These three types of austerities undertaken with complete faith and self control, and without any desire for fruit, are sattvic.

17.18

सत्कारमानपूजार्थं तपो दम्भेन चैव यत् । क्रियते तदिह प्रोक्तं राजसं चलमध्रुवम् ॥	Satkaaramaanapoojaartham tapo dambhena chaiva yat; Kriyate tadiha proktam raajasam chalamadhruvam.

Austerities undertaken with pride and ostentation to become famous and to be honored and revered are rajasic. Its results are uncertain and temporary.

17.19

मूढग्राहेणात्मनो यत्पीडया क्रियते तपः।	Moodhagraahenaatmano yat
परस्योत्सादनार्थं वा तत्तामसमुदाहृतम् ॥	peedayaa kriyate tapah;
	Parasyotsaadanaartham vaa
	tattaamasamudaahritam.

Austerities undertaken with deluded notions, that inflict pain on the self, or performed with the goal of harming others, are tamasic.

17.20

दातव्यमिति यद्दानं दीयतेऽनुपकारिणे।	Daatavyamiti yaddaanam
देशे काले च पात्रे च तद्दानं सात्त्विकं स्मृतम् ॥	deeyate'nupakaarine;
	Deshe kaale cha paatre cha
	taddaanam saattvikam smritam.

Charity given as a duty to the right person, at the right place and the right time, without expecting anything in return, is sattvic.

17.21

यत्तु प्रत्युपकारार्थं फलमुद्दिश्य वा पुनः।	Yattu pratyupakaaraartham
दीयते च परिक्लिष्टं तद्दानं राजसं स्मृतम् ॥	phalamuddishya vaa punah;
	Deeyate cha pariklishtam
	taddaanam raajasam smritam.

Charity made unwillingly, with the hope of reciprocation or some other gain, is rajasic.

17.22

अदेशकाले यद्दानमपात्रेभ्यश्च दीयते।	Adeshakaale
असत्कृतमवज्ञातं तत्तामसमुदाहृतम् ॥	yaddaanamapaatrebhyashcha deeyate;
	Asatkritamavajnaatam
	tattaamasamudaahritam.

Charity made reluctantly and contemptuously to an unworthy person at the wrong place and time is tamasic.

17.23

| ॐतत्सदिति निर्देशो ब्रह्मणस्त्रिविधः स्मृतः । ब्राह्मणास्तेन वेदाश्च यज्ञाश्च विहिताः पुरा ॥ | Om tatsaditi nirdesho brahmanas trividhah smritah; Braahmanaastena vedaashcha yajnaashcha vihitaah puraa. |

"OM, TAT, SAT" has been declared to represent Brahman, by which the Brahmanas, Vedas, and the sacrifices were originally created.

Commentary: The words OM TAT SAT are used either together or separately to represent Brahman. When a sacrificial rite is found to be flawed, it will be corrected by reciting any one of these symbols. OM represents the transcendental state. TAT means "That", the indefinable. SAT means reality.

17.24

| तस्मादोमित्युदाहृत्य यज्ञदानतपःक्रियाः । प्रवर्तन्ते विधानोक्ताः सततं ब्रह्मवादिनाम् ॥ | Tasmaadomityudaahritya yajnadaanatapahkriyaah; Pravartante vidhaanoktaah satatam brahmavaadinaam. |

Therefore, with the chanting of OM, the followers of the Vedas commence all acts of sacrifice, charity and austerities that are sanctioned by the scriptures.

17.25

| तदित्यनभिसन्धाय फलं यज्ञतपःक्रियाः । दानक्रियाश्च विविधाः क्रियन्ते मोक्षकाङ्क्षिभिः ॥ | Tadityanabhisandhaaya phalam yajnatapah kriyaah; Daanakriyaashcha vividhaah kriyante mokshakaangkshibhih. |

With the chanting of TAT, acts of sacrifice, austerity and charity are performed by the seekers of Moksha (liberation) without hoping for any material reward.

17.26

सद्भावे साधुभावे च सदित्येतत्प्रयुज्यते । प्रशस्ते कर्मणि तथा सच्छब्दः पार्थ युज्यते ॥	Sadbhaave saadhubhaave cha sadityetatprayujyate; Prashaste karmani tathaa sacchabdah paartha yujyate.

Arjuna, the word SAT is used to indicate *reality* and *goodness*. It is also used in the sense of an auspicious act.

17.27

यज्ञे तपसि दाने च स्थितिः सदिति चोच्यते । कर्म चैव तदर्थीयं सदित्येवाभिधीयते ॥	Yajne tapasi daane cha sthitih saditi chochyate; Karma chaiva tadartheeyam sadityevaabhidheeyate.

Solid devotion in the performance of sacrifice, practice of austerity and giving of gifts is called SAT. Also, the action for the sake of God is called SAT.

17.28

अश्रद्धया हुतं दत्तं तपस्तप्तं कृतं च यत् । असदित्युच्यते पार्थ न च तत्प्रेत्य नो इह ॥	Ashraddhayaa hutam dattam tapastaptam kritam cha yat; Asadityuchyate paartha na cha tatpretya no iha.

Arjuna, any action, be it sacrifice, charity or austerity, done without faith is called Asat. It is of no use either in this life or the next.

ॐ तत्सदिति श्रीमद्भगवद्गीतासूपनिषत्सु ब्रह्मविद्यायां योगशास्त्रे श्रीकृष्णार्जुनसंवादे श्रद्धात्रयविभागयोगो नाम सप्तदशोऽध्यायः	Om Tat Saditi Srimad Bhagavadgeetaasoopanishatsu Brahmavidyaayaam Yogashaastre Sri Krishnaarjunasamvaade Shraddhaatrayavibhaagayogo Naama Saptadasho'dhyaayah

Thus ends the seventeenth discourse entitled Shraddha Thraya Vibhaga Yoga in the Upanishad, the divine Bhagavad Gita, the knowledge of Brahman, the scripture on Yoga and the dialogue between Sri Krishna and Arjuna.

Chapter 18
Moksha Sanyasa Yoga

18.01	
अर्जुन उवाच | संन्यासस्य महाबाहो तत्त्वमिच्छामि वेदितुम् | त्यागस्य च हृषीकेश पृथक्केशिनिषूदन ||	Arjuna uvaacha: Sannyaasasya mahaabaaho tattvamicchaami veditum; Tyaagasya cha hrisheekesha prithak keshinishoodana.
Arjuna said: O Krishna, I would like to learn about Sanyasa and Tyaga.	

18.02

श्रीभगवानुवाच । काम्यानां कर्मणां न्यासं संन्यासं कवयो विदुः । सर्वकर्मफलत्यागं प्राहुस्त्यागं विचक्षणाः ॥	Sri Bhagavaan uvaacha: Kaamyaanaam karmanaam nyaasam sannyaasam kavayoviduh; Sarvakarmaphalatyaagam praahustyaagam vichakshanaah.

Bhagavan (Lord Krishna) said: The sages say that sanyasa means giving up actions motivated by selfish desires. Tyaga means giving up the fruits of action.

Commentary: A cursory glance at the words sanyasa and tyaga leaves the impression that they are synonyms. There is, however, a subtle difference between the two, and Lord Krishna makes this clear.

Sanyasa (renunciation) means abandoning all actions that are driven by selfish desire. A person practicing sanyasa does all he can to progress spiritually. He constantly seeks Self-knowledge and willingly shares his knowledge with others. He does not perform any action to become famous, to obtain material gains, to acquire power, or to get even. All his actions are devoid of ego. They are God centered and not self-centered.

Tyaga (relinquishment) means willingly giving up claims to the fruits of all actions. For example, holding a fundraiser and donating all proceeds to charity is a tyagic action. In some cases, desire for fruits may be the motivating factor for an individual to perform action. But if he then willingly gives up the fruits of that action for the benefit of all, he is still a tyagi. Tyaga gradually leads to sanyasa.

18.03

त्याज्यं दोषवदित्येके कर्म प्राहुर्मनीषिणः । यज्ञदानतपःकर्म न त्याज्यमिति चापरे ॥	Tyaajyam doshavadityeke karma praahurmaneeshinah; Yajnadaanatapah karma na tyaajyamiti chaapare.

Some sages say all action is evil and must be given up. Others say that acts of sacrifice, charity and austerity should never be given up.

18.04

निश्चयं शृणु मे तत्र त्यागे भरतसत्तम । त्यागो हि पुरुषव्याघ्र त्रिविधः सम्प्रकीर्तितः ॥	Nishchayam shrinu me tatra tyaage bharatasattama; Tyaago hi purushavyaaghra trividhah samprakeertitah.

Listen, Arjuna, to my explanation of tyaga. Arjuna, there are three kinds of tyaga.

18.05

यज्ञदानतपःकर्म न त्याज्यं कार्यमेव तत् । यज्ञो दानं तपश्चैव पावनानि मनीषिणाम् ॥	Yajnadaanatapah karma na tyaajyam kaaryameva tat; Yajno daanam tapashchaiva paavanaani maneeshinaam.

Performance of sacrifice, giving charity and practicing austerity should not be given up. By performing sacrifice, giving charity and practicing austerity, the wise become pure.

18.06

एतान्यपि तु कर्माणि सङ्गं त्यक्त्वा फलानि च । कर्तव्यानीति मे पार्थ निश्चितं मतमुत्तमम् ॥	Etaanyapi tu karmaani sangam tyaktvaa phalaani cha; Kartavyaaneeti me paartha nishchitam matamuttamam.

Arjuna, these acts must be performed without any attachment and desire for rewards. This is my firm conviction.

18.07

नियतस्य तु संन्यासः कर्मणो नोपपद्यते । मोहात्तस्य परित्यागस्तामसः परिकीर्तितः ॥	Niyatasya tu sannyaasah karmano nopapadyate; Mohaattasya parityaagas taamasah parikeertitah.

It is not right to give up one's duty. The abandonment of one's duty out of ignorance is considered tamasic.

18.08

दुःखमित्येव यत्कर्म कायक्लेशभयात्त्यजेत् । स कृत्वा राजसं त्यागं नैव त्यागफलं लभेत् ॥	Duhkhamityeva yat karma kaayakleshabhayaat tyajet; Sa kritvaa raajasam tyaagam naiva tyaagaphalam labhet.

One who forsakes duty to avoid physical discomfort or pain is practicing a rajasic form of tyaga. He does not benefit from such a tyaga.

18.09

कार्यमित्येव यत्कर्म नियतं क्रियतेऽर्जुन । सङ्गं त्यक्त्वा फलं चैव स त्यागः सात्त्विको मतः ॥	Kaaryamityeva yatkarma niyatam kriyate'rjuna; Sangam tyaktvaa phalam chaiva sa tyaagah saattviko matah.

Arjuna, when duty is performed because it needs to be done, without attachment, and when the benefits are given up, that is considered sattvic tyaga.

18.10

न द्वेष्ट्यकुशलं कर्म कुशले नानुषज्जते । त्यागी सत्त्वसमाविष्टो मेधावी छिन्नसंशयः ॥	Na dveshtyakushalam karma kushale naanushajjate; Tyaagee sattvasamaavishto medhaavee cchinnasamshayah.

One who has sattva guna and understands tyaga properly does not shirk from doing uncomfortable work, nor eagerly seek work that is comfortable.

18.11

न हि देहभृता शक्यं त्यक्तुं कर्माण्यशेषतः । यस्तु कर्मफलत्यागी स त्यागीत्यभिधीयते ॥	Na hi dehabhritaa shakyam tyaktum karmaanyasheshatah; Yastu karmaphalatyaagi sa tyaageetyabhidheeyate.

It is impossible for a human being to completely stop from working. Therefore, the person who completely gives up the fruits of action is considered a tyagi.

18.12

| अनिष्टमिष्टं मिश्रं च त्रिविधं कर्मणः फलम् ।
भवत्यत्यागिनां प्रेत्य न तु संन्यासिनां क्वचित् ॥ | Anishtamishtam mishram cha trividham karmanah phalam;
Bhavatyatyaaginaam pretya na tu sannyaasinaam kvachit. |

After death, those who did not practice tyaga accrue the fruit of their actions which is of three kinds: good, bad and mixed. Whereas sanyasis have none of these.

18.13

| पञ्चैतानि महाबाहो कारणानि निबोध मे ।
साङ्ख्ये कृतान्ते प्रोक्तानि सिद्धये सर्वकर्मणाम् ॥ | Panchaitaani mahaabaaho kaaranaani nibodha me;
Saankhye kritaante proktaani siddhaye sarvakarmanaam. |

Arjuna, according to the Sankhya system, there are five factors that contribute to success in all actions. Now, learn these from Me.

18.14

| अधिष्ठानं तथा कर्ता करणं च पृथग्विधम् ।
विविधाश्च पृथक्चेष्टा दैवं चैवात्र पञ्चमम् ॥ | Adhishthaanam tathaa kartaa karanam cha prithagvidham;
Vividhaashcha prithakcheshtaa daivam chaivaatra panchamam. |

They are: the body, the ego, various organs, various activities, and destiny.

18.15

| शरीरवाङ्मनोभिर्यत्कर्म प्रारभते नरः ।
न्याय्यं वा विपरीतं वा पञ्चैते तस्य हेतवः ॥ | Shareeravaangmanobhiryat karma praarabhate narah;
Nyaayyam vaa vipareetam vaa panchaite tasya hetavah. |

These factors are responsible for any action, right or wrong, performed by a person with the mind, speech or body.

18.16

| तत्रैवं सति कर्तारमात्मानं केवलं तु यः ।
 पश्यत्यकृतबुद्धित्वान्न स पश्यति दुर्मतिः ॥ | Tatraivam sati kartaaram aatmaanam kevalam tu yah;
 Pashyatyakritabuddhitvaan na sa pashyati durmatih. |

Therefore, one who thinks of one's self as the doer is mistaken, due to his total misconception of the truth.

18.17

| यस्य नाहंकृतो भावो बुद्धिर्यस्य न लिप्यते ।
 हत्वापि स इमाँल्लोकान्न हन्ति न निबध्यते ॥ | Yasya naahankrito bhaavo buddhiryasya na lipyate;
 Hatvaapi sa imaam llokaan na hanti na nibadhyate. |

One who is free from the sense of doership, and whose understanding is not deluded by attachment, does not really kill these people on the battlefield even if he kills all of them, and is not bound by his action.

18.18

| ज्ञानं ज्ञेयं परिज्ञाता त्रिविधा कर्मचोदना ।
 करणं कर्म कर्तेति त्रिविधः कर्मसंग्रहः ॥ | Jnaanam jneyam parijnaataa trividhaa karmachodanaa;
 Karanam karma karteti trividhah karmasangrahah. |

Knowledge, the object of knowledge, and the knower are the stimuli for action. The organs of action, the action itself and the doer of action are the constituents of action.

18.19

| ज्ञानं कर्म च कर्ताच त्रिधैव गुणभेदतः ।
 प्रोच्यते गुणसङ्ख्याने यथावच्छृणु तान्यपि ॥ | Jnaanam karma cha kartaa cha tridhaiva gunabhedatah;
 Prochyate gunasankhyaane yathaavacchrinu taanyapi. |

According to the science of gunas in Sankhya Philosophy, there are also three kinds each of knowledge, action, and doer. Hear them now.

18.20

सर्वभूतेषु येनैकं भावमव्ययमीक्षते । अविभक्तं विभक्तेषु तज्ज्ञानं विद्धि सात्त्विकम् ॥	Sarvabhooteshu yenaikam bhaavamavyayameekshate; Avibhaktam vibhakteshu tajjnaanam viddhi saattvikam.

Sattvic knowledge enables a person to see one imperishable being equally in all beings, undivided among the divided.

18.21

पृथक्त्वेन तु यज्ज्ञानं नानाभावान्पृथग्विधान् । वेत्ति सर्वेषु भूतेषु तज्ज्ञानं विद्धि राजसम् ॥	Prithaktvena tu yajjnaanam naanaabhaavaan prithagvidhaan; Vetti sarveshu bhooteshu tajjnaanam viddhi raajasam.

Rajasic knowledge leads a person to believe that the entity that dwells in everyone is different.

18.22

यत्तु कृत्स्नवदेकस्मिन्कार्ये सक्तमहैतुकम् । अतत्त्वार्थवदल्पं च तत्तामसमुदाहृतम् ॥	Yattu kritsnavadekasmin kaarye saktamahaitukam; Atattvaarthavadalpam cha tattaamasamudaahritam.

Tamasic knowledge instigates a person to latch onto something trivial and absurd without reason or basis, and to consider it as the be-all and end-all.

18.23

नियतं सङ्गरहितमरागद्वेषतः कृतम् । अफलप्रेप्सुना कर्म यत्तत्सात्त्विकमुच्यते ॥	Niyatam sangarahitam araagadveshatah kritam; Aphalaprepsunaa karma yattat saattvikamuchyate.

Action which is ordained by the scriptures and performed by a person without any sense of doership, without like or dislike, without any attachment, and without seeking any reward, is sattvic.

18.24

यत्तु कामेप्सुना कर्म साहंकारेण वा पुनः । क्रियते बहुलायासं तद्राजसमुदाहृतम् ॥	Yattu kaamepsunaa karma saahankaarena vaa punah; Kriyate bahulaayaasam tadraajasamudaahritam.

Action performed by a person keen on fulfilling selfish desires, with ego, and with a lot of effort, is rajasic.

18.25

अनुबन्धं क्षयं हिंसामनपेक्ष्य च पौरुषम् । मोहादारभ्यते कर्म यत्तत्तामसमुच्यते ॥	Anubandham kshayam himsaam anavekshya cha paurusham; Mohaadaarabhyate karma yattat taamasamuchyate.

Action performed by a person blindly, without considering personal ability and consequences, which involves loss and injury to others, is tamasic.

18.26

मुक्तसङ्गोऽनहंवादी धृत्युत्साहसमन्वितः । सिद्ध्यसिद्ध्योर्निर्विकारः कर्ता सात्त्विक उच्यते ॥	Muktasango'nahamvaadi dhrityutsaahasamanvitah; Siddhyasiddhyor nirvikaarah kartaa saattvika uchyate.

The agent who is without attachment and ego, who has perseverance, resolve and enthusiasm, and who is not affected by success or failure, is sattvic.

18.27

रागी कर्मफलप्रेप्सुर्लुब्धो हिंसात्मकोऽशुचिः । हर्षशोकान्वितः कर्ता राजसः परिकीर्तितः ॥	Raagee karmaphalaprepsur lubdho himsaatmako'shuchih; Harshashokaanvitah kartaa raajasah parikeertitah.

The agent who is very passionate, greedy, violent, unclean, who cares dearly for the fruits of labor, and who is susceptible to success and failure, is rajasic.

18.28

| अयुक्तः प्राकृतः स्तब्धः शठो नैष्कृतिकोऽलसः ।
 विषादी दीर्घसूत्री च कर्ता तामस उच्यते ॥ | Ayuktah praakritah stabdhah shatho naishkritiko'lasah;
 Vishaadee deerghasootree cha kartaa taamasa uchyate. |

The agent who is unsteady, vulgar, obstinate, deceitful, malicious, lazy, lethargic, and procrastinating, is tamasic.

18.29

| बुद्धेर्भेदं धृतेश्चैव गुणतस्त्रिविधं शृणु ।
 प्रोच्यमानमशेषेण पृथक्त्वेन धनञ्जय ॥ | Buddherbhedam dhriteshchaiva gunatastrividham shrinu;
 Prochyamaanamasheshena prithaktvena dhananjaya. |

O Dhananjaya (Arjuna), listen now, I will explain to you in detail the three types of buddhi (intellect) and the three types of dhriti (resolve) that are caused by the gunas.

18.30

प्रवृत्तिं च निवृत्तिं च कार्याकार्ये भयाभये । बन्धं मोक्षं च या वेत्ति बुद्धिः सा पार्थ सात्त्विकी ॥	Pravrittim cha nivrittim cha karyaakaarye bhayaabhaye; Bandhammoksham cha yaa vetti buddhih saa paartha saattvikee.

Arjuna, intellect that enables one to understand what is action and what is inaction, what should be done and what should not be done, what is fear and what is fearlessness, and what is bondage and what is liberation, is sattvic.

Commentary: Sattvic intellect enables a person to completely comprehend the consequences of any action before its initiation. It helps one to make correct decisions in a variety of confusing situations.

Pravritti is the path of action. This path can be binding if it is associated with selfish desires. On the other hand, if action is performed as a worship of God, without any ego and interest for the fruits, it is nonbinding and helps in spiritual progress.

Nivritti is the path of renunciation. It involves abstaining from all activities that lead to material enjoyments and constantly focusing on God.

Sattvic intellect enables us to do the right work, at the right place and at the right time, and avoid doing the wrong work, at the wrong place and time. We are exposed to a variety of fearful situations. Sattvic intellect enables us to recognize those fears that are unfounded. It helps us understand the actions that trap us in bondage and the actions that liberate us from bondage.

18.31

यया धर्ममधर्मं च कार्यं चाकार्यमेव च । अयथावत्प्रजानाति बुद्धिः सा पार्थ राजसी ॥	Yayaa dharmamadharmam cha kaaryam chaakaaryameva cha; Ayathaavat prajaanaati buddhih saa paartha raajasee.

Arjuna, intellect that leads one to the wrong understanding of what is dharma and what is adharma, and what should be done and what should not be done, is rajasic.

18.32

अधर्मं धर्ममिति या मन्यते तमसावृता । सर्वार्थान्विपरीतांश्च बुद्धिः सा पार्थ तामसी ॥	Adharmam dharmamiti yaa manyate tamasaavritaa; Sarvaarthaan vipareetaamshcha buddhih saa paartha taamasee.

Arjuna, intellect that is deluded and leads one to look at the world topsy-turvy like believing dharma as adharma and adharma as dharma, is tamasic.

18.33

धृत्या यया धारयते मनःप्राणेन्द्रियक्रियाः । योगेनाव्यभिचारिण्या धृतिः सा पार्थ सात्त्विकी ॥	Dhrityaa yayaa dhaarayate manah praanendriyakriyaah; Yogenaavyabhichaarinyaa dhritih saa paartha saattvikee.

Arjuna, resolve that enables one to practice the yoga of meditation and control the functions of the mind, life-breaths and sense organs, is sattvic.

18.34

यया तु धर्मकामार्थान्धृत्या धारयतेऽर्जुन । प्रसङ्गेन फलाकाङ्क्षी धृतिः सा पार्थ राजसी ॥	Yayaa tu dharmakaamaarthaan dhrityaa dhaarayate'rjuna; Prasangena phalaakaangkshee dhritih saa paartha raajasee.

Arjuna, resolve that leads one who seeks reward for his actions to hold on to his duties, wealth and pleasure, is rajasic.

18.35

यया स्वप्नं भयं शोकं विषादं मदमेव च । न विमुञ्चति दुर्मेधा धृतिः सा पार्थ तामसी ॥	Yayaa swapnam bhayam shokam vishaadam madameva cha; Na vimunchati durmedhaa dhritih saa paartha taamasee.

Arjuna, resolve by which a dull person does not give up excessive sleep, undue fear, constant grief, despair and excessive arrogance, is tamasic.

18.36

| सुखं त्विदानीं त्रिविधं शृणु मे भरतर्षभ ।
अभ्यासाद्रमते यत्र दुःखान्तं च निगच्छति ॥ | Sukham tvidaaneem trividham shrinu me bharatarshabha;
Abhyaasaadramate yatra duhkhaantam cha nigacchati. |

Arjuna, now you will hear from Me the three kinds of happiness. The happiness one feels by constant spiritual practice that ends all sorrow is sattvic.

18.37

| यत्तदग्रे विषमिव परिणामेऽमृतोपमम् ।
तत्सुखं सात्त्विकं प्रोक्तमात्मबुद्धिप्रसादजम् ॥ | Yattadagre vishamiva parinaame'mritopamam;
Tatsukham saattvikam proktam aatmabuddhiprasaadajam. |

The happiness that feels like poison in the beginning and feels like nectar in the end, due to the acquisition of Self knowledge, is sattvic.

18.38

| विषयेन्द्रियसंयोगाद्यत्तदग्रेऽमृतोपमम् ।
परिणामे विषमिव तत्सुखं राजसं स्मृतम् ॥ | Vishayendriya samyogaad yattadagre'mritopamam;
Parinaame vishamiva tatsukham raajasam smritam. |

The happiness that comes from the interaction of the senses with the sensory objects, that feels like nectar in the beginning but becomes like poison in the end, is rajasic.

18.39

| यदग्रे चानुबन्धे च सुखं मोहनमात्मनः ।
निद्रालस्यप्रमादोत्थं तत्तामसमुदाहृतम् ॥ | Yadagre chaanubandhe cha sukham mohanamaatmanah;
Nidraalasyapramaadottham tattaamasamudaahritam. |

The happiness that deludes the self from the beginning to the end, which comes from excessive sleep, lethargy and irresponsibility, is tamasic.

18.40

न तदस्ति पृथिव्यां वा दिवि देवेषु वा पुनः । सत्त्वं प्रकृतिजैर्मुक्तं यदेभिः स्यात्त्रिभिर्गुणैः ॥	Na tadasti prithivyaam vaa divi deveshu vaa punah; Sattvam prakritijairmuktam yadebhih syaat tribhirgunaih.

There is no one anywhere, either on earth or in heaven among the devas, who is free from the influence of the three gunas born of prakriti.

18.41

ब्राह्मणक्षत्रियविशां शूद्राणां च परन्तप । कर्माणि प्रविभक्तानि स्वभावप्रभवैर्गुणैः ॥	Braahmanakshatriyavishaam shoodraanaam cha parantapa; Karmaani pravibhaktaani swabhaavaprabhavairgunaih.

The duties of Brahmanas, Kshatriyas, Vaishyas and Shudras are classified by the gunas that are naturally inherited.

18.42

शमो दमस्तपः शौचं क्षान्तिरार्जवमेव च । ज्ञानं विज्ञानमास्तिक्यं ब्रह्मकर्म स्वभावजम् ॥	Shamo damastapah shaucham kshaantiraarjavameva cha; Jnaanam vijnaanam aastikyam brahmakarma swabhaavajam.

Calmness, self-restraint, austerity, patience, honesty, knowledge, wisdom, and faith in God are natural characteristics of Brahmins.

18.43

शौर्यं तेजो धृतिर्दाक्ष्यं युद्धे चाप्यपलायनम् । दानमीश्वरभावश्च क्षात्रं कर्म स्वभावजम् ॥	Shauryam tejo dhritirdaakshyam yuddhe chaapyapalaayanam; Daanameeshwarabhaavashcha kshaatram karmaswabhaavajam.

Courage, strength, resolve, dexterity, not running away from battle, generosity, and the capacity to rule are natural characteristics of Kshatriyas.

18.44

कृषिगौरक्ष्यवाणिज्यं वैश्यकर्म स्वभावजम् । परिचर्यात्मकं कर्म शूद्रस्यापि स्वभावजम् ॥	Krishigaurakshyavaanijyam vaishyakarma swabhaavajam; Paricharyaatmakam karma shoodrasyaapi swabhaavajam.

Interest in agriculture, raising cattle, and skill in trade are natural characteristics of Vaishyas. Shudras provide overall support to all the other castes.

18.45

स्वे स्वे कर्मण्यभिरतः संसिद्धिं लभते नरः । स्वकर्मनिरतः सिद्धिं यथा विन्दति तच्छृणु ॥	Sve sve karmanyabhiratah samsiddhim labhate narah; Swakarmaniratah siddhim yathaa vindati tacchrinu.

A person becomes perfect by doing his duty with total devotion. Listen now to how a person devoted to his duty attains perfection.

18.46

यतः प्रवृत्तिर्भूतानां येन सर्वमिदं ततम् । स्वकर्मणा तमभ्यर्च्य सिद्धिं विन्दति मानवः ॥	Yatah pravrittirbhootaanaam yena sarvamidam tatam; Swakarmanaa tamabhyarchya siddhim vindati maanavah.

A person can achieve perfection by worshipping the creator who is the source of all and who pervades the entire universe, through performing his duty properly.

18.47

श्रेयान्स्वधर्मो विगुणः परधर्मात्स्वनुष्ठितात् । स्वभावनियतं कर्म कुर्वन्नाप्नोति किल्बिषम् ॥	Shreyaanswadharmo vigunah paradharmaat swanushthitaat; Swabhaavaniyatam karma kurvannaapnoti kilbisham.

Doing one's duty imperfectly is better than doing another's duty well. He who performs action conducive to his nature does not incur sin.

18.48

सहजं कर्म कौन्तेय सदोषमपि न त्यजेत् । सर्वारम्भा हि दोषेण धूमेनाग्निरिवावृताः ॥	Sahajam karma kaunteya sadoshamapi na tyajet; Sarvaarambhaa hi doshena dhoomenaagnirivaavritaah.

Arjuna, one should not abandon one's natural duty, even though it may have some defects. All actions have defects, just as fire is covered by smoke.

18.49

असक्तबुद्धिः सर्वत्र जितात्मा विगतस्पृहः । नैष्कर्म्यसिद्धिं परमां संन्यासेनाधिगच्छति ॥	Asaktabuddhih sarvatra jitaatmaa vigatasprihah; Naishkarmyasiddhim paramaam sannyaasenaadhigacchati.

The person whose intellect is not attached to anything, who has subdued his self and who has no desire whatsoever, attains Brahman through sanyasa.

18.50

सिद्धिं प्राप्तो यथा ब्रह्म तथाप्नोति निबोध मे । समासेनैव कौन्तेय निष्ठा ज्ञानस्य या परा ॥	Siddhim praapto yathaa brahma tathaapnoti nibodha me; Samaasenaiva kaunteya nishthaa jnaanasya yaa paraa.

Arjuna, now learn from Me how a person who has attained perfection realizes Brahman, the supreme culmination of knowledge.

18.51-18.53

बुद्ध्या विशुद्धया युक्तो धृत्यात्मानं नियम्य च |
शब्दादीन्विषयांस्त्यक्त्वा रागद्वेषौ व्युदस्य च ||
विविक्तसेवी लघ्वाशी यतवाक्कायमानसः |
ध्यानयोगपरो नित्यं वैराग्यं समुपाश्रितः ||
अहंकारं बलं दर्पं कामं क्रोधं परिग्रहम् |
विमुच्य निर्ममः शान्तो ब्रह्मभूयाय कल्पते ||

Buddhyaa vishuddhayaa yukto dhrityaatmaanam niyamya cha;
Shabdaadeen vishayaanstyaktvaa raagadveshau vyudasya cha.
Viviktasevee laghwaashee yatavaakkaayamaanasah;
Dhyaanayogaparo nityam vairaagyam samupaashritah.
Ahankaaram balam darpam kaamam krodham parigraham;
Vimuchya nirmamah shaanto brahmabhooyaaya kalpate.

One who has reached perfection prepares himself to become fit to attain Brahman by the following process. He restrains the mind and senses with a purified intellect. He keeps away from sensory objects such as sound and others, and frees himself of likes and dislikes. He lives in seclusion, eats lightly of sattvic food, does not talk much, restrains his body and mind, and constantly engages in the yoga of meditation without any attachment. He gives up egoism, power, arrogance, lust, anger, possessiveness, the notion of "mine", and remains calm.

18.54

ब्रह्मभूतः प्रसन्नात्मा न शोचति न काङ्क्षति |
समः सर्वेषु भूतेषु मद्भक्तिं लभते पराम् ||

Brahmabhootah prasannaatmaa na shochati na kaangkshati;
Samah sarveshu bhooteshu madbhaktim labhate paraam.

Being Brahman and ever joyful, he does not grieve for anybody nor desire anything. He treats everyone alike and attains supreme devotion to Me.

18.55

| भक्त्या मामभिजानाति यावान्यश्चास्मि तत्त्वतः ।
ततो मां तत्त्वतो ज्ञात्वा विशते तदनन्तरम् ॥ | Bhaktyaa maamabhijaanaati yaavaanyashchaasmi tattvatah;
Tato maam tattvato jnaatvaa vishate tadanantaram. |

Through devotion to Me, he comes to know Me truly. Having known Me in essence, he becomes one with Me.

18.56

| सर्वकर्माण्यपि सदा कुर्वाणो मद्व्यपाश्रयः ।
मत्प्रसादादवाप्नोति शाश्वतं पदमव्ययम् ॥ | Sarvakarmaanyapi sadaa kurvaano madvyapaashrayah;
Matprasaadaadavaapnoti shaashvatam padamavyayam. |

Even while performing all actions, one who takes refuge in Me reaches the eternal and imperishable abode by my grace.

18.57

| चेतसा सर्वकर्माणि मयि संन्यस्य मत्परः ।
बुद्धियोगमुपाश्रित्य मच्चित्तः सततं भव ॥ | Chetasaa sarvakarmaani mayi sannyasya matparah;
Buddhiyogam upaashritya macchittah satatam bhava. |

Mentally dedicate all actions to Me and keep Me as your only goal. Keep your mind always fixed on Me, resorting to the yoga of equanimity.

18.58

| मच्चित्तः सर्वदुर्गाणि मत्प्रसादात्तरिष्यसि ।
अथ चेत्त्वमहंकारान्न श्रोष्यसि विनङ्क्ष्यसि ॥ | Macchittah sarvadurgaani matprasaadaat tarishyasi;
Atha chet tvam ahankaaraan na shroshyasi vinangkshyasi. |

Fix your mind on Me and you shall overcome all obstacles. If you do not listen to Me out of ego, you will be lost.

	18.59
यदहंकारमाश्रित्य न योत्स्य इति मन्यसे । मिथ्यैष व्यवसायस्ते प्रकृतिस्त्वां नियोक्ष्यति ॥	Yadahankaaram aashritya na yotsya iti manyase; Mithyaisha vyavasaayaste prakritistvaam niyokshyati.

If out of egotism you resolve not to fight, this resolve will be useless because your own nature will make you fight.

	18.60
स्वभावजेन कौन्तेय निबद्धः स्वेन कर्मणा । कर्तुं नेच्छसि यन्मोहात्करिष्यस्यवशोऽपि तत् ॥	Swabhaavajena kaunteya nibaddhah svena karmanaa; Kartum necchasi yanmohaat karishyasyavasho'pi tat.

What you do not like to do due to delusion, you will do against your will because your karma, born of your own nature, will force you to do it.

	18.61
ईश्वरः सर्वभूतानां हृद्देशेऽर्जुन तिष्ठति । भ्रामयन्सर्वभूतानि यन्त्रारूढानि मायया ॥	Eeshwarah sarvabhootaanaam hriddeshe'rjuna tishthati; Bhraamayan sarvabhootaani yantraaroodhaani maayayaa.

Arjuna, God dwells in every heart. He makes everyone move around as if they are mounted on a machine, by his power of Maya.

	18.62
तमेव शरणं गच्छ सर्वभावेन भारत । तत्प्रसादात्परां शान्तिं स्थानं प्राप्स्यसि शाश्वतम् ॥	Tameva sharanam gaccha sarvabhaavena bhaarata; Tatprasaadaatparaam shaantim sthaanam praapsyasi shaashvatam.

Arjuna, completely surrender yourself to Him. By his grace you shall attain supreme peace and reach his eternal abode.

18.63

| इति ते ज्ञानमाख्यातं गुह्याद्गुह्यतरं मया ।
विमृश्यैतदशेषेण यथेच्छसि तथा कुरु ॥ | Iti te jnaanamaakhyaatam guhyaad guhyataram mayaa;
Vimrishyaitadasheshena yathecchasi tathaa kuru. |

I have explained to you the most mysterious of all knowledge. Think it over carefully and do as you wish.

18.64

| सर्वगुह्यतमं भूयः शृणु मे परमं वचः ।
इष्टोऽसि मे दृढमिति ततो वक्ष्यामि ते हितम् ॥ | Sarvaguhyatamam bhooyah shrinu me paramam vachah;
Ishto'si me dridhamiti tato vakshyaami te hitam. |

Listen, once again, to my supreme word, the most mysterious of all. You are very dear to Me, and therefore I shall tell you this for your own good.

18.65

| मन्मना भव मद्भक्तो मद्याजी मां नमस्कुरु ।
मामेवैष्यसि सत्यं ते प्रतिजाने प्रियोऽसि मे ॥ | Manmanaa bhava madbhakto madyaajee maam namaskuru;
Maamevaishyasi satyam te pratijaane priyo'si me. |

Focus your thoughts on Me. Become my devotee. Worship Me and bow down to Me. You shall no doubt reach Me. I promise you this because you are dear to Me.

18.66

| सर्वधर्मान्परित्यज्य मामेकं शरणं व्रज ।
अहं त्वा सर्वपापेभ्यो मोक्षयिष्यामि मा शुचः ॥ | Sarvadharmaan parityajya maamekam sharanam vraja;
Aham tvaa sarvapaapebhyo mokshayishyaami maa shuchah. |

Abandon all your notions of duties and completely surrender to Me. I shall liberate you from all sins. Do not despair.

Commentary: Lord Krishna is not telling us here that one can commit all kinds of atrocities and gain absolution just by saying "God, I surrender to you". A person can truly surrender to God *only* when he has truly transcended his ego. Only people in a higher spiritual state can surrender and transcend dharma and adharma. Whatever actions these people perform will always be in accordance with dharma, although they do not consciously strive to follow any dharma. This is the grand finale of spiritual wisdom that Lord Krishna imparts to Arjuna.

18.67

| इदं ते नातपस्काय नाभक्ताय कदाचन ।
न चाशुश्रूषवे वाच्यं न च मां योऽभ्यसूयति ॥ | Idam te naatapaskaaya naabhaktaaya kadaachana;
Na chaashushrooshave vaachyam na cha maam yo'bhyasooyati. |

You should not disclose this to anyone who does not practice austerity, who has no devotion, who is reluctant to listen or who speaks ill of Me.

18.68

| य इदं परमं गुह्यं मद्भक्तेष्वभिधास्यति ।
भक्तिं मयि परां कृत्वा मामेवैष्यत्यसंशयः ॥ | Ya imam paramam guhyam madbhakteshvabhidhaasyati;
Bhaktim mayi paraam kritvaa maamevaishyatyasamshayah. |

Whoever reveals this sacred mystery to my devotees with devotion shall attain Me. There is no doubt about this.

18.69

| न च तस्मान्मनुष्येषु कश्चिन्मे प्रियकृत्तमः ।
 भविता न च मे तस्मादन्यः प्रियतरो भुवि ॥ | Na cha tasmaanmanushyeshu kashchinme priyakrittamah;
 Bhavitaa na cha me tasmaadanyah priyataro bhuvi. |

There is none among human beings who renders more devotional service than he. There will not be any other dearer to Me in the world than he.

18.70

| अध्येष्यते च य इमं धर्म्यं संवादमावयोः ।
 ज्ञानयज्ञेन तेनाहमिष्टः स्यामिति मे मतिः ॥ | Adhyeshyate cha ya imam dharmyam samvaadamaavayoh;
 Jnaanayajnena tenaaham ishtah syaamiti me matih. |

Whoever studies this sacred dialogue of ours, I consider that he has worshiped Me with Jnana Yagna (offering of knowledge). This is my promise.

18.71

| श्रद्धावाननसूयश्च शृणुयादपि यो नरः ।
 सोऽपि मुक्तः शुभाँल्लोकान्प्राप्नुयात्पुण्यकर्मणाम् ॥ | Shraddhaavaan anasooyashcha shrinuyaadapi yo narah;
 So'pi muktah shubhaamllokaan praapnuyaat punyakarmanaam. |

Anyone who listens to this with faith and without doubt will also be liberated from sins, and will reach the happy worlds of the pure.

18.72

| कच्चिदेतच्छ्रुतं पार्थ त्वयैकाग्रेण चेतसा ।
 कच्चिदज्ञानसम्मोहः प्रनष्टस्ते धनञ्जय ॥ | Kacchid etacchrutam paartha tvayaikaagrena chetasaa;
 Kacchid ajnaanasammohah pranashtaste dhananjaya. |

O Arjuna, did you hear what I said with full attention? Has your illusion born of ignorance been dispelled?

18.73

अर्जुन उवाच | नष्टो मोहः स्मृतिर्लब्धा त्वत्प्रसादान्मयाच्युत | स्थितोऽस्मि गतसन्देहः करिष्ये वचनं तव ||	Arjuna uvaacha: Nashto mohah smritirlabdhaa tvatprasaadaanmayaachyuta; Sthito'smi gata sandehah karishye vachanam tava.

Arjuna said: O Krishna, my delusion is gone by your grace and I have regained my memory. I stand firm without any doubts and am ready to follow your orders.

18.74

सञ्जय उवाच | इत्यहं वासुदेवस्य पार्थस्य च महात्मनः | संवादमिममश्रौषमद्भुतं रोमहर्षणम् ||	Sanjaya uvaacha: Ityaham vaasudevasya paarthasya cha mahaatmanah; Samvaadam imam ashrausham adbhutam romaharshanam.

Sanjaya said: Thus, I heard this wonderful and hair-raising dialogue between Vasudeva (Krishna) and the noble Arjuna.

18.75

व्यासप्रसादाच्छ्रुतवानेतद्गुह्यमहं परम् | योगं योगेश्वरात्कृष्णात्साक्षात्कथयतः स्वयम् ||	Vyaasaprasaadaacchrutavaan etadguhyamaham param; Yogam yogeshwaraat krishnaat saakshaat kathayatah swayam.

By the grace of Vyasa, I heard the supreme yoga from Krishna, the Lord of Yoga, directly speaking before me.

18.76

राजन्संस्मृत्य संस्मृत्य संवादमिममद्भुतम् | केशवार्जुनयोः पुण्यं हृष्यामि च मुहुर्मुहुः ||	Raajan samsmritya samsmritya samvaadam imam adbhutam; Keshavaarjunayoh punyam hrishyaami cha muhurmuhuh.

O King (Dhritarashtra), as I recollect this wonderful and sacred dialogue between Keshava (Krishna) and Arjuna, I rejoice again and again.

18.77

तच्च संस्मृत्य संस्मृत्य रूपमत्यद्भुतं हरेः । विस्मयो मे महान् राजन्हृष्यामि च पुनः पुनः ॥	Taccha samsmritya samsmritya roopamatyadbhutam hareh; Vismayo me mahaan raajan hrishyaami cha punah punah.

O Lord (Dhritarashtra), remembering again and again the awesome form of Hari (Krishna), I am filled with wonder and rejoice again and again.

18.78

यत्र योगेश्वरः कृष्णो यत्र पार्थो धनुर्धरः । तत्र श्रीर्विजयो भूतिर्ध्रुवा नीतिर्मतिर्मम ॥	Yatra yogeshwarah krishno yatra paartho dhanurdharah; Tatra shreervijayo bhootirdhruvaa neetirmatirmama.

Wherever there is Sri Krishna, the Lord of Yoga, and Arjuna, the great archer, there will be good fortune, victory, progress and righteousness.

ॐ तत्सदिति श्रीमद्भगवद्गीतासूपनिषत्सु ब्रह्मविद्यायां योगशास्त्रे श्रीकृष्णार्जुनसंवादे मोक्षसंन्यासयोगो नाम अष्टादशोऽध्यायः।	Om Tat Saditi Srimad Bhagavadgeetaasoopanishatsu Brahmavidyaayaam Yogashaastre Sri Krishnaarjunasamvaade Mokshasannyaasayogo Naama Ashtaadasho'dhyaayah

Thus ends the eighteenth discourse entitled Moksha Sanyasa Yoga in the Upanishad, the divine Bhagavad Gita, the knowledge of Brahman, the scripture on Yoga and the dialogue between Sri Krishna and Arjuna.

Bibliography

Bhavani, Sudhindra. *The Bhagavadgītā and its classical commentaries : a critical and comparative exposition*. 1st ed. Bangalore: Dvaita Vedānta Studies and Research Foundation, 1995.

Chandrasekharendra Saraswati, Swami. *Hindu Dharma: The Universal Way of Life*, 4th ed. Bombay: Bharatiya Vidya Bhavan, 2000.

Chidbhavananda, Swami. *The Bhagavad Gita*. Tirupparaithurai: Sri Ramakrishna Tapovanam, 2002.

Chinmayananda, Swami. *The Holy Geeta*. Bombay: Central Chinmaya Mission Trust, 2008.

Easwaran, Eknath. *The Bhagavad Gita for Daily Living: Commentary, Translation, and Sanskrit Text*. Berkeley, Calif: Blue Mountain Center of Meditation, 1975.

Gandhi, and Mahadev H Desai. *The Gospel of Selfless Action, or, The Gita According to Gandhi: Translation of the Original in Gujarati, with an Additional Introduction and Commentary*. 4th ed. Ahmedabad: Navajivan Pub. House, 1956.

Goyandka, Jayadayal. *Śrīmadbhagavadgītā: Tattvavivecanī (English commentary)*. Gorakhapur: Gita Press, 2008.

Jnanadeva. *Jñāneshwar's Gītā: A Rendering of the Jñāneśhwarī*. Albany, N.Y: State University of New York Press, 1989.

Majumdar, Sachindra Kumar. *The Bhagavad Gita: A Scripture for the Future*. Berkeley, Calif: Asian Humanities Press, 1991.

Malinar, Angelika. *The Bhagavadgītā: Doctrines and Contexts*. Cambridge: Cambridge University Press, 2007.

Nikhilananda. *The Bhagavad Gita*. New York: Ramakrisha-Vivekananda Center, 1944.

Padmanabhachar, C. M. *A Critical Study of Bhagavad Geeta*. Tiruchanur: Sri Madhwa Siddhanta Onnahini Sabha, 2007.

Prabhupada, A. C. Bhaktivedanta Swami. *Bhagavad-Gita As It Is*. Revised. Bhaktivedanta Book Trust, 1997.

Radhakrishnan, S. *The Bhagavadgītā, with an Introductory Essay, Sanskrit Text [transliterated]*. New York: Harper, 1948.

Ramanuja, and J. A. B. van Buitenen. *Rāmānuja on the Bhagavadgītā; a Condensed Rendering of His Gītābhāsya with Copious Notes and an Introduction*. Delhi: Motilal Banarsidass, 1974.

Ranganathananda, Swami. *Universal message of the Bhagavad Gītā : an exposition of the Gītā in the light of modern thought and modern needs*, 1st ed. Calcutta: Advaita Ashrama, 2000.

Ramdas. *Gita Sandesh (Message of the Gita)*. Bombay: Bharatiya Vidya Bhavan, 1966.

Sarasvatī, Madhusūdana and Sisir Kumar Gupta. *Madhusūdana Sarasvatī on the Bhagavad Gītā: Being an English Translation of His Commentary Gūḍhārtha Dīpikā*, 1st ed. Delhi: Motilal Banarsidass, 1977.

Schweig, Graham M. *Bhagavad Gītā: The Beloved Lord's Secret Love Song*. 1st ed. San Francisco: HarperSanFrancisco, 2007.

Shankaracharya, and Alladi Mahadeva Sastri. *The Bhagavad Gita: With the Commentary of Sri Sankaracharya*. 7th ed. Madras: Samata Books, 1977.

Shankaracharya, and Swami Gambhirananda. *Bhagavadgita with the Commentary of Shankaracharya*. Calcutta: Advaita Ashrama, 2006.

Sivananda, Swami. *Bhagavad Gita*. Shivanandanagar: Divine Life Society, 2000. Web.
<http://www.dlshq.org/download/bgita.htm>

Sreenivasaiah, Harave Narasimha. *Srimad Bhagavad Geetha*. Bangalore, 1997.

Sukhabodhananda, Swami. *Karma Yoga: The Inner Alchemy of Action*. Bangalore: Prasanna Trust, 2005.

Tapasyananda, *Srimad-Bhagavad-Gita, The Scripture of Mankind*. Madras: Sri Ramakrishna Math, 1984.

Tilak, Bal Gangadhar. *The Hindu Philosophy of Life, Ethics and Religion*. 5th ed. Poona: [Tilak Bros.] Saka year, 1905.

Varma, R. R. *The Bhagwat Gita: Symphony of the Spirit*. New Delhi: Prakash Books India, 2008.

Vinoba. *Talks on the Gita*. New York: Macmillan, 1960.

www.ingramcontent.com/pod-product-compliance
Lightning Source LLC
Chambersburg PA
CBHW051045160426
43193CB00010B/1076